AN AWAKENING TO HEALTH COOKBOOK

Omnibus Edition

CJ Ainsworth

Other Books by CJ Ainsworth

An Awakening: How I Defeated Cancer
without Chemotherapy or Radiation
ISBN 978-1522938439
ISBN 1522938435

An Awakening to Health Cookbook-Volume I
ISBN-13:978-1530234318
ISBN-10:153023431X

An Awakening to Health Cookbook-Volume II
ISBN-13:978-1530951161
ISBN-10:153095116X

Printed in the United State of America by Createspace

ISBN-13: 978-1532764639
ISBN-10: 1532764634

First Edition: April 2016

10 9 8 7 6 5 4 3 2 1

Dedication

This book is dedicated first, to my husband John Ainsworth, my caregiver throughout my entire cancer healing process. His relentless dedication helped me to achieve my healing goals throughout my two year alternative therapy program. He continues to keep me on track to ensure I have no cancer recurrence. I love him with all my heart.

I dedicate this book to Debbie Smith and Virginia Aguiles. God Bless you Virginia. Virginia was a trooper. I met both these wonderful women at an alternative medical clinic in California. They are my friends and we supported each other through our toughest ordeals. They inspired me to write my story "An Awakening: How I Defeated Cancer without Chemotherapy or Radiation" and my cookbook to enforce the importance of proper eating and to promote a new healthy lifestyle.

Acknowledgments

I would like to thank and acknowledge our children—Matthew Stoen, Melissa Ainsworth, Jens Stoen, John Ainsworth II and Elizabeth Ainsworth—for their continuing support of my cancer treatment decision and their constant love. I also thank the Gerson Therapy. Without the Gerson Therapy I would not be alive today or understand the meaning of true health.

Table of Contents

Table of Contents

Table of Contents

Table of Contents

Table of Contents

Table of Contents

Table of Contents

Introduction

Upon request, this book "An Awakening to Health Cookbook-Omnibus Edition" has combined "An Awakening to Health Cookbooks Volume I and Volume II". It has all the information of the previous volumes but now is in one book.

After healing from triple negative breast cancer, I wanted to emphasize the importance of a healthy lifestyle change. I am sharing these recipes and information for those who may have the desire to introduce healthy foods after or during certain therapies or to anyone who just want to be healthier. I am a chemotherapy and radiation-free cancer survivor and all my recipes have been developed during my alternative cancer treatment.

In my first book "An Awakening: How I Defeated Cancer without Chemotherapy or Radiation" I explain what I learned about breast cancer, what I went through, what changed my life and why I chose the alternative Gerson Therapy to heal from cancer rather than the "standard" cancer treatment. I explain what I learned and understand and believe to be true about chemotherapy and radiation and why I did not do it.

I have educated myself in healthy foods. I have applied what I learned that helped me heal to develop these healthy recipes by transforming my 50 years of cooking and baking recipes. They are healthier and have been modified to my new lifestyle. I have gathered juicing and smoothie recipes through the recent years which are healthy, nutritious and powerful without added sugar.

I believe that anyone can make healthy lifestyle changes; whether it is healing from cancer, diabetes, pancreatic disease, or any chronic disease. The main goal is to be healthy. Getting healthy and staying healthy is not easy. It takes work, hard work and commitment.

Disclaimer

The recipes in this book are not the authorized Gerson Therapy recipes unless otherwise stated. These are new and/or modified recipes I now use after the completion of my Gerson protocol.

Food Information

Organic and non organic foods

Organic produce is labeled organic when it has been grown, raised, harvested and packaged without the use of harmful chemicals, such as fertilizers, pesticides, insecticides, growth hormones or antibiotics. Organic also means the product has not been genetically modified (GM).

All recipes in this or any cookbook should be made with organic products or purchased from local farmers who do not use pesticides or GM products. GM products especially, use high amounts of pesticides to eradicate weeds which have become more resistant to pesticides and pesticides are a concern for 85 percent of Americans. According to the Reuters Group, which reports the latest news from around the world covering breaking news in business, politics and health, wrote an article about pesticides being tied to attention-deficit hyperactivity disorder (ADHD) in Children in the United States. Children exposed to pesticides could have a higher risk of ADHD and urges parents to always wash produce thoroughly.[1] In another study "Researchers tracked the pesticides' breakdown products in children's urine and found those with high levels were almost twice as likely to develop ADHD as those with undetectable levels." Children with higher pesticide exposure also have higher rates of IQ deficits and behavioral problems.[2]

Products that contain pesticides cannot be washed off or cooked out of fruit and vegetables. If pesticides are used in growing the food, the soil is contaminated and the food will grow with the pesticide. It is not just on the outside of the fruits or vegetables. Most alarming are the fruits and vegetables dubbed the "Dirty Dozen," which contain 47 to 67 pesticides per serving. For example, non-organic celery may contain up to 67 pesticides. These twelve foods are believed to be most susceptible because they have soft skin that tends to absorb more pesticides.

The Dirty Dozen include: celery, peaches, apples, domestic blueberries, nectarines, sweet bell peppers, spinach, cherries, potatoes, imported grapes, lettuce, and especially strawberries (must be organic). Consequently these foods should always be organically purchased. [3]

Not all non-organic fruits and vegetables have a high pesticide level. A number of non-organic fruits and vegetables dubbed the "Clean 15" contained little to no pesticides.

Food Information

The Clean 15 include: onions, avocados, sweet corn, pineapples, mango, sweet peas, asparagus, kiwi fruit, cabbage, eggplant, cantaloupe, watermelon, grapefruit, sweet potatoes, and broccoli. These are the only foods that would be permissible, however, it is recommended that all food should be organically grown or purchased from local farmers who do not use pesticides or GM products. [3]

It is also good to point out that there are a lot of organic processed foods. Care should be taken regarding all processed foods organic or not. Just because it says "organic" doesn't necessarily mean it is good for you. Get accustomed to reading labels for sugar, salt and fat content.

The most powerful foods to protect against cancer and other chronic diseases are; onions, beets, romaine lettuce, garlic cloves, purple cabbage, carrots, kale, Brussels sprouts, broccoli, celery, parsley, spinach, asparagus, turnips, tomatoes, fennel, lima beans, kidney beans, garden peas and adzuki. The most power herbs are; dill, basil, thyme, cayenne, coriander, peppermint, chamomile and anise. [4]

In my first book "An Awakening: How I Defeated Cancer without Chemotherapy or Radiation" Part III is research I have done on how we as consumers have been duped and manipulated about our food; how GM products are damaging our food which now require more pesticides; and what has happened to the meat we consume that is making us sick and why I do not eat meat and became a vegetarian.

Genetically Modified Food and Pesticides

The risk from pesticides on conventionally grown produce can vary from very low to very high, and it depends on the type of produce and the country where it's grown. Our food has been compromised with GM crops and carcinogenic pesticides. GMOs, genetically modified organisms, may be a potential cancer causing agent because of the high use of pesticides. GM crops are promoted as essential for an ever-growing population. However, the findings in the 2009 Failure to Yield Evaluating the Performance of Genetically Engineered Crops, by the Union of Concerned Scientists, reported in detail the overall, or combined, yield effect of GM food. After more than twenty years of research and thirteen years of commercialization in the United States, genetic modifications have done little to increase overall crop yields. Despite this, GM crops account for more than 80 percent of

North American crop acreage. Farmers do not choose GM crops. The industry destroys all options.

Mary Ellen Kustin, a senior policy analyst with Environmental Working Group (www.EWG.org) said "Instead of putting the brakes on the chemical treadmill, the government is on the fast track to approve more toxic weed killers. The USDA's decision to approve new varieties of genetically engineered corn and soybean seeds brings us one step closer to widespread use of a new toxic weed killer that would threaten children's health and the environment."

The American Academy of Pediatrics (AAP) points out that "Children encounter pesticides daily in air, food, dust, and soil and on surfaces through home and public lawn or garden application, household insecticide use, application to pets, and agricultural product residues. For many children, diet may be the most influential source, as illustrated by an intervention study that placed children on an organic diet (produced without pesticide). They observed drastic and immediate decrease in urinary excretion of pesticide metabolites."[3] Studies have shown that children exposed to pesticides have a greater risk of "preterm birth, low birth weight, congenital anomalies, pediatric cancers, neurobehavioral and cognitive deficits, asthma, and adverse neurodevelopment. Multiple case-control studies and evidence reviews indicate exposure to insecticides increase the risk of brain tumors and acute lymphocytic leukemia.[5]

Meat

The three most consumed types of animal protein in this country are beef, chicken, and pork. Animal feeding operations (AFOs) raise animals in confined situations. AFOs congregate animals, feed, manure and urine, dead animals, and production operations on a small land area. Feed is brought to the animals rather than the animals grazing or otherwise seeking feed in pastures, fields, or on rangeland. On these factory farms, animals eat commodity GM crops of primarily corn and soybeans. Millions of acres in the US produce animal feed from GM crops designed to resist weed killers such as Roundup.

In addition to pesticide laden feed, anabolic steroids are typically used in combinations. Measurable levels of growth-promoting hormones are found at slaughter in the muscle, fat, liver, kidneys and other organ meats, which according to the Food and Drug

Administration are "acceptable daily intakes" (ADIs) for these animal drugs.[6] Beef cattle are given anabolic steroids as well as estrogen, androgen and progestin, commonly called bovine growth hormones (BGH), developed by Monsanto, [7] to make them put on weight more quickly. The public health goals of regulation were to assure that drugs were safe and effective in animals and that any residues in food derived from such animals could be safely consumed by humans.[7] There has been more concern about industrial meat because of the environmental impact, inhumane animal conditions, and because too many antibiotics are fed to animals that are consumed for food.[8]

Regardless of warnings from scientists, such as Dr. Michael Hansen from the Consumers Union and Dr. Samuel Epstein from the Cancer Prevention Coalition, that milk or beef from rBGH (recombinant bovine growth hormone—a genetically engineered artificial hormone injected into dairy cows to make them produce more milk) injected cows contains substantially higher amounts of a potent colon and breast cancer tumor promoter called IGF-1, and despite evidence that rBGH milk or meat contains higher levels of pus, bacteria, and antibiotics, the FDA gave the hormone its seal of approval, with no real pre-market safety testing required.[9]

The conclusion is obvious to me. Americans need to promote good eating habits by making choices based on health, and moreover avoid harmful pesticides, and harmful drugs in our food. We need to "buy organic" and eat more fruits and vegetables. It is my belief that if everyone had a garden and were able to grow their own food without GM crops, we would have less pesticides and healthier food. It may sound idealistic but in my view, it could happen. There is an old saying "Rome wasn't built in a day."

Sulfites

Sulfites are a group of sulfur-based compounds that may occur naturally or may be added to food as an enhancer and preservative. In 1986, the FDA banned the use of sulfites on fruits and vegetables that are eaten raw, such as lettuce or apples. However, manufacturers can use sulfites in processed products but must list the compounds on their product labels. Sulfite also occurs naturally in the process of making wine and beer.

Food Information

In sensitive individuals, sulfites can cause allergic reactions. These allergic reactions can be relatively mild, such as hives, or more severe such as difficulty breathing and potentially fatal anaphylactic shock. For this reason, any food that contains sulfites in a ratio of at least 10 parts per million must include a warning on the label to enable sensitive individuals to avoid these foods. Some sensitive individuals also experience other side effects after eating sulfite-containing foods such as low blood pressure, flushed skin, stomach pain and diarrhea. When eating out, ask the chef or server if sulfites are used or added to food before or during preparation.

Webmd.com has listed the following foods that contain sulfites:

- Baked goods
- Soup mixes
- Jams
- Canned vegetables
- Pickled foods
- Gravies
- Dried fruit
- Potato chips
- Trail mix
- Beer and wine
- Vegetable juices
- Sparkling grape juice
- Apple cider
- Bottled lemon juice and lime juice
- Tea
- Many condiments
- Molasses
- Fresh or frozen shrimp
- Guacamole
- Maraschino cherries
- Dehydrated, pre-cut or peeled potatoes

If you are sensitive to sulfites, be sure to read the labels on all food items. These foods should be organic, sulfide and nitrate free when store-bought.

Food Information

Vitamin Supplements

Vitamins should be combined with your diet to maintain and improve your health. Remember to bring vitamin supplements with you while on vacation or on business trips. Dr. Russell Blaylock wrote *Natural Strategies for Cancer Patients* which speaks earnestly about vitamin supplements and nutrition. It is important to understand which supplements are healthy, especially for those who are dealing with cancer. Always try to use the form of supplements that most closely resembles the ones found in nature or those that have been known to have anticancer effects. The following are Dr. Blaylock's recommendations for the use of certain supplements.

Carotenoids found in certain plants and fruits that are red, orange or yellow serve as antioxidants and are a good source of vitamin A. Some allopathic (conventional) doctors state that an overdose of vitamin A can be harmful. That is true if it is consumed in supplements and not by juicing or eating these types of food.

Vitamin E comes in a gelatin capsule mixed with oil, which is usually soybean oil. Soy mimics estrogen and has been known to promote cancer growth and should be avoided. Never use vitamin E acetate as it is poorly absorbed and can cause problems with the liver and has very little anticancer effect. The most powerful form of vitamin E is vitamin E succinate. It is a white powder in a capsule.

Use vitamin C ascorbate rather than ascorbic acid. Ascorbic acid may cause stomach upset and cannot be absorbed well. High doses of ascorbic acid cause acid buildup and increase the risk of osteoporosis. Magnesium ascorbate and calcium ascorbate are the best in fighting osteoporosis. When vitamin C is taken, vitamin E should also be taken as they work well together. All nutrients interact in the body and this is especially true when dealing with cancer. It has been found that vitamin E reduces the risk of breast cancer and when selenium is added to the vitamin E, the risk reduces even more.

Selenium has attracted attention because of its antioxidant properties. It is a mineral found in soil, water, and some foods and is required in trace amounts for normal health, and is an essential element. The selenium antioxidants protect cells from damage. There is some evidence that selenium supplements may reduce the odds of prostate cancer. It is a safe mineral supplement and the general recommendation is 200 micrograms (mcg) a day. The safest limit for selenium is 400 mcg a day in adults. Anything above that is considered an overdose. Cancer patients should NOT take selenomethionine because of the methionine. Methionine is an amino acid that aids the liver in processing fats and it may cause conditions including recurrent bladder infections. Therefore, selenomethionine is not recommended for cancer or Parkinson disease patients. However, the body can typically meet the need for this nutrient through diet and would unlikely require supplementation for this purpose. The best source is *selenium-enhanced garlic.*

CoQ10 is a powerful nutrient and antioxidant that is a supplier of cellular energy and a cancer preventative. Cancer patients taking medicines must pay attention to CoQ10. Some medicines lower the body's supply of CoQ10. Statin drugs are prescribed to lower cholesterol; beta-blockers and clonidine are prescribed to lower blood pressure (clonidine is also used to treat ADHD); and anti-diabetic drugs for diabetics. All of these drugs cause damage to CoQ10 levels in the body and depletes other nutrients such as beta-carotene, folate, calcium, magnesium, zinc, phosphate, and vitamins A, B12, D, E, and K. It is important that a CoQ10 supplement be dissolved in an oil to be fully absorbed in the body. Empty the dry powder from a capsule onto a tablespoon of extra virgin olive or flax oil. It has very little taste.

Vitamin B Complex contains the essential B Vitamins - B1, B2, B3, B5, B6, B9, B12, plus vitamins Biotin, Choline, and Inositol. Vitamin B Complex is needed for the proper functioning of almost every process in the body. Vitamin B complex should be taken as a powder in capsule form with vitamin C as well as vitamin E. Used together these vitamins have been shown to assist each other.

All vitamins should be taken in a dry powder form in a capsule and never in a hard tablet. Tablets cannot be absorbed in the body because they contain binders like glue which keeps them from breaking and being damaged in shipping. Vitamins, important flavonoids, and antioxidants can come from a balanced diet. A balanced diet and taking the above vitamins are insurance to a healthy body.

Flavonoids

Flavonoids are found in the rind of green, citrus fruits and in rose hips and black currants. They are complex antioxidant chemicals and have been used in alternative medicine as an aid to enhance the action of vitamin C, to support blood circulation, treat allergies, viruses, arthritis and other inflammatory conditions. Flavonoids are often sold as an herbal supplement and work with other antioxidants to offer a system of protection.

Flavonoids numerous health benefit studies have shown their unique role in protecting vitamin C from oxidation in the body, thereby allowing the body to reap more benefits from vitamin C. Besides the important antioxidant effects, flavonoids help the body maintain health and function in many ways. They have been shown to be anti-mutagenic (reducing the frequency of mutation), anti-carcinogenic (tending to inhibit or prevent the activity of a carcinogen or the development of cancer), anti-aging, and promote structure and function in the circulatory system.

The main health benefits of flavonoids fall into two categories: health-promoting effects and therapeutic effects. The health-promoting effects include better eyesight, improved cardio-vascular health, increased capillary strength, improved structure of connective tissues and appearance of skin, and a stronger immune system. Flavonoids also offer the health-promoting effect of lowering the risk of some diseases, such as atherosclerosis, cancer, arthritis, and gastrointestinal disorders. Diets poor in fruit and vegetable intake deprive the body of important and vital antioxidants. The therapeutic applications include treating a variety of diseases and disorders. Several of these are coronary heart disease, allergies, inflammation, hemorrhoids, respiratory diseases, viral infections, some types of cancer, and peptic ulcers. Recent studies demonstrated that the powerful compounds of antioxidants in flavonoids can neutralize a host of dangerous free radicals and can chelate (remove) them which include dangerous free-radical generating metals as aluminum and some heavy metals including mercury, arsenic and lead. This is specifically important as we age because aluminum accumulation is common in disorders such as Alzheimer's and Parkinson's disease. These useful antioxidants may hold the key to controlling cancer as a preventative and treatment.[10]

Free radicals

I am not a chemist so the easiest way I know how to explain free radicals is that free radicals are unstable molecules. These molecules are responsible for aging, tissue damage, and diseases. These unstable molecules do not have an even number of electrons, so they are always searching for an extra electron to "steal" so they can become stable which destroys cell health.

Free radicals are "free" because they float around until they stabilize. They are "radical" in that these unstable molecules steal electrons from other molecules. A healthy molecule with an even number of electrons that had an electron stolen is now rendered uneven or unstable (missing an electron) so it becomes another free radical and has to steal electrons so they can become stable. This continuing effect can cause a lot of damage on healthy tissues. Once a molecule is damaged it needs to find another molecule to bond with and is further continuing the damaging process. In order to get free radicals under control, the body needs antioxidants.[11]

Antioxidants

Antioxidants are molecules found in fresh foods like vegetables and fruits, particularly in the vitamins found in these foods, including A, E, and beta-carotene. These antioxidants nutrients in our food can prevent or slow the oxidative damage to our body. When our body cells use oxygen, they naturally produce free radicals, a by-product, which can cause damage. Antioxidants act as "free radical scavengers" and prevent and repair damage done by free radicals. Health problems such as heart disease, macular degeneration, diabetes, cancer are all contributed by oxidative damage. Antioxidants also enhance the immune defense which lowers the risk of cancer and infection. [12]

Most Commonly Known Antioxidants:
- Vitamin A and Carotenoids Carrots, squash, broccoli, sweet potatoes, tomatoes (antioxidants are abundant in tomatoes), kale, collards, cantaloupe, peaches and apricots (bright-colored fruits and vegetables)
- Vitamin C Citrus fruits like oranges and lime etc., green peppers, broccoli, green leafy vegetables, strawberries (strawberries must be organic) and tomatoes
- Vitamin E Nuts & seeds, whole grains, green leafy vegetables, vegetable oil and liver oil (Whole grains are a good source of B vitamins, Vitamin E, magnesium, iron and

fiber, as well as other valuable antioxidants not found in some fruits and vegetables.)

- Selenium Fish and shellfish, red meat (limit red meat consumption), grains, eggs, chicken and garlic [12]

1. Pesticides Tied to ADHD in Children in U.S. Study May 17, 2010
   http://www.reuters.com/article/2010/05/17/us-adhd-pesticides-idUSTRE64G41R20100517
2. ADHD in kids tied to organophosphate pesticides
   http://www.reuters.com/article/us-adhd-pesticides-idUSTRE64G41R20100518
3. "Dirty dozen" produce carries more pesticide residue, group says By Danielle Dellorto, Senior Medical Producer June 1, 2010:
   http://www.cnn.com/2010/HEALTH/06/01/dirty.dounceen.produce.pesticide
4. Cancer Cure Foundation: http://www.cancure.org/12-links-page/37-cancer-fighting-foods-spices
5. Pesticide Exposure in Children-Sources and Mechanisms of Exposure-Chronic Effects:
   http://pediatrics.aappublications.org/content/130/6/e1757
6. Organic Consumers: https://www.organicconsumers.org/scientific/growth-hormones-fed-beef-cattle-damage-human-health
7. Richard A Merrill: Food Safety Regulation-Reforming the Delaney Clause
   http://aseh.net/teaching-research/teaching-unit-better-living-through-chemistry/historical-sources/lesson-2/Merrill-Food%20Safety%20Regulation-1997.pdf
8. Mother Earth News by Kim O'Donnell http://www.motherearthnews.com/real-food/food-policy/flexitarian-diet-zm0z14jjzmat.aspx
9. Pace Environmental Law Review by Sarah C. Wilson, "Hogwash! Why Industrial Animal Agriculture is Not beyond the Scope of Clean Air Act Regulation", 24 Pace Envtl. L. Rev. 439 (2010) Available at:
   http://digitalcommons.pace.edu/pelr/vol24/iss2/5
10. Bioflavonoids: Powerful Health Promoting Nutrients from Nature:
    http://www.metabolism.com/2014/02/16/bioflavonoids-powerful-health-promoting-nutrients-from-nature/
11. Health Check Systems: Understanding Free Radicals
    http://www.healthchecksystems.com/antioxid.htm
12. Health Castle: Simply Better Health: www.healthcastle.com/antioxidant.shtml

Food Information

Notes

Dos and Don'ts of Certain Foods

1. **Milk:** GIKids.org states that "Cow's milk protein intolerance (CMPI) is defined as an abnormal reaction by the body's immune system to protein found in cow's milk. The immune system normally protects our bodies from harm caused by bacteria or viruses. In CMPI the immune system reacts unusually to the protein found in cow's milk. This reaction can cause injury in the stomach and intestines." Cow's milk protein molecule has been linked to juvenile diabetes and closely resembles the islet cells of the pancreas that is responsible for insulin production; MSG also triggers this. If cow's milk products are used, it should only come from organic grass fed or flax meal fed cows that have not been injected or fed BGH (Bovine growth hormone) which induce more milk production. It is banned in Europe and Canada but not in the United States. The New England Journal of Medicine indicates that cows and chickens raised on corn contain twenty times more omega-6 than omega-3. Omega-6 increases inflammation, coagulation and the growth of cancer cells. Try goat milk or organic almond milk in lieu of whole milk if lactose intolerant and *avoid soy milk.*

Yogurt: Some people having problems digesting milk, i.e.; cramps, gas, diarrhea etc. are helped by eating yogurt a half hour prior to consuming milk. Yogurt is a fermented food. Fermented foods assist the stomach in creating good bacteria. Many yogurts are made using active, good bacteria, probiotics. Yogurt should be organic plain Greek yogurt. Four ounces of yogurt or other fermented milk products, i.e. buttermilk, can be consumed properly daily a half hour before eating or two hours after eating to get the most enzyme benefit.

Miguel Freitas, PhD, medical marketing manager for Dannon Co. says "The benefits associated with probiotics are specific to certain strains of these "good" bacteria. Many yogurts provide benefits by adjusting the micro flora (the natural balance of organisms) in the intestines, or by acting directly on body functions, such as digestion or immune function. However, keep in mind that the only yogurts that contain probiotics are those that say 'live and active cultures' on the label."

Also, remember that many yogurts come from cow's milk. So yogurt eaters will also get a dose of animal protein (about 9 grams per 6-ounce serving), plus several other nutrients found in dairy foods, like calcium, vitamin B-2, B-12, potassium, and magnesium. Yogurt should be purchased sugar free. Add your own fruit instead of purchasing it with fruit already processed in it. Fruit is a good natural sweetener and a little honey or 100% pure maple syrup can go a long way. If yogurt is not consumed, think about using probiotic supplements to the diet.

2. **Soy:**   Soy foods such as tofu, tempeh, edamame, miso, many veggie burgers, and other products made with soy flour contain isoflavones, which are chemically similar to estrogen. Two major types, genestein and daidzen, can act like estrogen in the body. These effects can be good or bad. While isoflavones may act like estrogen, they also have anti-estrogen properties. That is, they can block the more potent natural estrogens from binding to the estrogen receptor in cancer treatments. In addition, they stop the formation of estrogens in fat tissue and stimulate production of a protein that binds estrogen in the blood (to make it less able to bind to the receptor).

Like many plant-based foods, soy can be a healthy part of a nutritious diet. If you choose to eat soy, bear in mind two caveats; Soy is one of the most genetically modified foods in our country and 92 percent of the soybeans grown in the U.S. are genetically modified (that is likely not a healthy form); Genetically modified foods must be grown with more pesticides.

With the west's desire to mass-produce, shoyu has become tainted. Solvent processing takes the place of fermentation offering a faster way to get to the end product or so it seems. Unfortunately, according to the Food Standards Agency May 2010 report, the exposure to high temperatures during production incurs a group of chemicals known as chloropropanols. These contaminants have been found in high levels in acid-hydrolysed vegetable protein (vegetable protein processed with HCL or hydrochloric acid). Research has found a particular chemical, 3-monochloropropane-1,2diol (3-MCPD), which reacts with the human digestive lipase (lipase is an enzyme that catalyzes the hydrolysis of fats or lipids) which produce a carcinogenic compound. It has only been detected now because of the existence of more reliable methods. To top it off the chemical processing with hydrochloric acid produces glutamate in the form of MSG (mono-sodium glutamate) another infamous food additive.

Choose organic forms of soy instead

According to www.examiner.com/article/not-all-shoyu-is-good-for-you of Hawaii, traditional Chinese soy sauce or jiangyu were originally made with cooked soybeans (koji also known as huang and later ch'u) which is mixed with some wheat flour or wheat-flour based mold block. The koji is then fermented in large earthen pots that would store 12 to 60 gallons. Warming the pots in the sunlight accelerated the fermentation which assisted in improving color and aroma. After 3 to 6 months, a sieve or strainer made of bamboo was pushed down into the mash and held down with a stone. The liquid would then be ladled or siphoned out into smaller earthen jars covered with bamboo leaves or cloth. For 2 more weeks the pots are placed under the sun. This nutrient rich first grade soy sauce is not heated or pasteurized yet can be used. More salt and water is added to the mash and fermented for 1 to 2 months before a second lower grade drawing. This same method can bring forth more drawings producing much lower grades of soy sauce. This fermentation is able to produce health-boosting nutrients when eaten in moderation (recommended - no more than an ounce a day).

Avoid isolated soy protein

Isolated soy protein is found in a lot of bars, shakes, etc. as an ingredient and is in soy supplements. Soy protein is a protein that is isolated from soybean. It is made from soybean meal that has been hulled and defatted. Hulled and defatted soybeans are processed into three kinds of high protein commercial products: soy flour, concentrates, and isolates. Manufacturers take all of the other nutrients out of the soybean and retain only the protein as a cheap, easy way to increase the protein in these foods.

Dos and Don'ts of Certain Foods

Good soy products

Naturally fermented, unpasteurized keeping them a raw or "living food" containing probiotics, minerals, amino acids and enzymes:

Oshawa Organic Nama Shoyu

South River Miso

Eden Organics Shoyu Sauce

San J Tamari & Shoyu Sauce

Trader Joe's Soy Sauce

3. **Dried fruits:** Dried fruits are a healthy addition to a diet, but if portions sizes are not controlled they may have adverse effects on your weight. Portion sizes should be small, about 2 tablespoons. Snacking straight from the bag may lead to overeating. Read the nutritional facts on labels and avoid varieties that have added sugar or that is sweetened with fruit juice to minimize excessive calorie and sugar intake. All dried fruit must be organic, sulfide and nitrate free with no added salt as well. Sulfites can cause allergic reactions. So remember to buy organic, sulfide and nitrate free dried fruit.

4. **Sugars:**   The only sweeteners that should be used are; organic raw brown sugar, organic clear honey, organic 100% pure maple syrup, organic unsulfured molasses or organic Sucanat. Sucanat (or Rapadura) is dried, unrefined cane juice. Its primary benefit is that it is unrefined which means that it still has essential trace minerals and is nearly in its natural form. Because it is in its natural form, the body can metabolize it slightly slower; does not cause blood levels to sharply spike as white sugar does and the body will actually obtain some small nutritional benefit from consuming it.

White sugar is cane juice that has been separated, stripped and bleached to pull just the concentrated sugar out. This procedure makes white sugar highly concentrated and has absolutely no nutritional benefit and can be harmful when consumed regularly. The large quantities of highly refined sugar, changes in methods of farming and the exposure to large amounts of chemical products in our food have altered our food, which made our food lose its nutritional value, rendering them toxic. In the hunting and gathering era, food consisted of large amounts of vegetables and fruit and occasionally meat or eggs from wild animals. Those types of lifestyles provided a balance between fatty acids like omega-6 and omega-3 and there was very little sugar or flour.

Aspartame is a poor sugar substitute and is becoming a major substance in our diet and the health effects are profound, per Dr. Russell Blaylock, (board certified neurosurgeon, author and lecturer and an expert on nutrition and toxins in food, cookware, teeth, and vaccines). It should never have been approved but it was approved over the objections of some of the major neuroscientists and toxicologists who serve on the board of the FDA. It was approved for monetary reasons.

5. **Oils and Fats:** The research in today's Western diet or the SAD reveals that over half of the calories come from *refined sugars* (cane and beet sugar, corn syrup, etc.), bleached *refined flour* (white flour, white bread, white pasta, pastries, pizza, etc.) and *vegetable oils* (soybean, sunflower, corn and trans fats are found in margarine, processed foods such as cookies, crackers, potato chips, etc.). These three sources do not contain any proteins, vitamins, mineral, or omega-3 fatty acids which our bodies need to function properly and directly fuel the growth of cancer and promotes obesity.

To maintain proper oil content, limit saturated fats
- Avoid fried and barbecued foods cooked in fats that are solid at room temperature. These fats are typically saturated and raise the cholesterol more than anything else in the diet.
- Avoid fats such as margarines and vegetable shortenings, which are hydrogenated and are called trans-fats. (Use organic non-hydrogenated shortening substitute like palm oil.)

Dos and Don'ts of Certain Foods

- Include healthy fats (organic flax oil, hemp oil, canola oil, extra virgin olive oil, avocado oil, 100% pure natural, raw avocados, nuts, and seeds)
- Although butter is a saturated fat, it is healthier than other animal fats if it is organic butter that is made from organic grass fed or flax meal fed cows that have not been injected or fed BGH. It is still a good idea to limit any saturated fats.

Lately olive oil has come under scrutiny and label reading is a must to ensure you stay healthy. In September 2013 the U.S. International Trade Commission, released a report—"Olive Oil: Conditions of Competition between U.S. and Major Foreign Suppler Industries"—evidence of rampant fraud was found. "The United States does not have mandatory testing, nor does it impose penalties for noncompliance. This lack of enforcement has resulted in a long history of fraudulent practices (adulteration and mislabeling) in the olive oil sector." [1]

In the June 19, 2013 Consumer Reports News it was found that only 9 of the 23 olive oils from Italy, Spain and California tested, passed as being extra virgin olive oil even though all of them claimed so on the label. "Olive oil marketers aim to differentiate their products by brand and level of quality, but price remains one of the most important factors in U.S. consumer purchasing decisions. This is due, in part, to a lack of consumer awareness of quality differences. U.S. consumers are generally unfamiliar with the range of olive oil grades and uses".[1]

What is Extra Virgin Olive Oil?
- Oil must come from fresh olives that were milled within 24 hours of their harvest
- Oil must be extracted by mechanical means (cold-pressed), not from heat or chemicals
- Oil must not be treated chemically in any way
- Extra virgin oil is in fact fresh olive juice

- Olives are a fruit which contain natural antioxidants that protect the plant during its lifetime. When the olive tree is very old it contains more of these antioxidants. This is one of the reasons that olive trees are often hundreds of years old and create antioxidant rich products.[2]

In July 2010 the UC Davis Olive Center issued a report showing that 69 percent of imported olive oils labeled as "extra virgin" failed the International Olive Council (IOC) sensory standard — in other words, these oils were defective and failed to meet the international standard for extra virgin olive oil. In the months since the release of the study, similar quality problems have been found in Andalusia, the world's most productive olive oil region, by Spanish authorities. In the same report, 83 percent of the imported samples that failed the IOC/USDA sensory standards also failed the German/Australian 1,2-diacylglycerol content (DAGs) standard. Two additional imported samples that met the IOC/USDA sensory standard for extra virgin failed the DAGs standard.[3]

Tips to recognize real Extra Virgin Olive Oil from altered oil
- Ensure that the oil is labeled "extra virgin".
- Labels that read "pure" or "light" oil, "olive oil" and "olive pomace oil"—have undergone chemical refinement. Light olive oil or a blended olive oil isn't virgin quality and inexpensive extra virgin olive oil may not be real.
- Olive oil in dark bottles protects the oil from oxidation and is a sign it is real olive oil and real extra virgin olive oil must have the International Olive Oil Council (IOC) seal.
- Read the harvesting date on the label for freshness.
- Real extra virgin olive oil will become thick and cloudy as it cools completely in the refrigerator. However, some oils made from high-wax olive varieties may solidify so all the tips must be verified to ensure it is real extra virgin olive oil.

Dos and Don'ts of Certain Foods

These olive oils have met the extra-virgin standards:

- Corto Olive Oil
- Kirkland Toscano (Costco's brand)
- Kirkland Organic (Costco's brand)
- Cobran Estate Olive Oil (Australia's most awarded extra virgin olive oil)
- California Olive Ranch
- Lucero (Ascolano)
- McEvoy Ranch Organic
- Ottavio and Omaggio are good oils at reasonable prices
- Whole Foods California 365 olive oils

6. **Vegetable shortening:** Vegetable shortening is a common ingredient used in cakes, pies, breads, doughnuts and other baked goods. It is also typically used in fast food restaurants to prepare fried foods such as onion rings, breaded fish and chicken, and breakfast sausage. Although vegetable shortening features prominently in SAD, they are loaded with unhealthy trans-fats. Trans-fats are in deep-fried, processed, sodas, fast food, etc. These foods are not healthy, obviously, yet Americans are still eating them. In order to regain health Americans need to change. Add organic butter from animals grass fed or flax fed, not injected with BGH. Organic butter should be used in a slightly larger ratio in lieu of shortening for delicious flaky pastries and biscuits. Organic and low-fat butters are best. However, if you do not wish to use butter, go for an organic non-hydrogenated butter substitute. They're lower in saturated fat than butter and are completely free of cholesterol. But it must be "non-hydrogenated". Most butter substitutes such as margarines and shortenings are made with partially hydrogenated oil, which is code for trans-fat. Zero trans-fats means "non-hydrogenated".

Some non-hydrogenated shortening substitutes:

(I use either one of these and both are excellent and these shortenings are vegan and contain no dairy, soy or canola.)

- Spectrum Naturals Organic Shortening uses organic palm oil, extracted by manual pressing without the use of harmful chemicals. The oil is refined using a certified organic, chemical free process. The palm oil is then whipped using nitrogen, resulting in creamy consistency similar to conventional shortening.
- Nutiva's shortening is certified organic and non-GMO verified blend of cold pressed coconut and palm oils. It is the best choice for baked goods such as pie crusts, biscuits and cookies.

7. **Wheat:** A German biologist, Otto Heinrich Warburg won the Nobel Prize over 75 years ago for first uncovering cancer cells' massive dependence on sugar as a fuel source. He discovered that the metabolism of malignant tumors is largely dependent of glucose consumption. White flour turns into glucose. Sugar does not cause cancer but sugar feeds cancer! Physicians have been exposed to this information for 75 years, when most of your great grandparents were alive. Now Harvard researchers confirm this again, that some foods like sugar can increase the growth and spread of cancer. However, oncologists in many cases, allow their patients to eat these types of foods, especially sugar. Sugar feeds every cell in our body—even cancer cells. In my experience with oncologists there seems to be a consensus to negate this fact. On one of my visits to my oncologist I saw bowls of candy on the counters of the lobby area. I noted my observation to my oncologist as I was leaving his office. I asked why he had bowls of candy on the counters for cancer patients when it is known that sugar feeds cancer cells and should be removed from the cancer patient's diet. He preferred to stick to the fact that sugar does not cause cancer. I agreed that this was true and affirmed that sugar feeds it. He said I didn't know what I was talking about and there was no proof. I don't see him anymore.

Unfortunately, attitude has not changed the clinical protocols for the average oncologist. People must cut back the intake of white flour and refined sugar. Eating multigrain bread (bread with organic oatmeal, rye, flaxseed, barley, etc.) and sourdough bread (not common chemical baker's yeast as it raises the sugar level in bread) is essential in order to slow down the assimilation of the sugars coming from wheat.

William Davis, MD, author of "Wheat Belly" and a cardiologist states that today wheat is not the sturdy staple our forefathers ground into their daily bread. Today's wheat has been genetically modified (altered) to provide processed-food manufacturers the greatest yield at the lowest monetary cost. However, this "cost" is to the detriment of our health. Today's wheat causes blood sugar to spike more rapidly and has addictive properties that cause a roller coaster ride of hunger, overeating, and fatigue. This has connections to weight gain and adverse health effect from diabetes to heart disease. A loaf of bread, biscuits or pancake today is different from a thousand years ago as there are biochemical changes in the wheat protein structure. Be very wary of restaurant breads and what is contained in restaurant foods. If you must eat out, choose a restaurant that offers vegetarian and/or organic foods and stay away from fast food restaurants.

If you do not wish to use the any wheat, try this gluten free flour in recipes:
Gluten-Free Flour Blend: Combine 2 cups rice flour, 2/3 cup potato starch, 1/3 cup tapioca flour and 1 teaspoon xanthan gum. Use appropriate amount for the recipe and store the remainder in container with tight-fitting lid and stir before using.

8. **Gluten:**   Gluten causes inflammation in the small intestines of people with celiac disease. Eating a gluten-free diet helps people with celiac disease control their signs and symptoms and prevent complications. If you know you have a gluten problem, switching to a gluten-free diet is a big change and, like anything new, it takes some getting used to and is another life style change.

Many healthy and delicious foods are naturally gluten-free:
Beans, seeds, nuts, in their natural and unprocessed form, are naturally gluten-free. However it is important to know that organic almonds are always steam pasteurized treated, and truly raw almonds can still be purchased either at farmers markets or

farm stands. Some almond brand marked "natural" is treated with the toxic PPO gas[4] so label reading is important. Eggs are gluten-free and free range is more about their lower cholesterol content, high levels of vitamin D and choline, and omega-3 content. Make it a point to only choose high-quality organic, free range, omega-3 eggs, and buy local organic free range eggs as much as possible.

If gluten intolerant, it's important to make sure these foods are not processed or mixed with gluten-containing grains, additives or preservatives. Many grains and starches can be part of a gluten-free diet such as: amaranth, arrowroot, buckwheat, corn, cornmeal, flax, gluten-free flours (rice, corn, potato and bean, hominy—corn, millet, and quinoa) rice (brown or basmati rice—never use ordinary white or instant rice), sorghum, tapioca and teff—one of the earliest plants domesticated. In general, unless foods are labeled as gluten-free or made with corn, rice, or other gluten-free grain they should be avoided if grains are not tolerated. Also be alert for other products that may be eaten or that could come in contact with your mouth that may contain gluten.

Other gluten foods include:
Food additives, such as malt flavoring, modified food starch and others
Medications and vitamins that use gluten as a binding agent

9. **Pasta:** Pasta is included in some of the recipes, but never use pasta made from white refined flour even if you do not have a gluten problem. Try some of the following pastas:

Bean and legume pastas
- **Cellophane noodles:** Chinese: fen si, fun sie; Japanese: sarifun, harusame; Korean: dang myun; Vietnamese: bun tau. Cellophane noodles are made from mung bean flour, these semi-translucent noodles turn clear when cooked and often are called glass noodles or bean thread noodles. They can be quickly stir-

fried or braised with other ingredients. The noodles are nearly pure starch, containing almost no protein, vitamins, or minerals.

- **Lentil pasta:** Made from ground lentils, this pasta has a meaty, rich, slightly peppery lentil flavor.

Grain pastas

- **Amaranth pasta:** Light brown in color and resembling whole-wheat pasta, amaranth pasta has the bite and consistency of regular pasta.
- **Corn pasta:** Corn pasta has about half the protein of regular pasta, but otherwise is nutritionally comparable. It is a good alternative for people allergic to wheat.
- **Milo pasta:** Milo, also known as grain sorghum, produces pasta with a slightly sweet, interesting flavor.
- **Millet pasta:** Millet is ground into flour and used to make pasta, most often small macaroni.
- **Oat pasta:** Oat flour makes satisfying pasta, most often in small macaroni shapes.
- **Quinoa pasta:** Quinoa is ground into a flour to make pasta the color of whole-wheat pasta but with the consistency of regular pasta.
- **Rice noodles:** Chinese: sha he fen, sa ho fun, gan he fen, gon ho fun; Vietnamese: bun, banh pho, banh hoi. Dried Asian rice noodles, which are usually sold coiled in bags, are either thread-thin or spaghetti-like. The thinner form is usually sold as rice vermicelli; the thicker form is called rice sticks. Typically, they are boiled or stir-fried for use in salads or soups. Fresh rice noodles, a standard feature of the Chinese brunch called dim sum, are sold in wide sheets for making dishes similar to dumplings, or cut into ¾ inch-wide ribbons. They are precooked and are ready to eat once boiling water is poured over them. Like cellophane noodles, rice noodles are almost pure starch and are low in protein.
- **Rice papers (rice wrappers):** These round translucent sheets of dried rice noodle are used in Vietnamese cooking as a wrapper for food. They do not need to be cooked; they are softened in warm water until flexible and then wrapped around various fillings.

Dos and Don'ts of Certain Foods

- **Rice pasta:** Both white and brown rice are used to make rice pasta. These pastas tend to be fairly tender and may not hold up well when served with heavy sauces.
- **Teff pasta:** Generally made from a combination of teff flour and another grain, it can be used like regular pasta.
- **Barley pasta:** This slightly nutty-tasting pasta is made from barley flour.
- **Buckwheat noodles:** Chinese: qiao mian; Japanese: soba; Korean: naeng myun. These flat, gray Asian noodles are made from buckwheat and wheat flour, or just buckwheat flour. They are rich in protein. They may be served hot (usually in a broth) or chilled, accompanied by a dipping sauce. In Japan, soba noodles are eaten for lunch or as a snack, and are essential to a traditional dish prepared at New Year's.
- **Buckwheat pasta:** While buckwheat flour is used in Asian noodles, it is also used to make popular Italian pasta called pizzocheri. It has a rich, nutty flavor and a chewy texture.

Root and tuber pastas
- **Cassava pasta:** Made from the starchy tropical tuber known as cassava, this very white pasta tastes similar to wheat pasta. It does not expand a great deal when cooked.
- **Jerusalem artichoke pasta:** This pasta is made from a combination of Jerusalem artichoke flour and wheat flour. Organic pastas made with Jerusalem artichoke flour are rich source of protein and dietary fiber as compared to traditional pasta. Jerusalem artichoke flour also naturally contains inulin (found in plant foods as a water-soluble dietary fiber), a probiotic that stimulates the growth of beneficial bacteria in the digestive tract that in turn aids digestion and lowers blood pressure and cholesterol.
- **Malanga pasta**: The starchy tropical tuber Malanga resembles a potato. Malanga is used to make a pasta that closely resembles wheat pasta and has similar nutrients as potatoes

Dos and Don'ts of Certain Foods

- **Potato pasta**: Potato flour pasta sometimes has the addition of rice flour. This pasta is fairly sturdy and holds up well with rich sauces.
- **Shirataki pasta**: This root plant Shirataki grown in many parts of Asia. At times called the miracle noodle. These noodles are filled with fiber and claim to have no calories or carbohydrates.
- **White sweet potato pasta**: White sweet potato is starchy and has a slightly sweet flavor and can use these noodles in soups or stir-fries.
- **Yam pasta**: Like white sweet potato pasta, this has a slightly sweet flavor.

10. **Bread:**   Now that you understand wheat and gluten, if bread is eaten, its consumption should be held to a minimum and should **not** be a substitute for any items. Bread should be sourdough rye or plain sourdough. Sourdough bread is more digestible as the lactic acids make the vitamins and minerals more available to the body and slows down the rate at which glucose is released into the blood-stream. Sourdough is a bread product made by a long fermentation of dough using naturally occurring lactobacilli and yeasts. Individuals with grain allergies often tolerate wheat products that have first been soaked, sprouted or fermented like sourdough; but many must avoid wheat altogether even when it has been properly prepared.

If baking is enjoyed, follow the homemade sourdough and rye bread recipes. Use organic unbleached einkorn wheat flour or unbleached all purpose einkorn wheat flour or its evolutionary successor emmer wheat flour to replace the modern industrial wheat flours. This ancient einkorn or emmer wheat is a lower gluten wheat alternative. It can be purchased on-line or from organic or natural grocery stores in your area.

Homemade sourdough einkorn flour bread is a little heavier, but it has a richer flavor and I noticed that I don't have a bloated feeling or fatigue the next day. In the Sourdough and Breads section you will learn to appreciate rye and sourdough, how to make and care for your own sourdough starter.

For those who have neither the time nor the inclination for bread making, properly made sourdough breads are now commercially available. But please be a label reader, especially for salt content.

11. **Monosodium glutamate (MSG):** Glutamic acid is an amino acid that occurs naturally in many foods and can be broken down slowly during the digestive process. However, MSG is also called various types of other glutamates such as hydrolyzed protein, vegetable protein extract, autolyzed yeast extract or natural flavor. These are all toxic. During WWII American scientists analyzed the Japanese food rations to see why it tasted better than the American GI rations. The findings were that MSG was added and this information was passed to food manufacturers. The major food processors then began using this additive in processing the American food. MSG fools the brain into thinking something tastes better than it really does so manufacturers use it in lieu of quality ingredients. MSG does not have its own taste but it is a flavor enhancer and is used in virtually every canned, packaged and processed food sold in stores today.

MSG has been linked to obesity and adding aspartame with MSG greatly magnifies the bodies' toxicity in blood levels. MSG's can be labeled "contains no MSG" on food packages because the FDA says if it's not 99% pure, it can be labeled anyway the food manufacturers wish. In truth, there are no regulations that require the identification (labeling) of all processed free glutamic acid (MSG) present in processed food. Consumers have no way of knowing if there is MSG in the processed food they consume or if there is any, how much or how little there is. [5,6]

Some hidden MSG labeling:
- Glutamate anything
- Hydrolyzed anything
  - Hydrolyzed Soy Protein
  - Hydrolyzed Whey Protein

Dos and Don'ts of Certain Foods

    Hydrolyzed Corn Gluten

    Hydrolyzed Vegetable Broth

    Hydrolyzed Corn Protein Concentrate

    Hydrolyzed Whey Protein Concentrate

- Yeast Extract
- Malt Extract
- Soy Sauce Extract
- Yeast Nutrient
- Nutritional Yeast
- Torula Yeast (byproduct of the paper products) used as flavor enhancer
- Caseinate anything [5, 6]

A member of my family visited and brought a bag of organic Kettle Brand barbeque chips. I ate some and within 20 minutes I had sores on my tongue and inside of my cheek. I brushed my teeth as soon as my mouth became sore. My mouth did feel better.

Then I read label. Kettle Brand® Potato Chips Backyard Barbeque™ Ingredients: Potatoes, safflower and/or sunflower and/or canola oil, honey powder (dried cane syrup, honey), rice flour, sugar, salt, onion powder, yeast extract, tomato powder, paprika, torula yeast, garlic powder, chili pepper, citric acid, cayenne pepper, paprika extract (color), natural smoke flavor. This all looks good doesn't it? I thought so too until I researched "yeast extract and "torula yeast" – HIDDEN MSG! Remember: MSG's can be labeled "contains no MSG" on food packages because the FDA says if it's not 99% pure it can be labeled anyway the food manufacturers wish! Just because it says "organic" doesn't mean it is healthy! This manufacture chose not to say "contains no MSG" and they don't have to. This is what our children are eating most; Monosodium glutamate or MSG (often added to Chinese food) Soy and steak sauces.

Become a wise label reader! If children are consuming glutamates at an early age, they are destroying nerve cells in the brain. Now we know that glutamates during a child's growth period, the child becomes obese and there is also a strong link between obesity and Alzheimer's disease. Diabetes, cancer, and obesity, can be directly related to the intake of aspartame and MSG. If you want the body to function properly, do not use it!

12. **Salt:**   Like MSG, the same is true for salt. The Center for Science in the Public Interest is a nutritional lobbying group and claims that sodium chloride, common table salt, can be very dangerous to eat. They are so concerned; they are working to get the status of salt changed so that it can go from its current unregulated status to a status which the FDA has authority to regulate. Most common table salt and "fake sea salt" are made up of chemicals that pollute the body and wreak havoc on health. These salts have been altered in processing and stripped of its minerals which caused blood pressure fluctuations instead of stabilizing it. High levels of this salt in the diet can increase risk of developing cardiovascular events and chronic disease because of elevated blood pressure, arteriosclerosis and diabetes. It is about 97.5% sodium chloride and contains aluminum derivatives such as sodium solo-co-aluminate, an anti-caking additive which allows the table salt to flow easily without clumping (also found in dried egg-yolk products) and an excess of aluminum intake leads to neurological disorders. It also contains iodine to prevent goiters. However, not enough iodine can be obtained from table salt to maintain optimal health, unless a dangerous amount of sodium is consumed. Table salt and "fake sea salt" also contain MSG and/or white processed sugar to help stabilize the iodine. [7] If you really desire salt, think about healthy natural salts; Celtic and Himalayan salts.

Salt comparisons
Celtic Sea Salt has to pass rigid organic standards of the European and Australian Certification for purity. It has grayish hue and is naturally harvested in Brittany France near the Celtic Sea using a 2,000-year old Celtic method preserving its nutrition profile. Celtic Sea Salt retains all the minerals from sea water and sea water

contains the concentration of minerals washed down for thousands of years. The mineral content is better, more balanced, and has double the magnesium and 1/5 the sodium of Himalayan Salt.

Himalayan Salt has a translucent pink color and contains all of the 84 elements found in your body. It is however lower in electrolytes like magnesium than Celtic Sea Salt which is an important mineral for the body. It contains minerals that were washed down from the soil and deposited at the time of formation so it has a more salty taste than Celtic Sea Salt, more taste like refined salt. [8, 9]

These two salts contain *no* detectable toxins such as arsenic, cadmium, lead, nickel or mercury but have minerals and elements necessary for your optimal health.

People have a tendency to over salt foods. Consequently they become dehydrated and don't drink enough water for what is necessary in the body. Sodas have a high rate of sugar and also contain salt which makes a body thirsty and a desire to drink more. Regularly consuming too much salt can cause water retention and chronic health problems. Eight 8 ounce glasses of water should be consumed daily. Fresh squeezed juice or herbal tea can be substituted for water. Sodas, coffees and caffein-ated teas are not a substitute for hydrating the body. Some of the recipes in this book contain salt. Therefore if any salt is used it is recommended to be careful of salt intake.

Avoid high-salt foods

Salt and seasoned salt or salt seasonings; store-bought boxed mixes of potatoes, rice, or pasta; canned meats; canned soups and vegetables; cured or processed foods; ketchup, mustard, salad dressings, other spreads, and canned sauces; packaged soups, gravies, or sauces; pickled foods; processed meats; lunch meat, sausage, ba-con, and ham can also contain nitrates besides salt; salty snack foods also may have powerful toxins with high doses of MSG as well as sodium.

Dos and Don'ts of Certain Foods

Low-Salt Cooking Tips:

- Get in the habit of reading food labels.

- Use fresh organic ingredients and/or foods with no salt added.

- For favorite recipes, you may need to use other ingredients and delete or decrease the salt you would normally add. Salt can be removed from any recipe except from those containing yeast.

- Avoid convenience foods such as canned soups, entrees, and vegetables; pasta and rice mixes; frozen dinners; instant cereal; pudding, gravy, and sauce mixes; and fast food restaurants.

- Use organic fresh or frozen vegetables or organic no added salt canned vegetables and beans (well drain and rinse canned foods before they are prepared).

- Avoid mixed seasonings and spice blends that contain salt, such as onion or garlic salts. After about 2 weeks, your body will adjust and you will not miss the added salt in your diet. So be persistent and be patient, it can happen. And, you will actually taste your food!

1. Olive Oil: Conditions of Competition between U.S. and Major Foreign Supplier Industries (Inv. No. 332-537, USITC publication 4419, July 2013) is available on the USITC's Internet site at http://www.usitc.gov/publications/332/pub4419.pdf.

2. What is Real Olive Oil: http://realfoodforlife.com/which-olive-oil-to-buy-the-olive-oil-fraud

3. Tests indicate that imported "extra virgin" olive oil often fails international and USDA standards - UC Davis Olive Center, July 2010 http://olivecenter.ucdavis.edu/research/files/oliveoilfinal071410updated.pdf

4. Food Identity Theft: www.foodidentitytheft.com and search almonds

5. Complete listing and be amazed how manufacturers hide MSG from us www.saynotomsg.com/basics_list.php

6. Truth in Labeling: www.truthinlabeling.org/presentregulations.html

7. The Truth about Salt http://healthwyze.org/reports/115-the-truth-about-table-salt-and-the-chemical-industry

8. All Natural Health http://www.alnaturalhealth.com/blog/is-himalayan-rock-salt-better-than-celtic-sea-salt/

9. Dr Axe Food is Medicine: http://draxe.com/10-benefits-celtic-sea-salt-himalayan-salt/

Dos and Don'ts of Certain Foods

Notes

Lifestyle Diets

It is important to understand what a healthy diet is and how to keep your immune system viable. Lifestyle diets that reduce inflammation in the body to promote healthy disease fighting immune systems are Vegetarian diet, Mediterranean diet, Indian, Asian cuisine and now the Nordic Diet.

I first learned about the Mediterranean diet at my alternative cancer center that I could implement after completing my two years of the Gerson Therapy if I desired. I was reminded of the diet again at the University of Stanford's Cancer Center. I now do a combination of the Mediterranean diet (traditional dietary patterns of Greece, Southern Italy, Croatia and Spain) and the Nordic diet (seasonal dietary patterns of Norway, Sweden and Denmark). Both the Mediterranean diet and the Nordic diet encourage people to eat less red meat and more fish and tend to lean toward eating more vegetables. I have modified these diets for me to be primarily vegetarian. I do not eat beef, pork, or poultry but I do eat fish once in a while and enjoy an occasional glass of red wine. Neither vegetarians nor vegans eat meat. However, vegetarians tend to consume dairy products and eggs while vegan avoids all animal products, including eggs and dairy. Therefore, because I am a vegetarian, some of the recipes contain organic butter, free range eggs, low fat cottage cheese and low fat natural cheeses as well as wild fish—never use farmed fish due to contaminants.

The Mediterranean diet is a lifestyle not a short term fad diet. In his book *Health via Food*, William Howard Hay wrote, "First let us get rid of this accepted idea that any modification of conventional habit in foods is diet, for the diet is a restriction of eating for some definite purpose, as the relief from some specific diseased state. What we mean here by diet is nothing of the kind, but merely a normalizing of the daily intake of foods to bring this measurably toward the ideal."

These diets recommend eating fatty wild fish which are rich in omega-3, organic dairy products from animals fed on grass or flax meal, and eggs from hens grown in a natural environment (free range, cage free) or fed flax meal or non GMO food.

Red meat should only be eaten two times a month or once every two weeks and should be organic meats from animals fed grass or flax meal or hunted wild. Meat is high in Omega-6 fatty and even though Omega 6 fatty acids do not cause inflammation, the high intake in conjunction with the continuous daily exposures to exogenous toxins (chemicals that are made outside of your body and can harm your cells if they are ingested, inhaled, or absorbed into your bloodstream) will continuously initiate or promote the inflammatory response which prevent cell repair and eventually lead to disease.

If you eat meat, always eat vegetables when consuming meat without gravies or sauces made from meat fat. The flavonoids in the vegetables will neutralize the carcinogens in the meat, especially seared and charcoal BBQ'd meats. If BBQing is a choice it should be done on a gas grill. Meat is not recommended for cancer patients. In October, 2015 the World Health Organization has deemed that processed meats—such as bacon, sausages and hot dogs—can cause cancer. Although eating meat has known health benefits, it also points out that the cancer risk increases with the amount of meat consumed. Every beef eating American, for more than 50 years, has been exposed to steroids and growth hormones and now are additionally exposed to pesticide laden genetically modified crops that are fed to animals. Milk or beef cattle injected with growth hormones contain substantially higher amounts of potent cancer tumor promoting substances. According to articles in www.foodmatters/tv and mercola.com, conventionally raised cows and beef cattle have growth hormone laden milk or meat and contain higher levels of pus, bacteria, and antibiotics.

When a meal is prepared, raw and cooked vegetables should be added to the meal. Cooked vegetables should either be steamed or cooked at low heat enough to breakdown the plant cells but not as thoroughly as a fully cooked vegetable. Use only distilled water or purified water or use a reverse osmosis filter for cooking and cleaning fruits and vegetables.

Fruit should be eaten after you have finished a meal. Fruit in green juices makes the vegetable juice more palatable and sweeter. (Because of the sugar, cancer patients should only have small amounts of fruit until cancer is under control.)

Because the risks and the benefits vary by product—meat is different from produce. There are problems with E coli in organically grown and conventionally grown produce and with salmonella in organically raised and conventionally raised chicken and other meats. However, there are more concerns of high pesticide residue in conventionally grown produce and antibiotics and hormones in milk and meat products conventionally raised. Organic milk or organic meats do not contain antibiotics or hormones.

Mediterranean Diet Pyramid

A contemporary approach to delicious, healthy eating

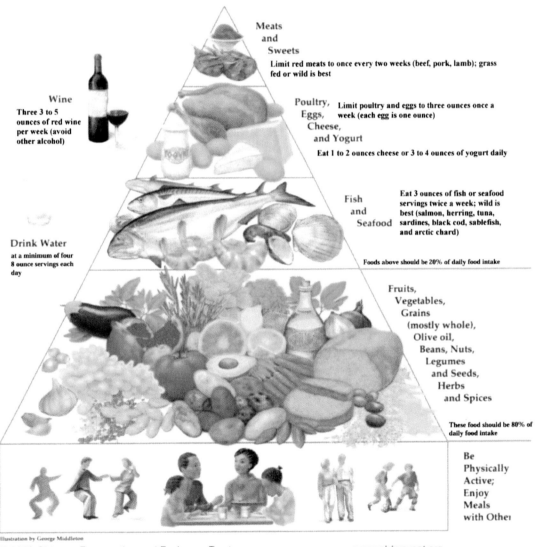

Meats and Sweets
Limit red meats to once every two weeks (beef, pork, lamb); grass fed or wild is best

Wine
Three 3 to 5 ounces of red wine per week (avoid other alcohol)

Poultry, Eggs, Cheese, and Yogurt
Limit poultry and eggs to three ounces once a week (each egg is one ounce)

Eat 1 to 2 ounces cheese or 3 to 4 ounces of yogurt daily

Fish and Seafood
Eat 3 ounces of fish or seafood servings twice a week; wild is best (salmon, herring, tuna, sardines, black cod, sablefish, and arctic chard)

Drink Water
at a minimum of four 8 ounce servings each day

Foods above should be 20% of daily food intake

Fruits, Vegetables, Grains (mostly whole), Olive oil, Beans, Nuts, Legumes and Seeds, Herbs and Spices

These food should be 80% of daily food intake

Be Physically Active; Enjoy Meals with Other

Illustration by George Middleton

Household Tips

Rid your house of as many chemicals as possible.

1. Air Freshener – Commercial air fresheners mask smells and coat nasal passages to diminish the sense of smell. Simmer a pot of water on the stove with herbs or pure essential oils for fragrance.

2. Aerosols – should be avoided, especially the use of pesticides. Spraying the yards with Roundup and other weed control, herbicides, and pesticides are dangerous. Even in extremely low doses these chemicals are powerful neurotoxins and they suppress immunity and some produce autoimmune disease and are carcinogens. Children and animals play in the yard with these toxins and bring them into the house on their feet. The toxins remain in the body for decades. The strong smell of tea tree oil naturally repels ants and other insects. I recommend making a natural insect repellent by mixing a few drops of tea tree oil with coconut oil in a spray bottle.

3. Baking Soda – cleans, deodorizes (including carpet), softens water and scours.

4. BonAmi – is the best cleanser as it is a biodegradable cleaning agent that is made from limestone, feldspar, coconut and corn husks and baking soda.

5. Cornstarch – can be used to clean windows as well as vinegar.

6. Hydrogen peroxide – can be used in lieu of chlorine in the laundry and when cleaning the kitchen or bathroom.

7. Isopropyl Alcohol – is an excellent disinfectant.

8. Lemon – is one of the strongest food-acids, effective against most household bacteria. Use it to wipe down bread boards after they are cleaned with soap and water.

9. Olive oil – can be used sparingly to clean stainless steel pots and pans with a scouring pad. When dusting furniture, use vinegar and olive oil on a rag and apply to any surface and wood.

10. Simple Green – is an effective, non-toxic, non-flammable, biodegradable and non-abrasive general house hold cleaner.

Household Tips

11. Soap – that is unscented in liquid form like Castile or other biodegradable liquids are excellent for cleaning. Biodegradable flakes or powders are great for laundry.

12. Tea Tree Oil – is an antiseptic. For skin conditions, simply crushed tea tree leaves can be applied to cuts, burns, and infections. If no leaves are available apply a few drops of oil to affected area. It is also good to stop itchy insect bites. Adding a few drops of this oil during the wash cycle will make your laundry smell crisper and kill organisms lurking in your washer.

13. White Distilled Vinegar – cuts grease, removes odors, some stains and wax build-up. Fabric softeners can cause asthma problems so it is recommended to use a ¼ cup of distilled vinegar be used in the laundry instead. I use it and it works great.

Juicing Tips

It's easy to make fresh juices and your health is important and needs to be taken seriously. All you need is high-quality organic or locally grown produce which is free of pesticides.

1. All produce should be washed using purified or distilled water with vinegar.
2. Remove all pits from fruits before juicing. Seeds are permissible. However, it has been recently discovered that apple seeds contain natural arsenic and deseeding is recommended.
3. Remove toxic greens from carrots and rhubarb before juicing. All other produce with stems and leaves can be juiced with other vegetables and fruit.
4. Citrus juicers can be used for oranges, grapefruits, lemons or limes. However if using a masticating juicer skins need to be removed but leave on the white pithy part of the peel; it contains valuable "bioflavonoid" and vitamin C. Kiwi and papaya should also be peeled. Generally fruits and vegetables from foreign tropical countries use carcinogenic pesticides and sprays which are still legal, therefore it is important to read labels and make sure they read "organic certified".
5. Bananas and avocados do not contain enough water content and cannot be used in a masticating juicer. They are better for smoothies in a blender with juice added. However, bananas can be frozen and used in the masticating juicer to make banana ice cream.
6. To obtain the maximum nutritional value of juices, they should be consumed within 20 minutes.
7. If trying to lose weight, avoid or limit produce highest in sugar content.
8. Clean all juicers well after every use to prevent food contamination. [1]

Juicers

To obtain the best juices from fruit and green vegetables require a masticating juicer, not extracting juicers. A masticating juicer can cost between $200 and $2,500.

In my opinion, the following are some of the better masticating juicers:

- Omega Juicers – Omega has a variety of masticating juicers, range from $230 to $500
- Breville masticating slow juicer, range from $230 to $500
- Campion heavy–duty commercial juicer, range from $230 to $350 (this is our travelling juicer)
- Super Angel All Stainless Steel Twin Gear Juicer, range from $1,230 to $1,500
- Norwalk Masticating Juicer and hydraulic press are about $2,300 to $2,500 (this is our main home juicer)

In my opinion, the following are some of the better citrus juicer

- To obtain the best juices for citrus and are least likely to breakdown can be purchased from $25 to $200.
- Black & Decker Citrus Juicer CJ625; $25 to $75
- Winco JC-19 Citrus Juicer; $80
- Alpine Cuisine Heavy Duty Citrus Juice; $50 to $150
- Omega - C-10W - White Electric Citrus Juicer; $150
- Breville 800CPXL Juicer, cast iron citrus press; $200

Juicing Tips

Eating and Other Juicing Tips

It needs to be stated that even though the above juicers are the best for juicing, in my opinion, it is more important to juice as much as possible. Even using a blender for making smoothies of fruits and vegetables are better than not juicing at all. Juicing should be a major part of a healthy diet and it is important that people wanting to heal to at least start juicing and integrating juicing into their daily new lifestyle. It is the only way to obtain the daily nutrients a body needs to repair a damaged body or maintain a healthy body.

Most juicing purists and I may be called one, believe that freshly made juice consumed within twenty minutes of juicing improves the body's ability to use the juice enzymes. This is also recommended by the Gerson Therapy. However, recent studies have shown that many enzymes are preserved if the juice is kept cold in the refrigerator. Enzyme survival is temperature dependent and heat can quickly destroy them.

Some cancer patients may not have someone to assist them with daily juicing. New studies have shown that freezing juices can preserve some of the enzymes. Therefore, preparing a batch of juice over the weekend when you may have more time or have someone to help may be an option. Pour the juice in ten ounce mason jars leaving ¼ inch from the top, apply light pressure to seal the lid, and then freeze the jars. Remove what is needed for the next day, the night before, to thaw in the refrigerator. Please note that these are my suggestions and **not** recommended by the Gerson Therapy.[2] I am a cancer survivor because of the Gerson Therapy nutrition regimen. However, I feel it is important that those who are unable to do the full therapy should start maximizing their immune system as soon as possible with a "salad drink" of at least five vegetables and only one fruit. A healthy diet should be highly considered for anyone receiving chemotherapy and/or radiation to keep the immune system as healthy as possible.

To include an extra 5-10 serving of fruit and vegetables in one large glass offers enormous health benefits. Consuming more fruit and vegetables increases well-being and reduces chronic disease. Juicing removes the indigestible fiber which enables us to ingest a large quantity of fresh fruit and vegetables which may not be possible when eating them whole or even as a smoothie. Eating raw vegetables limits the amount of nutrients that can

Eating and Other Juicing Tips continued

be absorbed because most people chew only a few times then swallow. Chewing vegetables allows only 30 percent of the nutrients to be absorbed which means you have to eat a lot more to get the full amount of the nutrients. Sitting down to eat a small handful of parsley, 4 carrots, 8 kale leaves, 1 celery sticks, 1 cucumber and an apple is certainly not possible for most people. By juicing these, our body is able to enjoy a huge benefit of nutrients we can take in.

The body requires very little effort to absorb these nutrients in juice when insoluble fiber is removed. This can be very beneficial in cases where people are convalescencing, suffering with an illness, fatigued, stressed, suffering with a digestive disorder or any other condition that may affect their ability to absorb nutrients and digest their food.

Blending or juicing releases 90 percent more nutrients which also mean you are consuming raw fruits and vegetables. Keep vigilant. Staying healthy is more than just practicing a few good techniques when you don't feel well. It involves regular exercise, plenty of healthy foods, and staying hydrated throughout the day and juicing is a good nutrient filled way to keep hydrated.

To assist in doing daily juices, we purchased a second refrigerator for $150 at a used appliance store just to store our juicing vegetables. After we do our grocery shopping on Saturdays, I prepare my vegetable storage containers. I prepare six glass cake dishes that have plastic lids. Each container has two 10 ounce serving for my most important green juice. If washed and sealed properly in glass they will last up to six days. I tried putting them in plastic bags but the vegetables, especially the lettuce, spoiled within three days. Glass works the best. If we want to add cucumber we add it at the time we juice to keep it from spoiling. Many times I will substitute different greens than the Gerson Green Juice recipe so I can get a variety of vegetables. I also add ginger and turmeric my juices.

Eating and Other Juicing Tips continued

This particular week I had kale, spinach, romaine lettuce, Swiss chard, bell pepper, a small beet or beet leaves, celery, red leaf lettuce, turmeric, ginger and a granny smith apple. I change it up each week so I don't become bored with my green juices.

Our refrigerator easily holds the six containers, carrot, apples and oranges which are ready for use.

1. Juicing for Life book has many healthy juices and tips
2. Healing the Gerson Way, Defeating Cancer and Other Chronic Diseases book outlines a cancer defeating program for those with cancer or any other chronic disease.

Juicing Tips

Notes

Juicing with Gerson

"Degenerative diseases render the body increasingly unable to excrete waste materials adequately, commonly resulting in liver and kidney failure. The Gerson Therapy uses intensive detoxification to eliminate wastes, regenerate the liver, reactivate the immune system and restore the body's essential defenses—enzyme, mineral and hormone systems. With generous, high-quality nutrition, increased oxygen availability, detoxification, and improved metabolism, the cells—and the body—can regenerate, become healthy and prevent future illness.

Fresh pressed juice from raw foods provides the easiest and most effective way of providing high-quality nutrition. By juicing, patients can take in the nutrients and enzymes from nearly 15 pounds of produce every day, in a manner that is easy to digest and absorb.

Every day, a typical patient on the Gerson Therapy for cancer consumes up to thirteen glasses of fresh, raw carrot-apple and green leaf juices. These juices are prepared hourly from fresh, raw, organic fruits and vegetables, using a two-step juicer **or** a masticating juicer used with a separate hydraulic press."[1] How the Gerson Therapy Works

"The Gerson Therapy has the potential to restore the body and enable the body to heal itself from a number of illnesses. However, the therapy does have its limits. There is no guarantee that *any* approach, conventional or alternative, will reverse every case of chronic disease or cancer." [1] Is the Gerson Therapy Right For You?

Juicing with Gerson

The following four juices are approved by the Gerson Therapy and was part, and still are, a part of my daily regimen. Since I have completed my two year Gerson Therapy, I now do one apple/carrot with breakfast and at least two 10 to 12 ounce vegetable juices a day. The most important juices are, according to the Gerson Therapy, apple/carrot, carrot, green juice and orange juice.

Not all the juices in this book are approved by the Gerson Therapy. However, it is my opinion that the juice recipes I am sharing are an excellent source of nutrition and juicing should remain fun and experimental. Green, leafy vegetables are rich in vitamins that help the body maintain a balanced diet and support a healthy immune system. Be creative when making juices. Make it fun and let kids help with more vegetables than fruit. If the vegetables taste great they'll drink them. I can't think of a better way to get kids to add vegetables to their diet than in a great tasting drink.

Whenever there is juicing, there will always be pulp and no one needs to waste it; compost it, feed it to chickens if you have them, mix them in pasta dishes, make dips from them or add them to soups, stews and broth and even breads or muffins. All it takes is imagination.

Gerson Apple Carrot Juice

Yield: 8-10 ounces

Ingredients

3 medium carrots, tops removed

1 large organic granny smith apple

(If travelling, this juice can be sealed: Pour the freshly made apple-carrot juice in an 8oz glass jar and let it overflow slightly, then place the lid. It will spill a little again as you push down to seal the lid. This method ensures there is no space for oxygen at the top of the jar to oxidize and interact with the juice.)

Directions

1. Wash carrots and apple in vinegar water, but do not peel
2. Core apple to remove seeds and slice to fit into juicer chute
3. Fill the juicer chute with the ingredients a little at a time
4. Start the machine and push them through completely and continue until all produce is juiced
5. Pour into glass and serve

Description

This juice is a good source of Thiamin, Niacin, Vitamin B6, Folate and Manganese, and a very good source of Dietary Fiber, Vitamin A, Vitamin K, Potassium and very high in Vitamin C.

Gerson Carrot Juice

Yield: 8-10 ounces

Ingredients

4 medium organic carrots, tops removed

(If travelling, this juice can be sealed: Pour the freshly made apple-carrot juice in an 8oz glass jar and let it overflow slightly, then place the lid. It will spill a little again as you push down to seal the lid. This method ensures there is no space for oxygen at the top of the jar to oxidize and interact with the juice.)

Directions

1. Wash carrots in vinegar water
2. Slice to fit into juicer chute
3. Fill the juicer chute with the carrots a little at a time
4. Start the machine and push them through completely and continue until all carrots are juiced
5. Pour into glass and serve

Description

Carrots alone are a good source of Thiamin, Niacin, Vitamin B6, Folate and Manganese, and a very good source of Dietary Fiber, Vitamin A, Vitamin C, Vitamin K and Potassium. Carrots are a great source of beta-carotene, a substance in plants that is converted into vitamin A in the body. Vitamin A plays an essential role in regulating the immune system and helps the body fight off infections, and helps keep enough T-cells, also known as fighter cells, in circulation. It also boosts the activity of white blood cells, which defend the body from foreign substances.

Gerson Green Juice

Yield: 8-10 ounces   **"The Most Important Juice"**

Ingredients

3 organic leaves of romaine lettuce

1 organic escarole leaf

3 organic leaves of green leaf lettuce

1/4 organic green bell pepper

1 organic leaf of green Swiss chard

1 organic leaf of red chard

2 organic leaves of red leaf lettuce

1 – 2 organic leaves of red cabbage

2 organic endive leaves

2 organic leaves young tender beet greens tops if available

1 small handful organic watercress, (depending on taste), raw

1 medium large organic granny smith apple

Directions

1. Wash all vegetables in vinegar water
2. Slice to fit into juicer chute
3. Fill the juicer chute with the ingredients a little at a time
4. Start the machine and push them through completely and continue until all produce is juiced
5. Pour into glass and rink immediately. Try to consume within 20 minutes for optimal benefit and to avoid oxidation. **Do not store**.

Gerson Green Juice

Description

It is recommended by Gerson to **not** substitute any of the ingredients for other vegetables or fruit during the Gerson Therapy. However after I finished my two year therapy I add or substitute other green vegetables such as kale, cucumber, spinach, broccoli, celery, parsley, or turnips. I now always add turmeric and ginger.

So many people who eat a high acid diet have trouble with acid reflux due to too much hydro-chloric acid stomach buildup. The stomach acid is meant to alkalize acidic intake. Those of us who constantly drink acidic drinks are actually making the stomach's job of breaking foods down with hydrochloric acid instead of processing food with the natural sodium bicarbonate. Consume natural, alkaline beverages. This green juice is a pH booster with Vitamin A, Vitamin C, Vitamin E (Alpha Tocopherol), Vitamin K, Thiamin, Riboflavin, Vitamin B6, Folate, Calcium, Iron, Magnesium, Phosphorus, Potassium, Copper and Manganese. Add ginger and turmeric to help with indigestion.

Orange Juice

Yield: 8-10 ounces

Ingredients

3 organic, oranges

(If travelling, this juice can be sealed: Pour the freshly made apple-carrot juice in an 8oz glass jar and let it overflow slightly, then place the lid. It will spill a little again as you push down to seal the lid. This method ensures there is no space for oxygen at the top of the jar to oxidize and interact with the juice.)

Directions

Using citrus juicers:

1. Wash oranges and slice in half
2. Place orange half on reamer, depress and turn squeezing orange
3. Pour into glasses and serve

Using masticating juicers:

1. Peel the oranges, leave the white on
2. Slice to fit into juicer chute
3. Fill the juicer chute with the oranges a little at a time
4. Start the machine and push them through completely and continue until all oranges are juiced
5. Pour juice into a glass and serve

Description

Oranges are a good source of Thiamin, Folate and Potassium, and Vitamin C.

Juicing with Gerson

After I completed my two year Gerson program and found using oregano, ginger and turmeric to be quite helpful and continue to use them daily. In fact, I should have added them during my program as they are very beneficial to me.

Oregano

Description

1. Oregano is a plant and the leaf is used to make medicine.
2. Oregano is used for respiratory tract disorders such as coughs, asthma, croup, and bronchitis. It is also used for gastrointestinal (GI) disorders such as heartburn and bloating.
3. Other uses include treating menstrual cramps, rheumatoid arthritis, urinary tract disorders including urinary tract infections (UTIs), headaches, and heart conditions.
4. The oil of oregano is taken by mouth (3 drops in 1 ounce water) for intestinal parasites, allergies, sinus pain, arthritis, cold and flu, swine flu, earaches, and fatigue.
5. A few drops of oil can be applied to the skin for skin conditions including acne, athlete's foot, oily skin, dandruff, canker sores, warts, ringworm, rosacea, and psoriasis; as well as for insect and spider bites, gum disease, toothaches, muscle pain, and varicose veins.
6. Oregano oil is also used topically as an insect repellent.
7. In foods and beverages, oregano is used as a culinary spice and a food preservative. [2]

Does it work? Oregano contains chemicals that might help reduce cough and spasms. Oregano also might help digestion by increasing bile flow and fighting against some bacteria, viruses, fungi, intestinal worms, and other parasites and per www.webmd.com and oregano is possibly effective for:

High cholesterol: Clinical research shows that taking oregano after each meal for 3 months can reduce low-density lipoprotein (LDL or "bad") cholesterol and increase high-density lipoprotein (HDL or "good") cholesterol in people with high cholesterol. However, total cholesterol and triglyceride levels are not affected.

Parasites in the intestines: Taking oil of oregano for 6 weeks can kill the parasites Blastocystis hominis, Entamoeba hartmanni, and Endolimax nana.[1]

Ginger

Description

1. Haven't been feeling hungry? Eat fresh ginger just before lunch to stoke a dull appetite and fire up the digestive juices.

2. Ginger improves the absorption and assimilation of essential nutrients in the body.

3. Ginger clears the 'microcirculatory channels' of the body, including the pesky sinuses that tend to flare up from time to time.

4. Feeling airsick or nauseous? Chew on ginger, preferably in a little honey.

5. Can't stop the toot-a-thon? Gas—oops—guess what?! Ginger helps reduce flatulence!

6. Tummy moaning and groaning under cramps? Munch on ginger.

7. Have joint pain? Ginger has wonderful anti-inflammatory properties—can bring relief. Float some ginger essential oil in your bath to help aching muscles and joints.

8. Just had surgery? Chewing ginger post-operation can help overcome nausea. (Have you heard of flattened ginger ale-no fizz?)

9. Stir up some ginger tea to get rid of throat and nose congestion. And when there's a nip in the air, the warming benefits of this tasty tea are even greater! Add ¼" of ginger while juicing too as it adds a little zip to your juice.[3]

Turmeric in Juices

Description

Try adding a ¼" turmeric root in a juice. Turmeric is a root plant. You probably know turmeric as the main spice in curry. It has a warm, bitter taste and is frequently used to flavor or color curry powders, mustards, butters, and cheeses. But the root of turmeric is also used widely to make medicine. The active ingredient in turmeric is called curcumin, which has been shown to have a variety of beneficial properties.

According to www.webmd.com Turmeric is used for arthritis, heartburn (dyspepsia), stomach pain, diarrhea, intestinal gas, stomach bloating, and loss of appetite, jaundice, liver and gallbladder disorders. [4]

It is also used for headaches, bronchitis, colds, lung infections, fibromyalgia, leprosy, fever, menstrual problems, and cancer. Other uses include depression, water retention, worms, kidney problems and Alzheimer's disease, and other chronic disorders. Some people apply turmeric to the skin for pain, ringworm, bruising, leech bites, eye infections, inflammatory skin conditions, soreness inside of the mouth, and infected wounds. The chemicals in turmeric might decrease swelling (inflammation).

In food and manufacturing, the essential oil of turmeric is used in perfumes, and its resin is used as a flavor and color component in foods. Don't confuse Indian turmeric (JIANGHUANG) with the Chinese/Japanese turmeric root (Curcuma zedoaria (YUJIN) grey in color).[3]

1. The Gerson Therapy— http://gerson.org/gerpress/the-gerson-therapy/
2. Dr Merola — http://articles.mercola.com/herbal-oils/oregano-oil.aspx
3. Food Matters—www.foodmatter.tv
4. Webmd: http://www.webmd.com/food-recipes/why-ls-turmeric-good-for-me

Juice Boosters for Health Help

Fruits and vegetables are great sources of the vitamins, minerals, and nutrients that can help you achieve optimal immune health.

Juice Boosters for Health Help

Anemia Booster Juice

Yield: 8-10 ounces

Ingredients

1 cup organic spinach leaves

6 ounces organic broccoli, florets

1 organic beet, whole

1 large organic granny smith apple

Directions

1. Wash produce in vinegar water
2. Slice to fit into juicer chute
3. Fill the juicer chute with the produce a little at a time
4. Start the machine and push them through completely and continue until all produce is juiced
5. Pour juice into a glass and serve

Description

The Anemia Booster is a good source of Dietary Fiber and Vitamin C, Protein, Vitamin E (Alpha Tocopherol), Thiamin, Riboflavin, Pantothenic Acid (Vitamin B), Calcium, Iron, Magnesium, Phosphorus and Selenium, Vitamin A, Vitamin K, Vitamin B6, Folate, Potassium and Manganese, Iron, high in Niacin, Zinc, and Copper.

Antioxidant Booster Juice

Yield: 8-10 ounces

Ingredients

1 cup organic blackberries

1 cup pitted organic Bing cherries

1 large organic granny smith apple

Directions

1. Wash fruit in vinegar water

2. Pit cherries before it is put into juicer chute

3. Fill the juicer chute with the fruit a little at a time

4. Start the machine and push them through completely and continue until all produce is juiced

5. Pour juice into a glass and serve.

Description

Berries are a very good source of Dietary Fiber, and a very good source of Vitamin C, Vitamin K and Manganese. This can be a very sweet drink so make sure to use only a granny smith apple.

Calcium Booster Juice

Yield: 8-10 ounces

Ingredients

1 cup or large handful of organic kale

2 ounces or small handful of organic parsley

4 medium organic carrots, tops removed

Directions

1. Wash produce in vinegar water

2. Remove tops from carrots and slice to fit into juicer chute

3. Fill the juicer chute with the produce a little at a time

4. Start the machine and push them through completely and continue until all produce is juiced

5. Pour juice into a glass and serve

Description

This is a good source of Dietary Fiber, Calcium, Protein, Thiamin, Riboflavin, Folate, Iron, Magnesium and Phosphorus, as well as Vitamin A, Vitamin C, Vitamin K, Vitamin B6, Potassium, Copper and Manganese.

Cleansing and Liver Assistance Juice

Yield: 8-10 ounces

Ingredients

1 medium organic beet, whole

4 medium organic carrots, tops removed

1 ounce organic ginger root

1 ounce organic turmeric

2 large organic granny smith apples

Directions

1. Thoroughly wash beets and carrots in vinegar water
2. Remove tops from carrots and slice beet to fit into juicer chute
3. Fill the juicer chute with the produce a little at a time
4. Start the machine and push them through completely and continue until all produce is juiced
5. Pour juice into a glass and serve.

Description

It is also a good source of Vitamin C, Iron and Magnesium, and a very good source of Dietary Fiber, Folate, Potassium and Manganese to assist the liver and aids in digestion.

Digestion Help Juice

Yield: 8-10 ounces

Ingredients

1 cup or handful of organic spinach leaves

4 medium organic carrots, tops removed

1 ounce organic ginger root

1 ounce organic turmeric

Directions

1. Wash produce, ginger root and raw turmeric in vinegar water

2. Slice carrots to fit into juicer chute

3. Fill the juicer chute with the produce a little at a time

4. Start the machine and push them through completely and continue until all produce is juiced

5. Pour juice into a glass and serve.

Description

This booster is a good source of Dietary Fiber and Vitamin C, Thiamin, Niacin, Vitamin B6, Folate and Manganese, Vitamin A, Vitamin K, Potassium, Zinc, Iron and Copper.

Juice Boosters for Health Help

Immune Booster Juice

Yield: 8-10 ounces

Ingredients

4 large organic celery stalks

1/2 medium organic beet, whole

2 medium organic carrots, tops removed

Directions

1. Thoroughly wash beets, carrots and celery in vinegar water

2. Remove tops from carrots and slice beet to fit into juicer chute

3. Fill the juicer chute with the produce a little at a time

4. Start the machine and push them through completely and continue until all produce is juiced

5. Pour juice into a glass and serve

Description

Apart from improving your immune system, it also benefits your health in other ways. Some nutrients that are found in beet juice include manganese, beta-carotene, sulfur, iron, vitamin C, potassium choline and calcium. Drinking this juice can improve the way the brain functions, strengthens the liver and gallbladder, and it is also known to cleanse the blood.

Ph Alkaline Booster Juice

Yield: 8-10 ounces

Ingredients

3 organic celery stalks

1/4 head organic green cabbage

Directions

1. Wash produce in vinegar water
2. Slice to fit into juicer chute
3. Fill the juicer chute with the produce a little at a time
4. Start the machine and push them through completely and continue until all produce is juiced
5. Pour juice into a glass and serve.

Description

This juice is a pH booster with it is also a good source of Thiamin, Riboflavin, Folate, Calcium, Iron and Magnesium, and a very good source of Dietary Fiber, Vitamin A, Vitamin C, Vitamin K, Vitamin B6, Potassium and Manganese.

Potassium Booster Juice

Yield: 8-10 ounces

Ingredients

1 cup or handful of organic parsley

1 cup or handful of organic spinach leaves

3 medium organic carrots, tops removed

2 organic celery stalks

Directions

1. Thoroughly wash beets, carrots, celery and parsley in vinegar water

2. Remove tops from carrots and slice beet to fit into juicer chute

3. Fill the juicer chute with the produce a little at a time

4. Start the machine and push them through completely and continue until all produce is juiced

5. Pour juice into a glass and serve

Description

One of the many health benefits of celery is that it is a great source of potassium. This makes it a great choice after a strenuous workout in the gym or after a run. It is a perfect way to replace lost electrolytes. Celery's ability to reduce high blood pressure has long been recognized by Chinese medicine practitioners. Celery has proven cholesterol-reduction capabilities but it must be organic. Leafy greens like spinach is excellent for a weight loss program because they are low in carbohydrates as well as calories while being loaded with fiber and potassium.

Vitamin A Booster Juice I

Yield: 8-10 ounces

Ingredients

4 medium organic carrots, tops removed

1 organic pear, cored

1 ounce organic ginger root

Directions

1. Wash, carrots, pear and ginger root in vinegar water
2. Remove tops from carrots and core pear; slice all to fit into juicer chute
3. Fill the juicer chute with the produce a little at a time
4. Start the machine and push them through completely and continue until all produce is juiced
5. Pour juice into a glass and serve

Description

High in very high Vitamin A, Thiamin, Niacin, Vitamin B6, Folate and Manganese, and a very good source of Dietary Fiber, Vitamin C, Vitamin K and Potassium.

Vitamin A Booster Juice II

Yield: 8-10 ounces

Ingredients

2 cups organic pumpkin, dice with skin

2 medium organic carrots, tops removed

Directions

1. Wash, carrots and pumpkin in vinegar water
2. Remove tops from carrot; remove seeds and dice pumpkin to fit into juicer chute
3. Fill the juicer chute with the produce a little at a time
4. Start the machine and push them through completely and continue until all produce is juiced
5. Pour juice into a glass and serve

Description

Stir in the juice ¼ teaspoon cinnamon and ¼ teaspoon nutmeg or to taste. High in very high Vitamin A, Thiamin, Niacin, Vitamin B6, Folate and Manganese, and a very good source of Dietary Fiber, Vitamin C, Vitamin K and Potassium.

Vitamin C Booster Juice

Yield: 8-10 ounces

Ingredients

1/2 cup organic pineapple

½ organic red bell pepper, sliced

3 organic broccoli, florets

2 medium carrots, organic with tops removed

1 medium organic orange, peeled

Directions

1. Wash fruit and produce in vinegar water
2. Remove tops from carrots; peel and core pineapple; peel orange, leave the white on; remove 3 large broccoli florets from head; slice all to fit into juicer chute
3. Fill the juicer chute with the produce a little at a time
4. Start the machine and push them through completely and continue until all produce is juiced
5. Pour juice into a glass and serve

Description

This juice is a not only high in Vitamin A and Vitamin C and also is a good source of Protein (especially broccoli), Vitamin E (Alpha Tocopherol), Thiamin, Riboflavin, Pantothenic Acid (Vitamin B), Calcium, Iron, Magnesium, Phosphorus and Selenium, and a very good source of Dietary Fiber, Vitamin K, Vitamin B6, Folate, Potassium and Manganese.

Juice Boosters for Health Help

Vitamin D in a Glass

Yield: 8-10 ounces

Ingredients

1 cup or large handful of organic kale

1 organic lemon, peeled

Directions

1. Wash kale and lemon in vinegar water; peel the lemon, leave the white on
2. Slice to fit into juicer chute
3. Fill the juicer chute with the kale and lemon a little at a time
4. Start the machine and push them through completely and continue until all produce is juiced
5. Pour juice into a glass and serve

Description

Thiamin, Riboflavin, Pantothenic Acid, Iron and Magnesium, and a very good source of Dietary Fiber, Vitamin C, Vitamin B6, Calcium, Potassium and Copper.

Vitamin K Drink

Yield: 8-10 ounces

Ingredients

3 leaves of romaine lettuce, organic

1/2 cup organic turnip greens

2 leaves organic red cabbage

1 cup or large handful of organic kale

1/2 cup or small handful organic spinach leaves

Directions

1. Wash all vegetables in vinegar water
2. Separate 2 leaves from cabbage; slice to fit into juicer chute
3. Fill the juicer chute with the ingredients a little at a time
4. Start the machine and push them through completely and continue until all produce is juiced
5. Pour into glass and serve

Description

Vitamin K and Copper Deficiency may be the cause of pain. Try this and Vitamin K Copper juices which may have promising results in pain management in a few short weeks. Turnip greens, spinach, red cabbage and kale are loaded with Vitamin A, Vitamin C, Vitamin K especially, Vitamin B6, Calcium, Potassium, Copper and Manganese. Add a half a granny smith apple for a little sweetener. It will also add more Vitamin C.

Vitamin K Copper Drink

Yield: 8-10 ounces

Ingredients

4 medium organic carrots, with tops removed

1 cup or large handful of organic kale

1/2 cup or small handful organic spinach leaves

1 organic garlic clove

1 ounce organic ginger root

Directions

1. Wash carrots in vinegar water
2. Remove carrot tops and slice to fit into juicer chute
3. Fill the juicer chute with the carrots, garlic and ginger root a little at a time
4. Start the machine and push them through completely and continue until all produce is juiced
5. Pour into glass and serve

Description

To help with pain try this and Vitamin K juice which may have promising results in pain management in a few short weeks. Carrots add a sweet flavor and are also a good source of Thiamin, Niacin, Vitamin B6, Folate and Manganese, and a very good source of Dietary Fiber, Vitamin A, Vitamin C, Vitamin K and Potassium.

Juices with Other Benefits

Juicing offers many life-enhancing health benefits including a faster, more efficient way to absorb immune boosting nutrients naturally found in fruits and vegetables. It provides a way to access digestive enzymes typically locked away in the fiber matrix of whole fruits and vegetables.

Juices with Other Benefits

Fruity Tea

Yield: 4-6 (8-10 ounce) glasses

Ingredients

1 medium organic orange, peeled

1/2 organic lemon, peeled

2 cups organic honeydew melon

Directions

1. Steep 1 quart green tea and let cool
2. Wash fruit in vinegar water; peel the orange and lemon, leave the white on; remove the melon seeds and cut up the flesh
3. Slice to fit into juicer chute
4. Fill the juicer chute with the fruit a little at a time
5. Start the machine and push them through completely and continue until all produce is juiced
6. Pour juice into a glass; add ice and desired amount green tea

Description

Juice the fruit and add to 1 quart cold green tea. Add fruit Popsicles in place of ice cubes. This is a refreshing summer drink on hot days that has a good source of Folate and Potassium, and a very good source of Vitamin C. Green tea is loaded with flavonoids and catechins, which function as powerful antioxidants. Catechins are a type of antioxidant found in tea, red wine, chocolate, and apples. These substances can reduce the formation of free radicals in the body, protecting cells and molecules from damage.

Juices with Other Benefits

Garden Protein Juice

Yield: 8-10 ounces

Ingredients

3 organic broccoli, florets

4 medium organic carrots, tops removed

2 large organic celery stalks

1/2 organic green bell pepper, remove top and seeds

Small organic handful of kale

Directions

1. Wash produce in vinegar water
2. Remove carrot tops; slice to fit into juicer chute; separate 3 florets from broccoli head; remove top and seed from pepper
3. Fill the juicer chute with the produce a little at a time
4. Start the machine and push them through completely and continue until all produce is juiced
5. Pour juice into a glass and serve

Description

This juice is a good source of Protein (especially broccoli), Vitamin E (Alpha Tocopherol), Thiamin, Riboflavin, Pantothenic Acid, Calcium, Iron, Magnesium, Phosphorus and Selenium, and a very good source of Dietary Fiber, Vitamin A, Vitamin C, Vitamin K, Vitamin B6, Folate, Potassium and Manganese.

Juices with Other Benefits

Healthy V8 Juice

Yield: 2 (10 ounce) glasses

Ingredients

4 organic carrots, tops removed

1 slice organic beet, raw

2 organic tomato

1 small organic cucumber

1 organic green bell pepper

2 organic celery stalk

1 organic lemon, peeled

1 organic garlic clove

Pinch cayenne pepper, (optional)

1 ½ cup organic spinach, (or any green can be substituted)

Directions

1. Wash produce in vinegar water and thoroughly scrub beet
2. Remove carrot tops and slice carrot and cucumber to fit into juicer chute; 1 slice of beet; remove top and seeds from pepper; peel the lemon, leave the white on
3. Fill the juicer chute with the produce a little at a time
4. Start the machine and push them through completely and continue until all produce is juiced
5. Pour juice into a glasses and serve

Description

Nutrient packed with Thiamin, Riboflavin, Pantothenic Acid, Calcium, Iron, Magnesium, Phosphorus and Selenium, and a very good source of Vitamin A, Vitamin C, Vitamin K, Vitamin B6, Folate, Potassium and Manganese.

Juice Fizzy

Yield: 2 (8 ounce) glasses

Ingredients

1 ounce organic ginger root

1/2 cup organic pineapple chunks

1 large organic granny smith apple

Directions

1. Wash and core apple and cut pineapple into chunks
2. Fill the juicer chute with the cut fruit and ginger root a little at a time
3. Start the machine and push them through completely and continue until all produce is juiced
4. Pour juice into a glass of sparkling water if desired

Description

This refreshing glass is a good source of Vitamin C, Magnesium, Potassium, Copper and Manganese.

Juices with Other Benefits

Lemonade

Yield: 2 (8 ounce) glasses

Ingredients

4 large organic granny smith apples

1 organic lemon, peeled

1 sprig of organic mint leaves, optional

Directions

1. Wash apples and lemon in vinegar water; core apples and peel the lemon, leave the white on
2. Slice to fruit fit into juicer chute
3. Fill the juicer chute with the fruit a little at a time
4. Start the machine and push them through completely and continue until all produce is juiced
5. Pour into iced glass and serve

Description

Lemon and apples a good source of Folate and Potassium, and a very good source of Vitamin C.

Juices with Other Benefits

Melonade

Yield: 2 (8 ounce) glasses

Ingredients

4 cups organic watermelons, cubed

1 cup organic cantaloupe, cubed

2 leaves of organic mint leaves, optional

Directions

1. Wash and cut melons into cubes to fit into juicer chute
2. Fill the juicer chute with the fruit a little at a time
3. Start the machine and push them through completely and continue until all produce is juiced
4. Pour into iced glasses and serve

Description

Cold melons are wonderful on hot days and are a good source of Potassium and a very good source of Vitamin A and Vitamin C.

Juices with Other Benefits

Very Berry Melon Juice

Yield: 2 (8 ounce) glasses

Ingredients

16 organic fresh strawberries

1 cup organic honeydew melon

1/2 cup organic blueberries

Directions

1. Wash fruit in vinegar water and cut melon into cubes to fit into juicer chute
2. Fill the juicer chute with the fruit a little at a time
3. Start the machine and push them through completely and continue until all produce is juiced
4. Pour into iced glasses and serve

Description

This is a hot day special with a good source of Folate and Potassium, and a very good source of Dietary Fiber, Vitamin C and Manganese.

Juicing Fruit for Desserts

Everyone likes something sweet once in a while and fruit is a healthier way to quench a sweet tooth. Like this banana ice cream.

Juicing Fruit for Desserts

Banana Ice Cream

Yield: 3 small bowls

Ingredients

4 medium frozen organic bananas

Directions

1. Peel the bananas and slice them in half-length wise
2. Lay them on a plate and freeze until solid, 2 to 4 hours
3. Break up the frozen bananas and put them in the blender or food processor to blend
4. Pulse until it spins; use spoon to loosen the mixture if it stops moving
5. It will be like soft-serve ice cream
6. Serve right away or store in the freezer in a lidded container

Description

No added sugar is needed. If you have a juicer that will accommodate making this ice cream, use it. We run this through our Norwalk juicer or our Champion juicer and have it drop into a dish for a creamy banana ice cream. Top with finely chopped nuts of choice. Bananas are a good source of Dietary Fiber, Vitamin C, Potassium and Manganese, and a very good source of Vitamin B6 and are a great healthy snack.

Juicing Fruit for Desserts

Berry and Grape Popsicles

Ingredients

1 large bunch organic fresh green seedless grape

1 large bunch organic fresh red seedless grape

1 qrt organic fresh blueberries

1 qrt organic fresh blackberries

Directions

1. Either juice or place in a blender, pour into molds or ice cube trays

2. Freeze until solid, about 4 hours or overnight

3. Once frozen, put ice cubes into sparkling water or organic herbal teas and juices

4. Or put them in Popsicle molds with a whole fruit slice of choice

Description

Any type of fruit makes wonderful pops. Plain frozen grapes are excellent on hot summer days. Kids love them and they are full of Vitamin C.

Juicing Fruit for Desserts

Gerson Popsicles

Ingredients

Mango Orange Banana:

1 ½ cups chopped fresh organic mango

1 medium organic banana, peeled

1/2 cup fresh squeezed organic orange juice

Watermelon Lime Mint:

2 ½ cups organic watermelons, chopped

2 teaspoon fresh organic mint leaves, chopped

2 teaspoon fresh squeezed organic lime juice

Cherry Yogurt:

2 cups fresh organic Bing cherries

1/2 cup low fat plain yogurt

Peach Banana Grape

1 cup large fresh organic peaches, chopped

1 medium organic banana, peeled

10 organic green seedless grapes, fresh

Directions

For each Popsicle put fruit of choice into a blender and purée until smooth

1. Add favorite cut up fruit for some texture
2. Pour into Popsicle molds, add tops or Popsicle sticks
3. Freeze until solid, about 4 hours or overnight

Description

These four Popsicle recipes are Gerson Therapy approved. They are healthy and contain no added sugar. We like to insert a piece of fresh fruit into the molds before freezing. Experiment with different fruits.

Juicing Fruit for Desserts

Tangy Sweet Slushy

Yield: 2 (8 ounce) glasses

Ingredients

2 cups organic pineapple, cut into chunks

1/2 cup organic cranberries, raw

1 cup frozen organic red seedless grape

4 ice cubes

Description

Full of vitamin C also add yogurt for a delicious smoothie with protein

Very Berry Slushy

Yield: 2 (8 ounce) glasses

Ingredients

2 cups frozen organic raw strawberries

2 cups frozen raw blueberries

5 1/2 cups frozen raw raspberries

1/4 cup Greek yogurt

4 ice cubes

Description

For a change up add soaked nuts for a delicious smoothie with added protein

Slushy Directions

1. Wash and freeze fruit
2. Place all frozen fruit in a blender a little at a time
3. Pulse; add ice, blend and Serve

Juicing Smoothies

These delicious healthy smoothie recipes make it easy to eat with fruit, milk, immune-boosting yogurt, and other nutritious ingredients. Smoothies are not really juices but they are healthy, fun and easy. All you need is a blender and like juicing, an imagination. The main ingredients are seeds, nuts, fresh fruits, fresh greens, or frozen fruits and vegetables and yogurt.

When adding milk or milk substitutes, such as almond milk (NOT SOY), pulse only a few times so the smoothie doesn't become frothy. Smoothies are thick shake type drinks filled mainly with fruit or vegetables and other nutrient dense ingredients. They make a wonderful snack when made with natural items.

Juicing Smoothies

Smoothie Information

About Nuts: Nuts like almonds, walnuts, pecans, hazelnuts, Brazil nuts, seeds and grains in cereals, have a natural component that repels predators while growing. This component is phytic acid (a saturated cyclic acid) and is indigestible. When something that contains phytic acid is eaten, the acid binds to minerals like zinc, iron, magnesium, calcium, chromium, and manganese in the gastrointestinal tract, which inhibits the digestive systems' ability to break the nut down properly. Therefore, in-home food preparation techniques can break down the phytic acid in all of these foods. Simply cooking the food will reduce the phytic acid but more effective methods are soaking. I have been doing this trick for years, and it helps.

Soaking Steps
1. Add nuts, seeds or cereal to a glass jar
2. Fill the jar with filtered water, being sure to cover nuts
3. Soak for 12 hours or overnight
4. When complete, discard the soak water and give them a good rinse
5. Refrigerate and consume within 24 hours

To make slushier smoothies, add ice. Caution is used with ice as it can also water down the smoothie. Adding organic frozen fruits and vegetables may be better. Adding organic, sulfide and nitrate free dried fruit will make the smoothie thicker but only add them a little at a time as they will plump up when hydrogenated. Yogurt, bananas, mango and avocados make the smoothies creamy. Avocados are bursting with vitamin C, which stimulates powerful healing and cleansing antioxidant production; and they help capture and eliminate heavy metal toxins!

Juicing Smoothies

Avocado Smoothie

Yield: 2 (8 ounce) glasses

Ingredients

2 large ripe organic avocados, halved and pitted

1 ½ cups coconut milk, canned (liquid expressed from grated meat & water)

1 cup low fat plain yogurt

3 tablespoons pure natural honey

1 cup ice cubes from filtered or distilled water

Directions

1. Wash, peel and cut avocado in half and remove seed
2. Place all ingredients a little at a time in blender while pulsing
3. Add ice and pulse
4. Pour into glasses and serve

Description

Avocados are a good source of pantothenic acid (vitamin B5) which breaks down fats and carbohydrates for energy. Vitamin B5 is critical to the manufacture of red blood cells, as well as sex and stress-related hormones produced in the adrenal glands, small glands that sit atop the kidneys. Avocados are also a good source of fiber, vitamin K, copper, folate, vitamin B6, potassium, vitamin E, and vitamin C.

Juicing Smoothies

Banana Avocado

Yield: 2 (6 ounce) glasses

Ingredients

1/2 cup Greek Yogurt

1 frozen medium organic banana

1 cup organic pineapple

1 organic avocado, peeled and seeded

1/2 cup crushed ice from filtered or distilled water

Directions

1. Wash, peel and cut avocado in half and remove seed
2. Break up frozen banana and cut fresh pineapple into cubes
3. Place all ingredients a little at a time and pulse in a blender
4. Add ice if desired and pulse; ice may make it a little on the watery side
5. Pour into glasses and serve

Description

Avocado with nonfat yogurt and a banana has 6 grams of protein per serving.

Green Avocado Smoothie

Yield: 2 (8 ounce) glasses

Ingredients

1¼ cups cold unsweetened almond milk or coconut milk

1 ripe avocado

1 ripe organic banana

1 sweet organic apple, sliced

1 organic celery stock, chopped

2 cups lightly packed organic kale leaves or spinach

1 inch piece peeled fresh ginger

8 ice cubes

Directions

1. Wash fruit and produce in vinegar water and pat dry
2. Peel and slice avocado, banana and ginger; core and slice apple
3. Place all ingredients a little at a time and pulse in a blender
4. Pour into glasses and serve

Description

This fast smoothie is full of vitamin K, copper, folate, vitamin B6, potassium, vitamin A, C and vitamin E.

Juicing Smoothies

In a Hurry Breakfast Smoothie

Yield: 2 (8 ounce) glasses

Ingredients

1 cup frozen organic strawberries

2 frozen medium organic bananas

1/4 cup Greek Yogurt

3 tablespoons organic raw sliced almonds, soaked

1/2 cup organic rolled oats, soaked

1 teaspoon 100% pure maple syrup

1/2 large organic avocado, seeded and peeled (optional)

Directions

1. Presoak nuts and oats
2. Break up frozen banana
3. Place all ingredients a little at a time and pulse in a blender
4. Add avocado if desired and pulse
5. Pour into glasses and serve

Description

Very filling, satisfying and full of protein and this is something that takes not time at all to make.

Orange Berry Breakfast Smoothie

Yield: 2 (8 ounce) glasses

Ingredients

2 organic oranges, peel and pith removed, cut into chunks

1 cup organic frozen blueberries

1 cup organic frozen raspberries

1/2 cup Greek Yogurt

3 tablespoons organic raw sliced almonds, soaked

Directions

1. Place all ingredients a little at a time and pulse in a blender
2. Pour into glasses and serve

Juicing Smoothies with Power

A good healthy smoothie should feed and nourish the liver with a delicious diet of cleansing, purifying SUPERFOODS and nutrients! Super food powders, flavorings and sweeteners can be added. These are organic fruit and root powders, whey protein powders, honey, Stevia and coconut oil. (Use caution when purchasing protein powders that they do not contain soy.) Try the following blended power smoothies and make juicing fun for the whole family by trying your own variations with juices and smoothies. Keep them healthy with no added sugars or salts.

Antioxidant Booster Smoothie

Yield: 2 (8 ounce) glasses

Ingredients

2 cups frozen organic blueberries

1 tablespoon ground, flaxseed

1 tablespoon Coconut Oil

2 cups organic almond milk

Directions

1. Wash berries, pat dry and freeze in plastic baggie (or frozen organic store-bought)
2. Place all ingredients a little at a time and pulse in a blender
3. Add ice and pulse
4. Blend until smooth and Serve

Description

Blueberries contain the unique antioxidants and resveratrol. Blueberries are a very good source of vitamin K, vitamin C, and manganese, fiber and copper.

Blackberry Protein Melon Smoothie

Yield: 2 (8 ounce) glasses

Ingredients

1/2 cup organic watermelon, chunks

2 cups organic baby spinach leaves

1/2 cup organic honeydew melon, chunks

1/2 cup organic cantaloupe, chunks

1/2 cup organic blackberries

1 organic banana

1 cup low fat cottage cheese

Directions

1. Wash spinach and berries in vinegar water and pat dry; cut up melons

2. Place all ingredients a little at a time and pulse in a blender

3. Add ice and pulse

4. Pour into glasses and serve

Description

Spinach is a great source of protein and is rich in vitamins A, C, B2, B6 E and K, manganese, folate, magnesium, iron, calcium, copper and potassium. Each cup of cottage cheese provides you with 28 grams of protein, or approximately 47 percent of the daily recommended protein intake.

Electrolyte Helper Smoothie

Yield: 2 (8 ounce) glasses

Ingredients

2 medium organic bananas

1 peeled organic lemon

1 cup coconut water (liquid expressed coconut)

1 ½ cups ice from filtered or distilled water

1 cup filtered or distilled water

Directions

1. Peel and slice bananas
2. Peel lemon and leave white on
3. Place all ingredients a little at a time and pulse in a blender
4. Add ice and pulse
5. Blend until smooth and Serve

Description

Coconut water is from young, green coconuts and is low in calories and a natural source of electrolytes including sodium and potassium. Eight ounces of coconut water has 46 calories, 9 grams of carbohydrates, 250 mg of sodium, 600 mg of potassium, 60 mg of magnesium, 45 mg of phosphorus, and 2 grams of protein.

Fiber Booster Smoothie

Yield: 2 (8 ounce) glasses

Ingredients

1 tablespoon flaxseed, raw

1/4 cup organic walnuts, pre-soaked and chopped

2 cups pitted organic dates

1/2 cup Greek Yogurt

1 cup coconut water (liquid expressed coconut)

1 tablespoon pure natural honey

1 cup ice from filtered or distilled water

Directions

1. Soak chopped nuts overnight; drain and rinse; chop dates and nuts
2. Place all ingredients a little at a time and pulse in a blender
3. Add ice and pulse
4. Blend until smooth and Serve

Description

Flax seed or linseed contains notable health benefiting nutrients, minerals, antioxidants, and vitamins that are essential for optimum health as well as being high in fiber. Walnuts are rich in omega-3 fats and contain higher amounts of antioxidants than most other foods as well as fiber. Eating walnuts may improve brain health while also helping to prevent heart disease and cancer.

Juicing Smoothies with Power

Green Power Smoothie

Yield: 2 (8 ounce) glasses

Ingredients

1 organic kiwi

1 organic orange, peeled

1 organic banana, peeled

½ cup frozen organic pineapple chunks

2 cups loosely packed organic baby spinach

1 tablespoons organic rice protein powder

Directions

1. Wash produce; slice the ends off the kiwi and peel
2. Peel orange and banana and slice
3. Place the kiwi, orange, banana, and frozen pineapple chunks in blender and blend until smooth
4. And spinach, blend on high until smooth
5. Reduce speed to low and add in the protein powder

Description

Chop the entire pineapple into bite size pieces then freeze. Pineapple is an excellent source of vitamin C and manganese. It is also a very good source of copper and a good source of vitamin B1, vitamin B6, dietary fiber, folate, and pantothenic acid. Spinach is one of wonderful green-leafy vegetable often recognized as one of the functional foods for its wholesome nutritional, antioxidants and anti-cancer composition. Just 100 g of spinach contains about 25% of daily intake of iron.

Heart Healthy Beet Smoothie

Yield: 2 (8 ounce) glasses

Ingredients

1 cup beet organic slices

2 cups organic arugula lettuce

4 leaves of organic sweet basil

2 medium organic bananas

Directions

1. Wash produce in vinegar water; pat arugula and basil dry
2. Slice well washed and peeled beets; peel and slice bananas to fit in blender chute and pulse
3. Place remaining ingredients a little at a time and pulse in a blender
4. Blend until smooth and Serve

Description

Beetroots and beetroot juice have been associated with numerous health benefits, including improved blood flow, lower blood pressure and increased exercise performance. They are packed with essential nutrients, a great source of fiber, folate (vitamin B9), manganese, potassium, iron and vitamin C.

Inflammation Reducer Smoothie

Yield: 2 (8 ounce) glasses

Ingredients

1 cup organic orange juice, fresh squeezed

1 cup Greek Yogurt

1/2 cup organic raspberries

1/2 teaspoon pure vanilla extract

1 tablespoon pure natural honey

1/2 cup coconut water (liquid expressed cocoanut)

1 ½ cups ice from filtered or distilled water

Directions

1. Wash fruit and squeeze juice from orange
2. Place all ingredients a little at a time and pulse in a blender
3. Add ice and pulse
4. Blend until smooth and Serve

Description

Inflammation reducer is full of Thiamin, Folate and Potassium, and a very good source of Vitamin C and is also good for the immune system.

Juicing Smoothies with Power

Power Protein Smoothie

Yield: 2 (8 ounce) glasses

Ingredients

1 ½ tablespoons dark chocolate 75-85%, shredded

1 ½ cups frozen organic raspberries

1/2 cup Greek Yogurt

1/4 teaspoon turmeric spice

1 tablespoon organic powdered chocolate whey protein

1 cup coconut water (liquid expressed coconut)

Directions

1. Wash raspberries; pat dry; place in a plastic baggie and freeze

2. Shred dark chocolate

3. Place all ingredients a little at a time and pulse in a blender

4. Blend until smooth and Serve

Description

Research points to flavonoids in dark chocolate. Flavonoid helps lower blood pressure, improves vascular function, cognitive function, and provides UV protection for our skin! A higher percentage of cocoa means a higher amount of flavonoids (milk chocolate doesn't do that).

Therapeutic Booster Smoothie

Yield: 2 (8 ounce) glasses or bowls

Ingredients

1/4 cup filtered organic flaxseed oil

1/2 cup cottage cheese, low fat (no BGH)

1/2 cup organic berries, of choice

1/4 cup soaked walnuts, chopped

1/4 cup soaked almonds, chopped or sliced

1 tablespoon pure natural honey

Directions

1. Soak nuts overnight, drain and rinse
2. Mix flax oil and cottage cheese well in a bowl and let the mixture sit for five to eight minutes
3. Transfer the mixture to a blender and add berries, nuts and honey to sweeten if desired and liquefy
4. Add some water if the mixture is too thick

Description

I love this but I do not liquefy as Dr. Budwig recommends but pulse the ingredients. I enjoy it thick and eat it in a bowl with a spoon. This is great for a mid-morning snack or a breakfast. Cancer patients should do this every morning per Johanna Budwig, PhD. Dr. Budwig discovered that eating a mixture of cottage cheese and flax oil can help in healing cancer. Yes, cottage cheese is a dairy product, but when you thoroughly mix it with flax oil it loses all of its dairy properties. People who suffer from lactose intolerance have no problem eating this cottage cheese and flax oil mixture.

Cooking Conversion Chart

Unit	Equals:	Also Equals
1 tsp	1/6 fl. oz.	1/3 tbs
1 tbs	1/2 fl. oz.	3 tsp
1/8 c	1 fl. oz.	2 tbs
1/4 c	2 fl. oz.	4 tbs
1/3 c	2 3/4 fl. oz.	1.4 c + 4 tsp
1/2 c	4 fl. oz.	8 tbs
1 c	8 fl. oz.	1/2 pt
1 pt	16 fl. oz.	2 c
1 qrt	32 fl. oz.	2 pts
1 liter	34 fl. oz.	1 qrt + 1/4 c
1 gal	123 fl. oz.	4 qrts

Cooking Oil Chart

Cooking Oil	Quality	SFA	MUFA	Shelf Life	Oil Smoke Point	
Canola	Expeller Press	6.60%	59.30%	12 mo	375-450°F	190-232°C
Coconut	Extra Virgin	86.00%	6.00%	12 mo	350°F	177°C
Corn	Unrefined	13.00%	28.00%	9-12 mo (opened)	252°F	178°C
Flaxseed	Unrefined	11.00%	21.00%	3-6 mo	-	-
Grape Seed		12.00%	17.00%	3-6 mo	420°F	216°C
Hemp		80.00%	14.00%	2-4 mo refrigerated 6 mo freezer	330°F	165°C
Olive Oil	Extra Virgin	14.00%	73.00%	6-12 mo	175°F	191°C
Palm	Virgin	49.00%	37.00%	12 mo	455°F	235°C
Peanut	Unrefined	17.00%	46.00%	6 mo (opened)	320°F	160°C
Rice Bran		20.00%	39.00%	6-12 mo	490°F	254°C
Safflower	Unrefined	3.70%	4.70%	6 mo	225°F	107°C
Sesame	Unrefined	14.00%	40.00%	2-4 mo	350°F	177°C
Sunflower	Unrefined	18.00%	46.00%	3 mo	225°F	107°C

saturated (**SFA**), a monounsaturated (MUFA)

Advance Food Preparation

Wash all fruit and vegetables in vinegar water prior to use. Water should be free of chlorine and fluoridation. This can be accomplished by the use of a reverse osmosis filtering system or distilling your water if you are able to purchase a distiller. This water should also be used for cooking meals. All cooked meals should be done using slow, medium low or low heat in stainless steel or glass (like Pyrex or ceramic) pots and pans to preserve the quality of the foods nutritional value.

Pressure cookers damage the food nutrients and should not be used. Also avoid using microwave ovens for the same reasons. In the summer of 2000, research in Switzerland by Hand Hertel and Bernard H Blanc, discovered that microwaves cause chemical reactions in food, damaging nutrients making natural amino acids toxic and emit radiation.

Researchers from Kinston University in Britain have studied the bioactive components of anticancer herbs and foods being cooked and frozen. Most cooking preserves the beneficial properties and in fact cooking tomatoes release anticancer properties better. Cooking soups and stocks are the most effective method to get the best out of herbs. Sautéing or grilling vegetables reduces some nutritional properties slightly but retains most. Steaming or simmering is preferred over boiling vegetables to retain more of the nutritional properties.

The beneficial properties of anticancer agents are preserved when foods are frozen with the exception of seafood. About 30% of the omega-3 fatty acids from frozen seafood are destroyed. Therefore, wild seafood should be freshly cooked using low heat, by steam or with slow oven baking for optimum nutritional value. Because steaming and freezing foods does lose a certain amount of nutritional value, the Gerson regime recommends against it. However, if you wish to purchase frozen seafood make sure it is wild caught, not farmed. There may be too many contaminates in farm raised fish and farming has raised concern about possible transfer of disease and controlling disease may require medication. If you wish to freeze fresh wild seafood, wrap it in single portion sizes with parchment paper then seal it in plastic. Always thaw frozen foods in the refrigerator and not on the counter or in a microwave.

Advance Food Preparation

Basic Beans (any kind)

Beans can be prepared in advance instead of using canned products. When cooking beans don't throw away any of the bean liquid! Home cooked bean liquid is full of flavor and good nutrients and can be saved for great base for soups and quick sauces. If beans are used in a soup, slightly undercook them as they will finish cooking in the soup.

Canned beans typically have the chemical BPA in them and usually contain large amounts of sodium. Therefore, if canned beans are used in recipes they should be organic low sodium or without sodium and should be drained and well rinsed before use as canned beans tend to have a slimy liquid in them.

Ingredients

One pound of dry beans makes about five cups of cooked beans which is equivalent to 3 cans of canned beans

Directions

1. Sort for rocks (yes rocks, it happens), shriveled and undesirable beans and rinse beans.
2. Transfer the cleaned beans to a large bowl, covering the beans with water 2" over beans and leave them on the counter to soak overnight
3. The next day, the beans will have absorbed most of the water; drain and rinse them.
4. Transfer the soaked beans to a large cooking pot and cover with water 2" over beans and cook over medium high heat.
5. Once to a boil reduce heat and simmer for 2 to 3 hours to almost tender (Leave the lid off for firm beans to be used for cold salads and pasta dishes. Cover the pot with the lid slightly ajar for creamier beans for soups, casseroles, and burritos.)
6. Add more water as needed to keep the beans submerged, and stir occasionally. Be patient and do not rush the simmering process. Test for doneness.
7. Transfer beans and liquid to a bowl, cover and store in refrigerator up to one week. If frozen, three months.

Description

Beans are high in fiber, low in fat, a good source of protein, vegan and vegetarian friendly and are gluten free.

Advance Food Preparation

Broth Information

Some vegetarians will use chicken and fish broth in cooking but not eat the meat. Therefore chicken and fish broth recipes are included. Broth is simple and inexpensive to make at home and can be used in a wide variety of leftovers.

Today Americans buy individual filets and boneless chicken breasts, or grab fast food on the run. Soup stock or broth has disappeared from the American tradition. Soup broth is made by simmering bones over low heat for an entire day that creates one of the most nutritious and healing foods there is. This broth can be used for soups, stews, or drinking straight. It can be also frozen for future use. Bone broth used to be a dietary staple just as fermented foods were once a staple. Now these are practically eliminated from our modern diet which is largely to blame for our increasingly poor health, and the need for dietary supplements.

Broth was used as a cure-all and in traditional households broth is made from bones of chicken and fish. When making broth, make sure the bones are from organically-raised, pastured or grass-fed animals. Animals raised in confined animal feeding operations (CAFOs) tend to produce stock that doesn't gel, and this gelatin has long been valued for its therapeutic properties. Homemade broth builds strong bones, helps the sore throat and nurtures the sick. If combating a cold, make the soup hot and spicy with plenty of pepper. Chicken broth contains a natural amino acid called cysteine and the spices will trigger a sudden release of watery fluids in your mouth, throat, and lungs, which will help thin down the respiratory mucus so it is easier to expel. Processed, canned soups will not work as well as the homemade bone broth. For best results, make up a fresh batch. Broth is easy to absorb, tastes good, and contains a rich concentration of nutrients and is a great way to replenish the body's likely depleted mineral reserves.

If suffering from GAPS (Gut and Psychology Syndrome) broth is therapeutic for individuals to heal the intestinal tract or the gut lining. It plays a critical role in soothing the gut allowing the body to absorb critical nutrition to assimilate in the body.[1] The following chicken and fish broth recipes are from Nourishing Broth by Sally Fallon Morell.

Basic Chicken Broth

Yield: approximately 16 cups broth

Ingredients

3-4 pounds bones, neck, backs and wing tips (request pastured chickens bones from the butcher) thoroughly cleaned in cold water

8 quarts cold filtered water

4 tablespoons raw organic apple cider vinegar

2 large organic onions, coarsely chopped

1-2 whole organic heads of garlic, smashed and peeled

4-6 organic carrots, coarsely chopped

6-8 organic celery stalks, coarsely chopped

1 organic leek, trimmed and cut into large chunks

4 bay leaves

1 or 2 bunches of organic parsley

Directions

1. Wash vegetables in vinegar water; slice leek length wise in half and wash between sections with vinegar water; cut off and discard the tough greens and slice the remaining tender part of the leek; coarsely chop all vegetables
2. Place the chicken pieces and bones in a large stainless steel stockpot with the filtered water, vinegar and all the vegetables (minus the parsley)
3. Let stand 1 hour (the vinegar will help to draw the minerals out of the bones)
4. Bring to a boil, and remove any scum that rises to the top
5. Add the bay leaves and reduce heat, cover and simmer for 6 to 24 hours (this can also be done in an electric crock pot and always do a full 24 hours as the longer it cooks the richer the flavor will be)
6. 10 minutes before the broth is finished add the parsley
7. Remove all the bone with tongs and a slotted spoon and strain the stock through a fine mesh strainer and let the broth cool before pouring into glass jars to refrigerate up to 5 days

Basic Chicken Broth continued

8. If freezing the broth, leave 2 inches of head space and allow cooling fully before placing in the freezer

Description

Bone broths contain minerals such as calcium, silicon, sulphur, magnesium, phosphorous and trace minerals. Keep in mind that the "skin" that forms on the top contains valuable nutrients such as sulfur and other healthy fats and should be stirred it back into the broth. If canned broth is used in recipes they should be organic low sodium or without sodium.

Basic Fish Broth

Yield: approximately 16 cups broth

Ingredients

4 pounds non oily fish bones and/or heads from sole, flounder, halibut, rockfish, snapper or turbot, cut into 2-inch pieces; rinsed and thoroughly cleaned in cold water

2 tablespoons butter

1/2 cup dry white wine or vermouth

About 4 quarts cold filtered water

2 medium organic onions, coarsely chopped

4 organic celery stalks, coarsely chopped

2 medium organic carrots, coarsely chopped

1 cup mushrooms, coarsely chopped (optional)

Tie in a cheese cloth; 1/4 cup roughly chopped fresh parsley leaves and stems

6 to 8 sprigs fresh thyme and 2 dried bay leaves

Directions

1. Over medium-low heat melt butter in an 8 quart stockpot and add onions, carrots, optional mushrooms and cook stirring occasionally for 30 minutes, until vegetables are softened

2. Add wine and increase heat to medium and bring to a boil

3. Add fish carcass and/or heads and add enough filtered water to cover the bones

4. Lower heat to simmer and carefully skim off any scum that rises to the top

5. Add tied herbs and turn heat down to low to cook at a bare simmer with the lid off for about 1 hour occasionally skimming off the scum (to ensure the bones remain covered with water, add more as needed during cooking time)

6. Remove all the bone with tongs and a slotted spoon and strain the stock through a fine mesh strainer into a 2 quart glass heatproof bowl and allow to cool or use immediately for a recipe

Basic Fish Broth continued

7. If not using right away, when cooled refrigerate uncovered for several hours or until the fat rises and congeals

8. Skim off fat and transfer to lidded bowl to refrigerate for up to five days or freeze for several months

Description

Fish bone broth is helpful in treating digestive disorders and the cartilage (aka-broth) can be considered for use in the following conditions: arthritis, inflammatory bowel disease such as Crohn's disease and ulcerative colitis, cancer, decreased immune system, and malnutrition. Bone broth is loaded with collagen and can be considered for drinking in the following conditions: poor wound healing, soft tissue injury (including surgery), cartilage and bone injury (including dental degeneration).[1]

Advance Food Preparation

Basic Vegetable Broth

Yield: 12 cups broth

Ingredients

10 cups filtered water

1 medium-sized organic onion, coarsely chopped

2 organic cloves of garlic, mashed and peeled

2 organic celery stocks with leaves, cut into large chunks

2 organic carrots, unpeeled and cut into large chunks

2 organic leeks, trimmed and cut into large chunks

2 medium organic tomatoes, quartered

4 medium organic new red potatoes, halved

8 fresh organic parsley sprigs

1 bay leaf

Directions

1. Wash vegetables in vinegar water; Slice leek length wise in half and wash between sections with vinegar water; cut off and discard the tough greens and slice the remaining tender part of the leek; coarsely chop all vegetables and add to pot of water

2. Bring to a boil, reduce the heat and simmer, uncovered, for 1 hour (Adjust the seasonings to taste and simmer for 30 minutes longer)

3. Strain the broth through a fine mesh strainer into a 2 quart glass heatproof bowl and allow to cool or use immediately for a recipe; discard the bay leaf

4. Reserve the vegetables to purée them and use to thicken soups or sauces for stews

5. Let the broth cool to room temperature and then refrigerate, covered, in a glass container up to five days or freeze for several months (this recipe is easily doubled)

Basic Vegetable Broth continued

Description

If you don't have any of these vegetables, use any fresh vegetables you have on hand, as well as any vegetable scraps, and make up your own vegetable broth. Make sure to cut off the green leafy tops of carrots and the skins of onions as these can make the broth bitter. When making your own recipes limit the salt or skip it altogether. Make sure to include onion, garlic and other lots of herbs like parsley or thyme to add flavor without sodium. Homemade vegetable broth is rich and delicious and the peel adds color and vitamins and has much less salt. Vegetable broth doesn't contain many calories and is a good source of vitamin A.

Store-bought broth contains high amounts of sodium so be a label reader and look for a vegetable broth labeled "low sodium," as these broths can contain no more than 5 percent of the daily value or 140 milligrams of sodium per serving. Consuming too much sodium increases your risk for high blood pressure, heart disease and stroke.[1,2]

1. Nourishing Broth By Sally Fallon Morell
2. Healing the Gerson Way by Charlotte Gerson with Beata Bishop

Advance Food Preparation

Basic Rice

Ingredients

Use a 1:2 ratio of rice and water—one cup of rice to two cups of water. A good practice for measuring rice is a half cup of uncooked rice per person. Wild, brown or basmati rice should be used and *never* use ordinary white or instant rice. For one to two cups of uncooked rice use a 2 qrt pot

Directions

1. Rice should be rinsed in a strainer before cooking to rinse off surface starch and to remove other particles
2. Bring the water to boil in a saucepan large enough to accommodate for rice expansion
3. When the water has come to a boil, stir in the well rinsed rice and reduce to a gentle simmer
4. Cover the pot and don't remove the lid while rice is cooking
5. Check the rice at rice cooking time in description; when done, the rice will be firm but ender, not crunchy, slightly sticky but not gummy
6. Drain off excess water if any
7. When the rice is done, turn off the heat and remove lid. Fluff the rice with a spoon or a fork and let it sit to rest a few minutes. It should be just a steamed texture

Description

Rice cooking times

- Basmati Rice: 18 to 25 minutes
- Brown Rice: 30 to 40 minutes
- Wild Rice: 45 to 60 minutes

Rice keeps well in the refrigerator for several days, so you can make extra ahead to serve later. You can also freeze cooked rice. Rice can be stored in the freezer up to 1 month. To freeze, place plastic wrap on top of a cup and invert the cup onto the wrap. Remove the cup and wrap the rice and seal it in a freezer bag. Label and date the bag. Freezing the rice in one cup measurements makes it easier for use later. Rice is high in fiber, low in fat, vegan and vegetarian friendly and is gluten free.

Advance Food Preparation

Hard Boiled Eggs

Eggs are no longer on the list of bad foods. Although eggs are high in cholesterol, researchers now know that cholesterol in food doesn't raise blood cholesterol levels, saturated fat does. So if you like hard-boiled eggs include them in your diet a few days a week. Hard-boiled eggs are low in calories and a good source of protein. They are also a good source of vitamin D, B12 and E, folic acid, iron and zinc. Eggs also provide all of the essential amino acids, which make them a high-quality source of protein. Protein is essential to life and occurs in every cell in your body.

The egg is a powerhouse of disease-fighting nutrients like lutein and zeaxanthin. These carotenoids may reduce the risk of age-related macular degeneration, the leading cause of blindness in older adults. And brain development and memory may be enhanced by the choline content of eggs.

But the full health benefits of eggs can only be realized if stored properly in the refrigerator and cook thoroughly to kill any potential bacteria. Hard-cooked eggs in the shell can be refrigerated up to one week and peeled they can be stored in the refrigerator in a bowl of cold water, covered for about one week (change the water daily)—or in a sealed container without water covered with damp paper towel for the same length of time.

Directions

1. Place desired amount of eggs in a single layer at the bottom of a saucepan with enough cold water to cover eggs
2. Bring to a full rolling boil and add a teaspoon of vinegar if an egg is cracked to keep the egg from seeping (It will also help to peel a fresh egg)
3. Remove the pan from the heat as soon as the water comes to a rolling boil and let the eggs set for 10 to 12 minutes in the hot water (for higher elevations boil eggs 3 minutes before removing from heat)
4. Drain the water and let them set in ice water to stop the cooking and until the eggs can be handled with bare hands
5. Crack each egg and peel under cold running water; use or store as described above

Advance Food Preparation

Canning Information

Most people today, who like to cook, have no clue about canning and how cheap food can truly be if they are homemade. Sure canning takes time, but one day spent canning probably wouldn't need to done for another year or so. Canning is an important and safe method for preserving and advance food preparation if it is done properly.

In canning, foods are placed in jars which are heated to a temperature that destroys micro-organisms that cause food to spoil. There are two safe ways to process food; the boiling water bath and the pressure canner method. Pressure processing is necessary for low acidic foods like meats and vegetables which can form deadly botulinum toxins (poisons). Foods that are low acid have a pH higher than 4.6 and because of the danger of botulism; they must be prepared in a pressure canner. Since I am a vegetarian, I only pressure cook vegetables. However low acidic foods for pressure canning include:

meats

- seafood
- poultry
- dairy products
- all vegetables

The boiling water bath method is safe for tomatoes, fruits, jams, jellies, pickles and other preserves. Since I have included some tomato and pickle recipes in this book, this method is used. Jars of food in this method are heated completely covered with boiling water (212°F at sea level) and cooked for a specified amount of time.

High acid foods have a pH of 4.6 or lower and contain enough acid so that the botulinum spores cannot grow and produce their deadly toxin. Therefore, acidic foods can be safely canned use the boiling water bath method. The high acidic foods for water bath method include:

- fruits
- properly pickled vegetables

Canning Information continued

To do home canned foods you need the following

- Tongs
- Wooden spoon
- Ladle
- Hot pads
- A wide-mouth funnel
- A variety of measuring cups
- A jar lifter (a jar lifter is a tong designed for lifting jars from hot water with minimal effort.)
- Boiling water bath canner or a large deep saucepot with a lid, and a rack or a pressure canner depending on the type of canning being done
- Glass preserving jars, lids and bands (always start with new lids)
- Fresh organic produce and other quality ingredients

A water bath canner is a large stock pot, with a lid and a wire or wooden rack that keeps jars from touching the bottom or each other which help keep the jars from bumping into each other that could cause cracking or breaking while boiling. The diameter of the canner should be no more than 4 inches wider than the diameter of your stove's burner to ensure proper heating of all jars. It is not recommended for a pot to fit over two burners because the middle jars do not get enough heat. Canners used on an electric stove must have a flat bottom. Canners can be used in outdoor fire pits with a solid grate but use a thermometer to insure proper boiling temperature is reached.

Pressure canners are a specially-made heavy pot with a lid that can be closed steam-tight. The lid is fitted with a vent, a dial or weighted pressure gauge and a safety fuse. Newer models have an extra cover-lock as an added precaution and also have a rack to protect the jars from bumping into each other and braking. Because each type is different, be sure to read the directions for operating.

Canning Information continued

When canning, these steps are important to understand.

1. **Find** a recipe using a reliable source from a cookbook with tested recipes or the Ball website at http://www.freshpreserving.com where these instructions were retrieved. When canning fruits, fruit juices, jams, jellies and other fruit spreads, salsas, tomatoes with added acid, pickles, relishes, chutneys, sauces, vinegars and condiments use a water bath method. These foods are high in acid.

2. **Read** the recipe and all its instructions and make sure all the equipment and ingredients needed are ready before canning is started. Follow the recipe preparation, jar size, preserving method and processing time.

3. **Check** the jars, lids and bands for proper functioning. Mason jars with nicks, cracks, uneven rims should be discarded. The underside of lids should not have scratches or uneven or incomplete sealing compound to prevent sealing. Bands should fit the jars. Wash jars, lids and bands in hot, soapy water; rinse well and dry the bands.

4. **Heat** the home canning mason jars in hot water, not boiling, until they are ready to be used. Fill a large saucepan or stockpot half-way with water; place jars in the water and fill the jars with water to prevent them from floating. Bring to a simmer over medium heat. Keep jars hot until ready for use. A dishwasher may also be used to wash and heat jars. Keeping jars hot prevents them from breaking when hot food is added. Leave lids and bands at room temperature for easy handling.

5. **Prepare** the boiling water bath canner: A boiling water bath canner is simply a large, deep saucepot equipped with a lid and a rack. The pot must be large enough to fully surround and immerse the jars in water by 1 to 2 inches and allow for the water to boil rapidly with the canner lid on. Fill the canner half-full with water and simmer covered with lid. Place prepared hot jars in canner; fill jars with water and cover the jars with water. Be sure the rack in resting on the rim of the canner or on the bottom, depending on the type of rack you are using. Boil the jars for 30 minutes to sanitize properly.

6. **Prepare** the preserving recipe using fresh organic produce and other quality ingredients as instructed by the recipe.

Advance Food Preparation

Canning Information continued

7. **Remove** the hot jar from the boiling water, using a jar lifter, emptying the water inside jar. Fill the jar one at a time with prepared food using a wide mouth jar funnel leaving 1/4 inch from the rim of the jar for soft spreads such as jams and jellies and fruit juices; 1/2 inch for fruits, pickles, salsa, sauces, and tomatoes. Remove air bubbles, if stated in recipe, by pushing a rubber spatula down in the jar on top of the food to release trapped air and ensure proper headspace during processing. Repeat 2 to 3 times to rid the jar of all bubbles.

8. **Clean** the jar rim and threads of jar using a clean, damp cloth to remove any food residue. Center lid on jar to allow the sealing compound to come in contact with the jar rim; apply the band and adjust until the fit is fingertip tight. Place filled jars back in the canner until canner is full of all filled jars; lower the rack with jars into water. Make sure water covers the filled jars by 1 to 2 inches. Place the lid on water bath canner and bring the water to a full rolling boil to begin the processing time.

9. **Process** the jars in the boiling water for the processing time indicated in recipe, adjusting for altitude. (1000 to 3000 feet increase time by 5 minutes; 3001 to 6000 feet increase time by 10 minutes; 6001 to 8000 feet increase time by 15 minutes; 8001 to 10000 feet increase time to 20 minutes). When processing time is complete, turn off the heat and remove the canner lid and allow the jars to stand in canner for 5 minutes to get adjust to the outside temperature.

10. **Remove** the jars from canner with a jar lifter and set upright on a towel to prevent jar breakage that can occur from temperature differences. Bands should not be retightened as this may interfere with the sealing process. Leave the jars undisturbed for 12 to 24 hours.

11. **Check** the jars lids for seals. A popping noise may occur as lids seal. Lids should not flex up and down when the center is pressed. Remove bands and try to lift lids off with fingertips. If the lid cannot be lifted off, the lid has a good seal. If a lid does not seal within 24 hours, the product can be immediately reprocessed or refrigerated. Clean mason jars and lids. Label and store in a cool, dry, dark place up to 1 year.

Canning Information continued

After one year foods natural chemical changes occur that could lessen the quality. Therefore it is a good practice that foods stored the longest period of time should be used first.

Canned food should not be stored in areas subject to freezing. Freezing causes the food to expand and break the seal. Storing home canned foods between 50°F and 70°F is ideal and may help preserve the food for a longer period of time.

Light hastens oxidation and destroys certain vitamins. Light will also cause certain foods to fade in color. To protect home canned foods from the deteriorating effects of light, store jars in a place that does not receive direct sunlight. Therefore, it is best to keep home canned foods in a cool, dry, dark place.

(Refer to http://www.canning-food-recipes.com/canning.htm for additional tips)

Advance Food Preparation

Notes

Dill Pickles

Yield 7 Pints

Ingredients

4 pounds organic cucumbers, cleaned and cut in half
or in slices

12 garlic cloves for kosher dills

3 cups white vinegar

3 cups distilled water

1/4 cup Celtic, Himalayan or kosher salt

14 tablespoons dill seeds

21 peppercorns

Organic dill sprigs

7 pint canning jars

Directions

1. See Advance Food Preparation – Canning Information
2. Wash cucumbers in vinegar water and slice length-wise for spears or cross-wise for pickle rounds; if a more crisp pickle is desired try soaking the cucumbers in ice water for 4 hours before processing them into pickles
3. Fill the canner half-full with water and simmer covered with lid
4. Wash jars in hot water, rinsing well before placing jars in canner using a jar lifer; fill jars with hot water and cover jars with water until complete submerged in canner pot. Add lids and rings to the water and boil for 30 minutes to sanitize properly
5. While jars, rings and lids are sanitizing, combine in a separate stock pot with distilled or filtered water, vinegar and salt to a boil
6. For Kosher Dills, without the benefit of clergy, add 12 peeled garlic cloves to the mixture and bring to a boil

Dill Pickles continued

7. When the pickling liquid reaches the boiling point, remove the garlic (just as with all onion family, garlic is very susceptible to bacterial activity, so be sure to remove the garlic)
8. One at a time using a jar lifter, remove a sanitized jar and dump the water filled jar back into the bath water and place it on a towel
9. Drop 2 tablespoons dill seeds, 3 peppercorns and a sprig of dried dill into each hot sanitized jar; pack with sliced cucumbers
10. Fill the jars to ¼ inch from the top with the hot pickling liquid
11. Immediately place the lids and rings on each jar and finger tighten
12. Using the jar lifter replace packed jars back into canner pot of boiling water and process in the boiling water bath for 15 minutes and turn off the burner
13. Allow the jars to rest for 5 more minutes in the water before removing the jars
14. Remove and pickle jars and set aside to cool; retighten the lids and let set overnight (lids should make a pop sound when cooled and sealed)
15. When cool, remove the bands and check the seals; if the lids can be lifted from the jar with fingers, there is no seal and the jar needs to be reprocessed
16. Date the side of the cooled jar with a permanent marker and store in a dark place between 50º and 70ºF

Description

Adjust the recipe to the pounds of cucumber harvested. Here's an easy tip for dill pickle relish to add to your condiments on hand. Simply drain the jar of pickles, reserving some liquid, and place in a food processer with a tablespoon or two of red bell pepper and pulse. If there is not enough juice in the relish, add some of the liquid that was reserved and discard the rest of the liquid. The relish can be stored in the refrigerator for up to 3-4 weeks.

Advance Food Preparation

Basil Pesto

Yield: 2 ½ cups

Ingredients

2 cups fresh organic basil

1/2 cup extra virgin olive oil

1/2 cup organic Romano or low fat organic parmesan cheese, grated

1/3 cup pine nuts

2-3 medium organic garlic cloves, minced

Directions

1. Rinse basil leaves and pat dry
2. Pulse in food processor nuts and basil several times
3. Add oil and blend until smooth
4. Add remaining ingredients and pulse several more times
5. Pour into 8 oz glass canning jars and leave 1/4" space at top of jar and add 3 tablespoons of olive oil on top before securing lid
6. Label, date, cover and store in refrigerator for 4 weeks

Description

This recipe can easily be doubled or tripled depending on your use. If freezing is intended, do not add cheese. Transfer pesto to an 8 oz glass canning jars. Leave 1/4" space at top of jar and pour 3 tablespoons of olive oil on top before securing lid. Freeze for up to 3 months; thaw in refrigerator, then stir in cheese. Canning pesto is not recommended because cheese and garlic can create an environment for botulism to thrive even when pressure canned. If pesto is canned follow canning information, **do not add cheese and garlic.** Leave 1/4" space at top of jar and pour 3 tablespoons of extra virgin olive oil on top and store in a cool, dry, dark place up to 1 year. To use, open jar and place in food process and add minced garlic and grated cheese and store in refrigerator for up to 4 weeks.

Advance Food Preparation

Tomato Pesto

Yield: 2 cups

Ingredients

4 ounces organic sun-dried tomatoes

2 tablespoons fresh organic basil, chopped

2 tablespoons fresh organic parsley, chopped

1 tablespoon fresh organic garlic cloves, chopped

1/4 cup fresh organic pine nuts, chopped

3 tablespoons fresh organic onions, chopped

1/4 cup balsamic vinegar

1 ½ tablespoons organic tomato paste, no added salt

1/3 cup organic tomato, crushed

1/2 cup extra virgin olive oil

1/2 cup low fat organic parmesan cheese, grated

1/4 teaspoon Celtic or Himalayan salt

Directions

1. Place sun-dried tomatoes in a stainless steel saucepan and cover with water, just enough to submerge tomatoes
2. Over low heat simmer for 5 minutes or until tender
3. In a food processor or blender combine sun-dried tomatoes, basil, parsley, garlic, pine nuts and onion; process until well blended
4. Add vinegar, tomato paste, crushed tomatoes, and process until well combined
5. Mix in olive oil and parmesan cheese; season with salt to taste
6. Pour into 8 oz canning jars and leave 1/4" space at top of jar and add 3 tablespoons of olive oil on top before securing lid.
7. Label, date, cover and store in refrigerator for 4 weeks

Tomato Pesto continued

Description

This recipe can easily be doubled or tripled depending on your use. If freezing is intended, do not add cheese. Transfer pesto to an 8 oz glass canning jars. Leave 1/4" space at top of jar and pour 3 tablespoons of olive oil on top before securing lid. Freeze for up to 3 months; thaw and then stir in cheese. Canning pesto is not recommended because of the cheese and garlic which can create an environment for botulism to thrive in, even when pressure canned. If pesto is canned follow the canning information, **do not add cheese and garlic**. Leave 1/4" space at top of jar and pour 3 tablespoons of extra virgin olive oil on top and store in a cool, dry, dark place up to 1 year. To use, open jar and place in food process and add minced garlic and grated cheese and store in refrigerator for up to 4 weeks.

Advance Food Preparation

Tomato Sauce

14 - 16 Pints

Ingredients

15 pounds organic tomatoes

6 organic garlic cloves, minced

3 large organic onions, chopped

1/3 cup sucanat (organic unrefined sugar)

3 tablespoons oregano, dried

2 tablespoons basil, dried

1 teaspoon pepper

14 to 16 pint jars or 7-8 qrt jars

Directions

1. See Advance Food Preparation - Canning
2. Sanitize jars in boiling water for 30 minutes using a canner pot
3. Wash tomatoes well in vinegar water, discard any that are badly bruised, cut off tomato stem ends and slice into large chunks.
4. Mix in food processor or blender until juicy, but not puréed
5. In a stainless steel stock pot in medium heat bring tomatoes to boiling; stir frequently
6. Add remaining ingredients; reduce heat to medium low; simmer 30 minutes
7. Remove all foam that may have formed while simmering
8. One at a time using the jar lifter, remove a sanitized jar and dump the water filled jar back into the bath water and place it on a towel
9. Ladle sauce into clean sanitized canning jars leaving over a ¼" space at top of jar
10. Wipe the rims clean using a damp towel and cap with sanitized lids and screw on the bands using medium finger pressure
11. Return capped jars using the jar lifter into the boiling water bath to process in the canner pot for 45 minutes

Tomato Sauce continued

12. Turn off the heat and allow the jars to adjust to the water temperature change for 10 minutes
13. Remove jars with the jar lifter and secure the lids tighter; let set to seal over night

14. Remove the bands and check the seals; if the lids can be lifted from the jar with fingers, there is no seal and the jar needs to be reprocessed or stored in the refrigerator to be used within 2 weeks
15. Label and date jars and store in dark cool place 50º to 70º F

Description

Foods canned properly using correct processing methods and processing time can be safely stored for one year. Homemade tomato sauce has many uses:

Cocktail Sauce

Mix ½ cup tomato sauce with desired amount of horseradish and honey to taste in a small bowl; serve with deveined cooked shrimp

Seafood Marinara

Sauté sliced garlic in olive oil in stainless steel skillet; add 1/2 cup white wine, 2 cups tomato sauce,1 pound cleaned coarsely chopped mussels, 1 pound clean, coarsely chopped and deveined shrimp, 1 pound cleaned coarsely chopped crab meat; cover and cook 5 minutes; serve over cooked organic noodles of choice

Spaghetti Sauce

Add to tomato sauce desired amount of Italian seasoning, onion and garlic; voilà spaghetti sauce

Tomato Sauce continued

Zesty Vegetable Chip Dip

Combine equal parts Greek yogurt and tomato sauce in a bowl; stir in grated Parmesan cheese and oregano

Quick Minestrone Soup

Boil 1 jar tomato sauce and 5 cups water; stir in cooked small organic pasta of choice, chopped mixed organic vegetables and canned well rinsed organic beans; cook until vegetables are tender; grate parmesan cheese over top and serve

Spanish Rice

Cook 1 cup rice, 1 cup faltered or distilled water and 1 cup tomato sauce covered over medium low heat until rice is soft but firm (about 15 minutes); stir in capers or peas, chopped organic olives and chopped organic scallions; serve hot as a side dish

Shrimp & Tomato Capellini

Sauté 1 pound cleaned, coarsely chopped and deveined shrimp in garlic and butter. Add 1 cup tomato sauce, chopped fresh herbs and toss with capellini (thinner than spaghetti, angel hair) for a simple supper.

Grilled Vegetable Gratin

Grill softer vegetables such as peppers, zucchini, eggplant, or asparagus. Place in a casserole dish, top with 1 cup tomato sauce and fresh mozzarella. Broil until cheese is melted.

Baked Cauliflower or Zucchini

Pour 1 cup tomato sauce over cauliflower florets or chopped zucchini and bake in a casserole dish until vegetables are tender. Sprinkle with Parmesan and return to oven a few minutes more, if desired. Also serve sourdough bread with garlic-infused olive oil.

Advance Food Preparation

Notes

Condiments

Before food preservation techniques were developed, strong spices and condiments were used to make the food more appetizing and improve the taste of spoiling food. Today condiments are all about tasty flavors.

Condiments

Condiment Information

The exact definition of what a condiment is varies. Some definitions include spices and herbs, including salt and pepper. Condiments may include such items as sauces, spreads, vinegars, flavored and unflavored oils, relishes and pickled items and many food items can be both a condiment and an ingredient. Ketchup and mustard are often used as ingredients in baked bean recipes. Sauces such as mayonnaise and pesto can be used as a condiment on French fries or sandwiches even though their chief purpose is to be an ingredient. Hummus and guacamole are used as dips and are food items but can also be used as a condiment on sandwiches or burgers. Almost every cuisine has its own range of unique condiments however; mustard and vinegar have a tendency to be used worldwide. Condiments can be sweet or savory like caramelized onion, relishes or cranberry sauces.

Some condiments are healthier than others and some may add large amounts of calories, fat, or sodium to a meal. One of the best ways to add flavor and keep calories and fat lower is to stock up on lighter condiments and what is better than homemade. Homemade spice blends not only save money, particularly if purchased in bulk, but homemade condiments help in avoiding harmful ingredients that are in many pre-mixed packaged seasonings like MSG, sugar, saturated fat, tans fats and salt. When shopping for ketchup, mustard, mayonnaise and other condiments, pay attention to information about calories, fat, sodium and sugar—be a label reader.

All the following condiments can be made ahead of time to have on hand and ready to use. How much is made depends on your condiment use.

Baking Powder

Yield: 1 cup

Ingredients

1/4 cup organic baking soda

1/4 cup organic arrowroot

1/2 cup organic cream of tartar

Directions

Mix all ingredients well stored in an airtight glass jar

Description

Homemade baking powder is very simple to do and takes less than 10 minutes to make and has no harmful chemicals.

Condiments

Better Butter

Yield 1/2 pound

Ingredients

1/2 cup softened organic unsalted butter

2 tablespoons organic filtered flax oil

2 tablespoons organic extra virgin olive oil

Directions

1. In a food processor pulse all ingredients until well blended and smooth
2. Store in butter crock or a covered small bowl in the refrigerator; this is a softer butter and will spread more easily straight from the refrigerator

For Herb Butter add:

2 tablespoons organic parsley

1 tablespoon organic tarragon

1 teaspoon organic thyme

Blend well and chill in a crock

Description

Flaxseed oil is an excellent source of omega-3 and omega-6 fatty acids. Flaxseed oil is nutritionally superior to olive oil and tastes better with the butter. The Harvard School of Public Health states that replacing saturated fats with unsaturated fats increases HDL, "good," cholesterol and decreases LDL, "bad," cholesterol. This decreases the risk of cardiovascular health problems, such as heart disease, stroke and hardened arteries.

Condiments

Horseradish Creamy Style

Yield: 1 ½ cups

Ingredients

1/2 cup horseradish root, peeled and diced

1/2 cup vinegar

2 teaspoons sucanat (organic unrefined sugar)
or pure natural honey

1/2 cup Greek Yogurt

Directions

1. Combine all ingredients in a food processor or blender; process until puréed
2. Carefully remove cover of processor or blender, keeping face away from container as the horseradish can be very pungent
3. Cover and store in a labeled and dated glass container in the refrigerator up to 2 months

Ghee or Clarified Butter

Yield 1 Pound

Ingredients

1 pound organic unsalted butter

Directions

1. Cut butter into cubes
2. Melt over medium heat in a heavy stainless steel saucepan
3. When the butter has melted, reduce to a simmer and after 5 minutes, stirring continually (butter will form a whitish froth on top and will bubble and pop until all the moisture is evaporated)
4. Simmer about another 10 minutes and the froth will sink to the bottom and form a golden brown crust
5. Turn off the heat and skim off the remaining froth on top with a spoon and let the butter sit for about 15 minutes
6. The butter should be clear and is now ghee
7. Place cheese cloth over the pan and carefully pour the ghee to sieve into a jar leaving the residue at the bottom of the pan
8. Cover the jar and store at room temperature on the counter to be used frequently
9. Spices can be added for flavor

Ghee or Clarified Butter continued

Description

The process of creating traditional clarified butter is complete once the water is evaporated and the fat, clarified butter is separated from the milk solids. Simmering the butter so the milk solids caramelize makes it nutty-tasting and aromatic. What remains is basically a pure combination of fats without any milk residue so it does not need to be refrigerated. Ghee can last for months or even years without refrigeration which made it very popular before modern refrigeration. However, always use a clean spoon when taking ghee from the jar to prevent contamination.

The ghee will turn a deep opaque yellow color when cooled and is excellent for sautéing vegetables. The French use the ghee for making sauces and it has been said that ghee has many nutritional healing benefits and is the most stable of all oils. Ghee like other fats needs to be consumed in moderation but it is safe for those with dairy allergies. That is because the casein and lactose have almost been entirely removed during the clarification process. Other ghee benefits are its ability to protect the gastrointestinal system, strengthen your immune system, and even prevent certain types of cancer. A study published in September 2012 in "The Indian Journal of Medical Research" reported that ghee, when compared to soybean oil, decreases enzyme activity responsible for activating carcinogens in the liver. The study also showed that ghee helped increase carcinogen detoxification.

Some restaurants and store processed foods may use partially hydrogenated vegetable oil or "vegetable ghee" in place of real ghee because of its lower cost. This "vegetable ghee" contains trans-fats. Trans-fats have been shown to increase the risk of coronary heart disease even more so than saturated fats. If purchasing ghee in lieu of making it at home make sure to read the labeled ingredients.

Chili Powder Seasoning

Yield: 1 cup

Ingredients

2 tablespoons cayenne pepper

1/4 cup organic garlic powder

3 tablespoons organic onion powder

1/4 cup organic oregano

2 tablespoons organic paprika

1/4 cup organic cumin

1 tablespoon organic thyme

Directions

1. Using mortar and pestle grind all ingredients well
2. Place in an airtight labeled and dated container
3. Adjust cayenne pepper to taste for a hot or mild blend

Description

This is great to keep on hand for making quick chili on a busy night. It is also great to add into omelets and roasted veggies.

Condiments

Italian Seasoning

Yield: 1/2 cup

Ingredients

2 tablespoon dried organic oregano

2 tablespoon dried organic marjoram

2 tablespoon dried organic thyme

2 tablespoon dried organic basil

2 tablespoon dried organic rosemary

2 tablespoon dried organic sage

Directions

1. Using a mortar and pestle course grind the rosemary
2. Combine remaining ingredients and course grind together
3. Transfer to a jar with a lid and label of contents and date

Description

Herbs and spices have very low calorie content and are good to keep on hand when needed. They are relatively inexpensive particularly if purchased in bulk and are a great way to turbo-boost the natural antioxidant and anti-inflammatory power of your diet as well as enhance the flavor of food.

Condiments

Mayonnaise

Yield: 1 ½ cups

Ingredients

1 organic free range egg (cold)

1/4 teaspoon dried organic mustard

1/4 teaspoon sucanat (organic unrefined sugar)

1 tablespoon organic lemon juice or organic apple cider vinegar

1¼ cups organic canola or organic avocado oil, 100% pure natural (cold)

Dash cayenne pepper, if desired

Directions

1. In food processor or blender add egg, mustard, pepper, lemon juice and sugar
2. While the machine is blending SLOWLY add ½ the cold oil
3. Stop and scrape down the mixture and continue blending adding the remaining oil SLOWLY
4. Blend until well combined creamy and thick
5. Store ingredients in a labeled and dated pint jar in the refrigerator for one week to two weeks

Description

Homemade mayonnaise can also be made into Aioli simply by adding 1 to 2 cloves of minced garlic and an added ½ teaspoon dried organic mustard. Here's another mayo idea. Try using Greek yogurt and add different herbs and spices that create fantastic flavors like garlic, basil, black pepper, chives, lime, and cilantro or just add lemon juice. These work well as a tasty sandwich topping or as a creamy dip.

Condiments

Mustard, Hot

Yield: 1 cup

Ingredients

4 tablespoons organic mustard seeds

1/2 cup dried organic mustard powder

1/2 teaspoon garlic powder

1/4 teaspoon organic allspice

2 tablespoons organic minced shallot or
dried organic onions

1/4 teaspoon Himalayan or Celtic salt

1/4 cup white wine vinegar

1/4 cup white wine or water

2 tablespoons pure natural honey

Directions

1. Grind the whole mustard seeds for a few seconds in a spice or coffee grinder or by hand with a mortar and pestle
2. Pour ground seeds into food processor or blender
3. Add remaining ingredients blending well
4. Pour into a labeled and dated glass jar and refrigerate overnight
5. Mustard will last several months if refrigerated

Description

This recipe can easily be doubled or tripled to have on hand and readily available. Mustard seeds are an excellent source of selenium and a very good source of omega-3 fatty acids and manganese. They are also a good source of phosphorus, magnesium, copper, and vitamin B1.

Condiments

Mustard, Mild

Yield: 1 cup

Ingredients

1/2 cup dried organic yellow mustard powder

1/2 cup filtered or distilled water

1/3 cup organic apple cider

1 teaspoon potato flour

1/4 teaspoon Himalayan or Celtic salt

1/4 teaspoon organic turmeric

1/4 teaspoon organic garlic powder

1/4 teaspoon organic ground paprika

Directions

1. Mix all ingredients in food processor or blender until smooth
2. Pour into a labeled and dated glass jar and refrigerate overnight
3. Mustard will last several months if refrigerated

Description

Depending on how much mustard wanted on hand, this recipe can easily be doubled or tripled to have readily available.

Condiments

Peanut Butter

Yield: 1 ¼ cups

Ingredients

2 ½ cups lightly roasted organic peanuts, shelled

Directions

1. Place shelled peanuts in a food processor
2. Process 5 minutes, stop and scrape sides
3. Continue processing until mixture is smooth and creamy, about 15 minutes; stop occasionally to scrape sides during processing
4. Label and date covered jar and store peanut butter in refrigerator for up to 8 weeks
5. Substitute peanuts for cashews or almonds

Description

Peanuts are an excellent source of biotin (B complex vitamin). They are also a very good source of copper as well as a good source of manganese, niacin, molybdenum, folate, vitamin E, phosphorus, vitamin B1, and protein.

Taco Seasoning

Yield: 1/2 cup

Ingredients

2 teaspoon organic potato flour

4 teaspoon organic chili powder

2 teaspoon organic paprika

2 teaspoon dried organic minced onion

1 teaspoon cumin

1/2 teaspoon cayenne pepper (if desired)

1 teaspoon organic garlic powder

1 teaspoon organic ground oregano

Directions

1. Combine all of the ingredients in a mortar and pestle and grind together
2. Transfer to a jar with a lid and label of contents and date

Description

Not only is this homemade taco seasoning more nutritious, it's also cheap! It has no chemicals or MSG. This recipe can easily be doubled or tripled to have on hand, readily and available.

Condiments

Tomato Ketchup

Yield: 1 cup

Ingredients

1 (6-ounce) can organic tomato paste, no salt added

1/2 teaspoon organic lemon juice, fresh squeezed

1 teaspoon organic garlic powder

1 teaspoon organic onion powder

1/4 teaspoon organic clove powder

1 teaspoon dried organic yellow mustard

1/4 teaspoon Celtic or Himalayan salt

1 teaspoon organic Worcestershire sauce (no soy)

2 tablespoons organic black strap molasses

1 teaspoon organic red wine vinegar

1/4 cup filtered or distilled water

Directions

1. Purée in all ingredients in food processor or blender
2. In stainless steel sauce pan over medium low heat simmer gently, stirring occasionally, until a thick consistency is reached, about 30 minutes; taste to adjust flavor if necessary
3. Reduce to low and simmer for 5 minutes and continue stirring
4. Remove from heat and cool
5. Spoon into glass container, label, date, cover and store in refrigerator for up to 2-3 weeks

Description

This recipe can easily be doubled or tripled to have on hand, readily and available. Homemade tomato ketchup tests carried out by Finnish scientists found that ketchup could cut low-density lipoprotein, aka "bad cholesterol". Homemade has no refined sugar, higher in vitamin C and has no MSG. This ketchup can also be used for a seafood cocktail sauce just by adding a little horseradish.

Salad Dressings

In homemade dressings you know what's actually in them and they are easy to make and cheaper on the pocket. They even can be made in advance and ready for use.

Cheeses and milk are in some of the recipes. Make sure cheeses and milk are from animals not fed BGH, are grass or flax fed. As with all cheese, pay attention to its frequent use.

Salad Dressings

Salad Dressing Information

Most of the oils used in nonorganic salad dressings today come from genetically engineered soy or canola. These crops have never been tested for their impact on human health which is grown using massive amounts of pesticides that can wind up inside of the food as well.

Titanium dioxide which is in paint, make colors brighter and is a common ingredient in salad dressings and supposed to seem fresher. Titanium dioxide is sometimes contaminated with lead. Watch out for red fruit color which is from Red #40, an artificial food dye linked to ADHD in children. Yellow #5, a fake food dye, causes allergic reactions in certain people and could harbor cancer-causing substances like benzidine. Many salad dressing flavors like honey mustard, Caesar, or creamy balsamic may rely on caramel coloring to give them their rich brown or golden hue. Some of these caramel colors have been linked to cancer. Trans-fats are required to be labeled, but there are loopholes and food manufacturers are capitalizing on it as only .5 grams of trans-fat per serving are not required to disclose this on the label. Read the label and if it lists "partially hydrogenated," "shortening," or "interesterified", watch out. Avoid products listing MSG or monosodium glutamate; other ingredients hidden MSG labeling like natural flavoring and hydrolyzed vegetable protein could also contain glutamate, according to CSPI (Center for Science in Public Interest).[1]

Opt for organic when buying dressing at the supermarket if you want, but homemade dressings are better than any processed kind.

1. Rodales Organic Life: http://www.rodalesorganiclife.com/wellbeing/6-shocking-facts-about-salad-dressing

Salad Dressings

Blue Cheese Dressing

Yield: 1 ½ cup

Ingredients

1/2 cup Greek Yogurt

1/2 cup milk, whole organic vitamin D

1 cup mayonnaise homemade

(See recipe-Condiments) or store-bought organic mayonnaise

4 ounces blue cheese, crumbled

1/8 teaspoon onion powder

Directions

1. Combine all ingredients into a bowl and mix well to incorporate
2. Pour into glass jar, date and store in refrigerator
3. Use within 10 days

Salad Dressings

Caesar Garlic Dressing

Yield: 1 cup

Ingredients

2 organic cloves garlic, minced

1/4 cup low fat organic parmesan cheese, grated

1/2 teaspoon dry mustard

2 tablespoons organic fresh squeezed lemon juice

1 organic free range egg

1 teaspoon Worcestershire sauce (with no Soy)

2 tablespoons organic red wine vinegar

1/2 cup flaxseed oil or cold pressed olive oil

4 tablespoons Greek Yogurt (depending on desired dressing thickness)

Directions

1. Juice lemon; mince garlic
2. Mix egg, vinegar, Worcestershire sauce, garlic, dry mustard, and lemon juice in blender or food processor and blend well
3. Add oil slowly to blend all ingredients together
4. Add yogurt and parmesan cheese (add more yogurt for a thicker dressing)
5. Pour into glass jar, date and store in refrigerator for 10 days

Celery Seed Dressing

Yield: 1 cup

Ingredients

1/4 cup pure natural honey

2 teaspoons dry mustard

1 teaspoon celery seeds

1 tablespoon organic onion, chopped

1/3 cup organic red wine vinegar

1 cup flaxseed oil or cold pressed extra virgin olive oil

1/4 teaspoon thyme, dried organic

Directions

1. Chop a small slice of onion for one tablespoon

2. In a food processor or blender combine all ingredients and blend well

3. Pour into glass jar, date and store in refrigerator for 10 days

Salad Dressings

Old Fashioned French Dressing

Yield: 1 ½ cup

Ingredients

1/4 cup distilled or filtered water

1/4 cup organic red wine vinegar

1 tablespoon organic fresh squeezed lemon juice

1 teaspoon Worcestershire sauce (without soy)

1 teaspoon dry mustard

1 organic garlic clove, minced

1 cup flaxseed oil or cold pressed extra virgin olive oil

Directions

1. Juice lemon; mince garlic
2. Place all ingredients in blender or food processor and blend
3. Pour into glass jar, date and store in refrigerator for up to 10 days
4. Shake before serving

Creamy French:

Follow recipe above

1. Add 1 teaspoon pure natural honey
2. 3 tablespoons Greek yogurt

Yield: 1 ½ cup

Spicy French:

Follow recipe above

Add 1 tablespoon finely chopped horseradish

Yield: 1 ½ cup

Salad Dressings

Onion Garlic or French Style Vinaigrette Dressing

Yield: 1 cup

Ingredients

1 large organic onion, minced

3 organic garlic cloves, minced

2 tablespoons organic red wine vinegar

1/2 teaspoon coarsely ground rosemary, dried

1/2 teaspoon oregano, dried

1/2 teaspoon basil, dried

1/2 teaspoon thyme, dried

1/2 teaspoon marjoram, dried

Directions

1. Mince onion and garlic; process all ingredients in a blender or food processor; mix to a thick consistency
2. This is the base for the dressing and is stored and dated in a glass covered bowl in the refrigerator for up to 2 weeks. You can also use the base on individual pizzas

Yield: about 1 cup

Onion Garlic Dressing:

1. Spoon ¼ cup dressing base into a pint glass jar
2. Add ¼ cup organic red wine vinegar and ½ cup flax seed oil or cold pressed extra virgin olive oil and shake vigorously
3. Date jar and store in refrigerator up to 10 days

Yield: about 1 cup dressing

Onion Garlic or French style Vinaigrette Dressing continued

French style vinaigrette:
1. Spoon ¼ cup dressing base into a glass pint jar
2. Add ¼ cup organic red wine vinegar, 1 teaspoon Dijon type mustard and ½ cup flax seed oil or cold pressed extra virgin olive oil and shake vigorously
3. Date jar and store in refrigerator

Yield: 1 cup dressing

Marinade: Excellent for gas fired BBQ veggies
1. Process in blender ¼ c dressing base
2. Add ¼ cup organic red wine vinegar
3. ½ c flax oil or cold pressed extra virgin olive oil
4. Add another ¼ teaspoon of each of the herbs and another minced garlic clove
5. Pour into a large bowl with desired sliced veggies, cover and refrigerate for 2 hours
6. Remove veggies and BBQ on a gas grill or stove top griddle for 2 minutes on each side

Peanut Dressing

Yield: 2/3 cup

Ingredients

1/3 cup distilled or filtered water

3 tablespoons homemade peanut butter (see recipe-Condiments) or reduced-fat creamy organic store-bought peanut butter

2 tablespoons Oshawa Nama Shoyu (organic fermented unpasteurized soy)

1 tablespoon pure natural honey

1/4 teaspoon ground ginger, dried

1/8 teaspoon ground red pepper or cayenne

1 organic garlic clove, minced

1 tablespoon organic red wine vinegar

Directions

1. Mince garlic
2. In a small saucepan, combine all ingredients
3. Whisk continually over medium-low heat about 3 minutes or until smooth and slightly thickened (mixture will appear curdled but will become smooth as whisking continues)
4. Pour into glass jar, date and store in refrigerator for up to 10 days

Salad Dressings

Pumpkin Vinaigrette Dressing

Yield: 1 cup

Ingredients

1/2 cup organic pumpkin

1/2 cup organic apple cider vinegar

1/2 cup flaxseed oil or cold pressed extra virgin olive oil

1 tablespoon organic garlic clove, minced

1 tablespoon organic store-bought Dijon style mustard or mild homemade mustard

(see recipe-Condiments)

Directions

1. Wash and quarter small pumpkin; remove seeds and bake at 425° F for 30 minutes or until the pumpkin is soft; if pumpkin frozen, thaw and measure 1/2 cup (organic unsweetened store-bought pumpkin can be used if fresh pumpkin is unavailable)
2. Cool, peel off skin and cut into small cubes; measure 1/2 cup and freeze remaining pumpkin for future use
3. Transfer pumpkin to a food processor or blender
4. Add remaining ingredients with pumpkin and blend together
5. Date and store in refrigerator for up to 10 days

Salad Dressings

Ranch Dressing

Yield: 1 cup

Ingredients

1 cup low fat plain yogurt

3 tablespoons Greek Yogurt (or more for desired thickness)

1 teaspoon parsley, dried

1 teaspoon organic onion, minced

1/2 teaspoon dill weed, dried

1 teaspoon organic fresh squeezed lemon juice

2 teaspoons onion powder

2 teaspoons garlic powder

6 low sodium organic saltine crackers

Directions

1. Mince onion; squeeze juice

2. Mix all together in food processor or blender

3. Pour into glass jar, date and store in refrigerator for up to 10 days

Salad Dressings

Sweet Tomato Dressing

Yield: 1 cup

Ingredients

2 medium organic tomatoes

2 teaspoons pure natural honey or 100% pure maple syrup

1 tablespoon organic red wine vinegar

1/2 cup flaxseed oil or cold pressed extra virgin olive oil

1 teaspoon garlic powder

1 teaspoon onion powder

1 teaspoon ground, rosemary, dried

1 teaspoon oregano, dried

1 teaspoon ground thyme, dried

Directions

1. Wash tomatoes with vinegar water and cut into chunks
2. Transfer to a blender or food processer and liquefy all ingredients together
3. Pour into glass jar, date and store in refrigerator for up to 10 days

Salad Dressings

Tomato Base and Dressing

Yield: 1 ¼ cup base; 1 cup dressing

Ingredients

14 sundried tomatoes halves

1 cup organic vegetable stock

2 tablespoons flaxseed oil or cold pressed
extra virgin olive oil

2 tablespoons organic red wine vinegar

1/2 cup organic onion, chopped

2 organic garlic cloves, minced

1 teaspoon coarse ground rosemary, dried

1 teaspoon oregano, dried

1 teaspoon coarse ground thyme, dried

Directions

Dressing base; prepare ahead

1. Bring 1 cup vegetable stock to a boil and remove from heat and add 14 sundried tomato halves and let cool (If no sundried tomatoes are available use a 6ounce can with no salt added organic tomato paste – no stock or cooking required)
2. Mince garlic and chop onion
3. When tomatoes are cooled transfer tomatoes and stock to food processor or blender and mix all ingredients to a tomato paste consistency
4. Store in glass jar, date and refrigerate for up to 2 weeks until needed to make the dressing. You can also use the base on individual pizzas

Tomato Dressing:

1. Spoon ¼ cup tomato dressing base into pint glass jar
2. Add ¼ cup red wine vinegar
3. Add ½ cup flax seed oil or extra virgin olive oil and shake vigorously
4. Date jar and store in refrigerator for up to 10 days

Salad Dressings

Yogurt Cucumber Dressing

Yield: 1 ½ cup

Ingredients

1 organic cucumber, sliced

1/2 teaspoon marjoram, dried

1/2 teaspoon dill weed, dried

1 teaspoon organic fresh squeezed lemon juice

1/2 teaspoon organic onion, finely chopped

1 tablespoon Greek Yogurt, more if thicker dressing is desired

Directions

1. Wash cucumber and slice; mince onion and juice lemon

2. Mix all together in food processor or blender

3. Pour into glass jar, date and store in refrigerator for up to 10 days

Sauces and Dips

In cooking, sauces are also used in preparing other foods and are not normally consumed by themselves. Store-bought sauces and dips are often overloaded with sodium and sugar so become a label reader and opt for organic. However, it is better to make your own healthy sauces for satisfying and healthy meals.

Sauces and Dips

Sauce and Dip Information

The encyclopedia defines sauce, seasoning or flavoring composition, usually in liquid or semi-liquid form, used as an appetizing accompaniment for meat, fish, vegetables, and desserts.

Sauces add flavor, moisture, and visual appeal to another dish and are an important feature of quality cookery, especially in France. Sauces have often been named for the chefs who created them. Sauces may be classed as hot and cold. The hot is usually white and brown and the cold such as a mayonnaise type are used for coating cold foods and often contain gelatin. Hot sauces are typically made with a flour base, fat, and milk or broth. Hot sauces may be varied by seasonings and added ingredients. Stewed fruits, such as apple and cranberry, are sometimes classified as sauces. Commercial sauces, which are finely blended extracts of various fruits and vegetables with vinegar and condiments, include Worcestershire sauce, Leicester sauce, chili sauce, Creole sauce, soy sauce like Nama Shoyu, and Tabasco.

A dip or dipping sauce is a common condiment for many types of food and are used to add flavor or texture to a food. Sauces are applied to the food; with dips, the food is put in or dipped into the food. Dips are generally finger foods, appetizers, or other hand held foods. Thick dips based on sour cream, crème fraiche, milk, yogurt, mayonnaise, soft cheese, or even beans are a staple of American hors d'oeuvres and are thinner than spreads to make dips. Alton Brown, a food show presenter, author, and actor, suggests that a dip is defined based on its ability to "maintain contact with its transport mechanism over three feet of white carpet". Dips in various forms are eaten all over the world and people have been using sauces for dipping for thousands of years.

Sauces and Dips

Cranberry Apple Sauce

Yield: 1 ½ cups

Ingredients

1 lb organic fresh cranberries

1 cup sucanat (organic unrefined sugar)

1/2 cup organic apple juice

2 tablespoons organic lemon juice, fresh squeezed

1/2 teaspoon grated lemon peel, zest

2 organic apple, cored and diced

1/2 teaspoon cinnamon

1/8 teaspoon allspice

1/8 teaspoon ground cloves

Directions

1. Wash fruit in vinegar water; core, peel and dice apple; squeeze juice; zest citrus
2. Sort shriveled and undesirable cranberries after washing
3. Place cranberries in a 2 quart saucepan over medium heat and add diced apples, apple juice, sugar and cover
4. When the cranberry mixture starts to bubble, reduce heat to low and cook for 12 minutes or until cranberries burst; remove from heat and cool
5. Transfer cooled cranberry apple mixture to a food processor; stir in the spices; pulse until well blended; pulse in freshly squeezed citrus juice and add grated citrus peel (zest)
6. Transfer to a jam jar labeled and dated and stored in the refrigerator for up to 3 weeks

Description

Phytonutrients in cranberries offer antioxidant, anti-inflammatory and anti-cancer health benefits.

Sauces and Dips

Cranberry Orange Marmalade Sauce

Yield: 1 cup

Ingredients

2 cups fresh organic cranberries, coarsely chopped

1/4 cup organic orange juice, fresh squeezed

1/4 cup 100% organic cranberry juice

(not cocktail juice)

3/4 cup organic orange marmalade

1/4 teaspoon ground ginger

1/3 cup pecans, finely chopped

Directions

1. Sort shriveled and undesirable cranberries; rinse well; coarsely chopped, squeeze juice
2. Add juices and marmalade in a 2 qrt stainless steel saucepan over medium-high heat; bring to a boil; at boiling point reduce heat to medium-low and simmer for 5 minutes
3. Add cranberries to juice mixture; cook for 15 minutes, stirring occasionally until the cranberries burst and mixture thickens
4. Stir in nuts and remove from the heat to cool
5. Transfer to a jam jar labeled and dated and stored in the refrigerator for up to 3 weeks

Description

This sauce is great in the mornings to spread on toast. Cranberries are a very good source of vitamin C, dietary fiber, and manganese, as well as a good source of vitamin E, vitamin K, copper, and pantothenic acid.

Sauces and Dips

Cranberry with Dried Apricots Sauce

Yield: 2 cups

Ingredients

2 cups fresh organic cranberries

1/2 teaspoon ground cardamom

1¾ cups organic apricot nectar

1/2 cup sucanat (organic unrefined sugar)

1/2 cup apricot preserves

1/2 cup dried apricots, dice

1/3 cup organic lemon juice, fresh squeezed

1½ teaspoons grated lemon peel, zest

1/4 cup unrefined honey

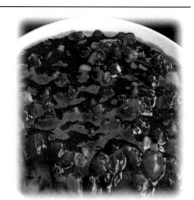

Directions

1. Sort shriveled and undesirable cranberries and rinse well; diced dried apricots
2. Bring nectar, cardamom, sugar, preserves, juice and honey to a boil in stainless steel saucepan over medium heat; stir until sugar dissolves
3. Add diced apricots; cook 2 minutes
4. Add cranberries; cook until berries pop, stirring occasionally, about 10 minutes; mix in lemon zest; remove from heat at cool
5. When cooled to lukewarm; transfer to a jam jar labeled and dated and stored in the refrigerator for up to 3 weeks

Description

The nice thing about cranberry sauces is that it goes well with potatoes as a side dish or on top of pancakes for a tangy sweet delightful taste. Cranberry sauce is also wonderful in Greek yogurt and can be added until you get the intensity of flavor desired.

Sauces and Dips

Dill Sauce

Yield: 1 cup

Ingredients

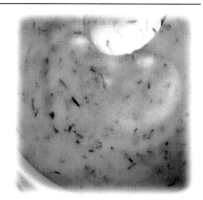

1 cup milk, whole organic Vitamin D

2 tablespoons Greek Yogurt

1 tablespoon organic butter

1 tablespoon organic arrowroot or non GMO corn
starch

2 teaspoons dill, dried

1/2 teaspoon garlic powder

1/2 teaspoon onion powder

Directions

1. Melt butter in small stainless steel saucepan over low heat
2. Add dill and seasonings
3. Whisk yogurt and milk together in a small bowl and add to butter slowly stirring
4. Add 1 teaspoon filtered water in a cup with arrowroot; stir to dissolve
5. Stir in dissolved arrowroot; increase heat to medium low and continue to stir until thickened; remove from heat
6. Use immediately hot or transfer to a glass container; label and date, cover and refrigerator up to 2 weeks; reheat if desired

Description

This is a perfect sauce to complement any fish dish.

Sauces and Dips

Enchilada Sauce

Yield: 6 cups

Ingredients

1/4 cup extra virgin olive oil

4 tablespoons potato flour

4 cups homemade tomato sauce or 1 (28-oz) store-bought organic tomato sauce, no added salt

2 cups vegetable or chicken broth (see recipe-Basic Broth) or organic low sodium store-bought

1 (10-ounce) can organic tomato paste, no salt added

1½ teaspoons garlic powder

1½ teaspoons oregano, dried

1½ teaspoons onion powder

1½ teaspoons cumin

1 teaspoon basil, dried

4 tablespoons chili powder (more for spicy hot sauce)

Directions

1. Add flour to oil in stainless steel saucepan over medium heat and stir for 1 minute; combine broth and stir 1 minute
2. Stir in remaining ingredients and bring to a boil; at boiling point reduce heat to low and simmer for 15 minutes until smooth and thick, stirring occasionally
3. Use the sauce immediately or let cool completely before refrigerating in an air tight container for up to 2 weeks or freeze up to 4 months

Description

Enchilada sauce can be used for so many other dishes besides enchiladas. It also makes a wonderful dressing. It just takes imagination.

1. Mix 1/2 cup of sauce with 2 tablespoons organic red wine vinegar in a lidded jar
2. Add 1/2 cup flaxseed oil or cold pressed extra virgin olive oil and shake vigorously

Sauces and Dips

Hot Artichoke Dip

Yield: 2 cups   Preheat oven 425°F

Ingredients

1 cup homemade mayonnaise or organic store-bought

1 cup low fat organic parmesan cheese, grated

1 jar artichoke hearts, drained and mashed

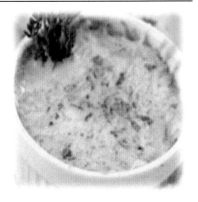

Directions

1. Drain and mash artichokes and prepare homemade mayonnaise
2. Combine all ingredients to a bowl and mix well
3. Transfer to a well oiled baking/serving dish
4. Bake for 20 minutes or until bubbly
5. Remove and serve with cleaned cut up vegetables or small pieces of sourdough bread for dipping as an appetizer

Description

The phytonutrients in artichokes provide potent antioxidant benefits. In a 2006 study conducted by the US Department of Agriculture and published in the American Journal of Clinical Nutrition showed that a serving of artichokes provides greater antioxidant benefits per serving than many other foods traditionally considered to be antioxidant-rich such as dark chocolate, blueberries and red wine.

Anthocyanins, quercetin, rutin, and many other antioxidants contained in **fresh artichokes** offer a range of health benefits from cancer prevention and immune support to protection against heart disease. When using a store-bought marinated artichoke it is very important to read the label. Watch the sodium, calorie and fat count.

Sauces and Dips

Hummus

Yield: 2½ cups   Preheat oven to broil

Ingredients

1 organic red bell pepper

4 organic garlic cloves

1 small organic onion

2 cups cooked organic chickpeas or well drained
organic store-bought chickpeas

1/3 cup organic sesame tahini

1 tablespoon organic lemon juice, fresh squeezed

1 tablespoon Worcestershire sauce (without soy)

Directions

1. Wash, core and deseed red pepper; peel garlic and onion
2. Line cookie sheet with parchment paper and spray lightly with avocado oil
3. Roast pepper, garlic and small onion on cookie sheet
4. Vegetables should be soft and slightly browned when done
5. Remove and place covered in bowl so the ingredients sweats and cools
6. When cooled to the touch, remove from bowl and peel the skin from red pepper
7. Place in food processor and add remaining ingredients and blend until smooth; if the hummus is too dry add a little water
8. Hummus can be refrigerated up to 2 weeks in covered glass bowl

Description

Chickpeas, also called garbanzo beans, belong to the legume family, which includes a variety of beans, peanuts, and lentils. Chickpeas also provide a vegetarian-friendly source of protein and fiber. Another idea for dip is to add Greek yogurt to tahini. Use it as a veggie sandwich spread or a veggie dip.

Sauces and Dips

Salsa

Yield: 2 cups   Preheat oven to broil

Ingredients

3 organic large tomatoes, roasted

1 organic red pepper, roasted

1 large organic Anaheim pepper (Anaheim pepper is a mild variety; use jalapeños if more spice is desired)

1 large organic yellow onion, roasted

4 organic garlic cloves, roasted

1/4 cup fresh organic cilantro, chopped

1 tablespoon organic lime juice, fresh squeezed

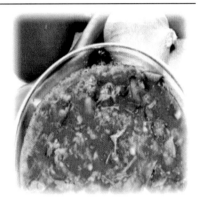

Directions

1. Wash tomatoes, peppers and cilantro in vinegar water; pat dry; coat tomatoes with extra virgin olive oil to aid in peeling after roasting; peel onion and garlic

2. Roast tomatoes, peppers, garlic and onion on a parchment covered cookie sheet until lightly browned in boiler

3. Remove and place covered in bowl so the ingredients sweats and cools

4. When cooled, peel tomatoes and peppers (wear rubber gloves when using a spicier or hot pepper and keep away from skin and eyes); deseed peppers

5. Place cooled roasted onion and garlic in food processor and pulse

6. Add all remaining cooled ingredients and pulse (do not over pulse to make salsa mushy)

7. Transfer to a covered glass container to cool or use immediately; label and date container covered in refrigerator for up to 3 weeks or store in freezer up to 4 months

Description

This is a great sauce to serve with any meal to add rich flavors

Salsa II

Yield: 2 cups   Preheat oven to broil

Ingredients

1 organic roasted tomato, chopped

1 small organic zucchini, finely chopped

1/2 organic roasted yellow bell pepper, chopped

1/2 organic roasted orange bell pepper, chopped

1/2 organic red onion, roasted, chopped

1 garlic clove, minced

1 tablespoon fresh organic cilantro, chopped

1 tablespoon organic lime juice, fresh squeezed

2 teaspoons extra-virgin olive oil

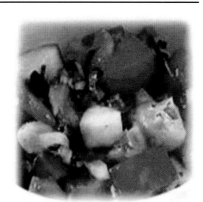

Directions

1. Wash tomatoes, peppers and cilantro in vinegar water; pat dry
2. Roast tomatoes, peppers, garlic and onion on a parchment covered cookie sheet until lightly browned in boiler
3. Remove and place covered in bowl so the ingredients sweats and cools
4. When cooled, peel tomatoes and peppers; chop roasted tomato, peppers, onion and garlic; chop zucchini and cilantro
5. Combine all ingredients in a small bowl and mix together with juice and oil
6. Store salsa in the refrigerator for up to 3 days

Description

Nice for a Mediterranean meal.

Sauces and Dips

Spaghetti Sauce

Yield: 6 cups

Ingredients

2 tablespoons extra virgin olive oil

1 tablespoon organic low sodium store-bought vegetable or chicken base (bouillon)

 3 organic garlic cloves, minced

1 large organic onion, chopped

1 organic green pepper, chopped and deseeded

2 (14-ounce) organic store-bought stewed tomatoes with no salt added (do not drain)

2 cups homemade tomato sauce or 1(14-ounce) organic store-bought tomato sauce

1 (16-ounce) organic store-bought tomato paste, no salt added

2 tablespoons sucanat (organic unrefined sugar)

2 teaspoons basil, dried

2 teaspoons oregano, dried

2 teaspoons marjoram, dried

2 teaspoons thyme, dried

1/4 cayenne pepper, if desired

Directions

1. Wash pepper in vinegar water, pat dry; deseed and chop pepper and onion, mince garlic
2. Sauté onion and green pepper in a stainless steel stock pot with olive oil until onions are transparent; add garlic and vegetable base and sauté 1 minute
3. Add remaining ingredients and simmer 1 hour, mashing tomatoes and stirring occasionally

Spaghetti Sauce continued

4. Serve immediately with cooked spaghetti squash, homemade noodles (see Pasta Dough recipe-Main Dishes) or other organic store-bought noodles of choice and a green salad
5. Or, transfer to a covered glass container after cooled; label and date container covered in refrigerator for up to 2 weeks or store in freezer up to 4 months

Description

This is also delicious served with Vegetarian Sausage/Meatballs (see recipe-Main Dishes) Tomatoes are a fruit but are commonly eaten as a vegetable. Tomatoes are low in calories and fat contents and have zero cholesterol levels. They are an excellent source of antioxidants, dietary fiber, minerals, and vitamins.

Sauces and Dips

Tartar Sauce

Yield: 1 cup

Ingredients

1 cup mayonnaise homemade
(see recipe-Condiments) or organic store-bought low
sodium mayonnaise

Homemade dill pickles or 1/2 cup organic store-
bought dill pickles, finely chopped

2 tablespoons organic green onions, finely chopped

2 tablespoons organic parsley, fresh finely chopped

1 tablespoon organic lemon juice, fresh squeezed

Directions

1. Chop pickles, green onion and parsley
2. Blend all ingredients in a food processor
3. Transfer to a glass container; label and date, cover and refrigerator up to 2 weeks

Description

Not only does tartar sauce complement fish, it is also a great to substitute plain
mayonnaise for tartar sauce in potato salads.

Sauces and Dips

Tangy White Sauce

Yield: 2 cups

Ingredients

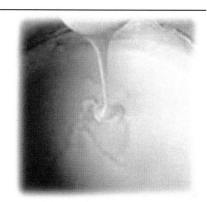

2 tablespoons ghee

3 tablespoons organic potato flour

1 tablespoon organic low sodium store-bought
vegetable or chicken bouillon

1 tablespoon organic lemon, fresh squeezed

1/2 cup water

1/2 cup organic low fat yogurt

1 cup milk, whole organic Vitamin D

Directions

1. Melt ghee in a saucepan over medium low heat; stir in flour and bouillon until roux is well blended; continue to cook and stir until thickened and lightly browned, about 5 minutes.
2. Increase heat to medium and whisk water into roux until smooth
3. Whisk together yogurt and milk and into roux; cook and stir until thickened, about 2 minutes more and add squeeze lemon into sauce; stir until well combined

Description

This can be an eggless hollandaise or don't add the lemon and mix with vegetables or any pasta dish.

Vegetable Dill Dip

Yield: 1 cup

Ingredients

1/2 cup Greek Yogurt

1/2 cup homemade mayonnaise (see recipe-Condiments) or organic low sodium store-bought

Juice from half organic lemon

2 teaspoons dill, dried

1/2 teaspoon parsley, dried

2 organic garlic clove, minced

1 tablespoon organic onion, minced

Directions

1. Whisk all ingredients together in a small bowl
2. Use immediately or transfer to a glass container; label and date, cover and refrigerator up to 2 weeks

Description

Serve with a plate of fresh organic chopped vegetables of choice as an appetizer. To make this thicker creamier dip, add 1/2 cup organic cream cheese.

Sourdough and Breads

Wheat breads, pasta, crackers, bagels, cereal all spike blood sugar levels, which signals the body to store fat and age faster. Some of these side effects include inflammation, cramps, and bloating. These symptoms can be very frustrating! If you want to lose substantial amounts of weight and keep your pH at a premium level, then gluten should be reduced to a minimum in your diet. For those who have neither the time nor the inclination for bread making, properly made sourdough breads are now commercially available. But please be a label reader, especially for salt content.

Sourdough and Breads

Appreciating and Understanding Rye and Wheat

There is a lot of information about sourdough and starter cultures. I find that www.culturesforhealth.com or www.kingarthur.com seem to have the best information and products. Another wonderful site I love is www.thenourishingcook.com and their book "Nourishing Traditions" as it challenges politically correct nutrition.

Sourdough rye bread is traditional bread throughout the Scandinavian countries. Many different types of rye grain have come from north-central and eastern Europe, many parts of Central Europe, and Germany. Dark rye bread was considered a staple through the middle ages.

The gluten in rye is inferior to wheat which makes rye tricky to bake. To assist with this problem most bakers mix rye with wheat flour to give the dough more structure. Learning and working with sourdough, takes practice and practice makes perfect. But first, to make a great loaf of bread there needs to be an understanding of some of the flours.

Rye and wheat grains both contain enzymes that break down their starches and a loaf of baked bread needs these starches. Water and heat gelatinized starch and make it susceptible to the action of enzymes. Rye enzymes are more heat stable than wheat. The heat stable rye bread made with only rye flour tends to be flat from the action of the enzymes on the starch. Adding wheat flour to the dough gives the bread more structure as more of the enzyme has been inactivated which leaves more starch to gelatinize. The acidic pH of naturally fermented dough also helps to inhibit the action of rye enzymes. That may be why all traditional rye breads are made from sourdough.

The correct proportion of wheat to rye flour depends on what kind of bread you want to make. If you want a light sandwich type of bread, limit the rye flour to about 20% of the total flour. Most traditional German rye breads contain around 30% rye, but they ferment the bread which lowers the pH to inhibit the action of enzymes. One of the traditional European rye breads, Vollkornbrot, contains 100% coarse rye meal. It takes a long time to rise and ferment and produces heavy, dense, and chewy loaves. They are delicious, although not generally what the American palate is accustomed to.

Sourdough and Breads

Appreciating and Understanding Rye and Wheat

Individuals with grain allergies often tolerate wheat products that have first been soaked, sprouted or fermented; but many must avoid wheat altogether even when it has been properly prepared. Those who are allergic to milk products can use water and add a small amount of whey or yogurt, but it may not have as satisfactory results. Some baked good recipes soak flour in sour or cultured milk, buttermilk or cream which helps with digestion. If using a soaked method, flour products should be soaked at room temperature for at least from 4 to 12 hours but better results may be obtained with a 24-hour soaking. Because grains are acidic, buttermilk, cultured milk, yogurt and whey (as well as lemon juice and vinegar) activate the enzyme phytase, which works to break down phytic acid in the bran of grains. However this is not necessary for sourdough.

Sourdough breads take more dedication and time than regular breads. They must be made with high gluten flours, such as spelt, kamut, hard winter wheat or rye. Older wheat varieties, such as einkorn, emmer, spelt and kamut, are the first choice for substitutes because they mimic the properties of modern hybrid or genetically modified (GM) wheat; and no special adjustments are needed when substituting them for wheat in most recipes. (For those who have neither the time nor the inclination for bread making, properly made sourdough breads are now commercially available. But please be a label reader, especially for salt content.)

Everyone should avoid two grain products considered to be health foods which are bran and wheat germ. Bran is high in phytates and wheat germ is extremely susceptible in becoming rancid. Eating the bran and germ separate from the starchy portion of grain, presents as many problems as eating the starchy portion of germ separated from the bran and the germ. Traditionally people consume all parts of grain together but they are freshly ground or milled and properly prepared.

Many alternative flours are also available, not only those that contain gluten, such as rye, barley or oat, but also non-gluten flours like corn, rice, millet, buckwheat, amaranth, quinoa, potato, tapioca, bean and tuber flours. All of these may be used for baked goods, such as muffins, pancakes, waffles and soda breads; but certain adjustments must be made to the recipes because these flours are heavier than wheat flour and do not rise as well.

Sourdough and Breads

Appreciating and Understanding Rye and Wheat

Specific recipes for alternate flours are beyond the scope of this book. However you should add baking soda and baking powder (see homemade baking powder recipe under Condiments) to alternative grain recipes in the proportion of 2 level teaspoons per cup of flour. You may wish to add guar gum to your batter if it seems too runny as alternative flours do not absorb water as well as wheat or spelt. Use ½ teaspoon guar gum per cup of flour.

Soy flours should not be used. Soy contains high phytate content as well as potent enzyme inhibitors. These are not inactivated by ordinary cooking methods, such as soaking. Soy needs a long slow fermentation process for proper results that are used in the traditional fermented soy products. The anti-nutrients in modern soy products and soy flour can inhibit growth and cause intestinal problems, swelling of the pancreas and even cancer tumor growth. In addition, soy contains a high omega-3 content that quickly goes rancid when the bean is made into flour. Soy flour has a disagreeable taste that is difficult to mask (nature's way of telling us to avoid it). The phytoestrogens in soy have been promoted as panaceas (a solution or remedy for all difficulties or diseases) but soy actually depresses the thyroid function causing hormonal problems.

Sourdough and Breads

Make Your Own Sourdough Starter

Make sure all ingredients purchased are organic. When wheat is referred to, use organic einkorn wheat or its evolutionary successor emmer wheat to replace the modern industrial wheat. Always use a glass, wooden or plastic containers and utensils. Never use metal storing or mixing sourdough starter. Sourdough is naturally acidic and long exposure to specific metals, such as copper and aluminum, may damage sourdough. Therefore it's advised to keep starters in glass jars or plastic containers. However, brief contact with metals mixing the starter with a stainless steel utensil for recipes will not cause detrimental effects to the metal or sourdough. When water is referred to, use chlorine-free, filtered, distilled or purified water.

Your sourdough starter can be researched and/or purchased online. Before I knew how to make starter I purchased mine from www.kingarthurflour.com. If you decide to make your own let's get started.

Day 1: Depending on which starter you wish to make and have on hand, both rye and wheat are made using the same process. Combine 1 cup flour with 1/2 cup cool water (it's also important to feed your starter with chlorine-free, filtered, distilled or purified cool water from now on) in a 4 cup non-reactive container, such as glass or crockery. I use a small ceramic cookie jar which has a loose lid. Whole grain flour (wheat or rye) is used because whole grains contain more nutrients and sourdough friendly microorganisms than all-purpose flour.

Stir everything together thoroughly; make sure there's no dry flour anywhere. Cover the container loosely and let the mixture sit in a warm room temperature (about 70°F) for 24 hours. A cooler environment causes your starter to grow more slowly. If the normal temperature in your home is below 68°F, use a smaller, warmer spot to develop your starter or place it on top of a water heater or any appliance that may generate a small amount of heat or place it on top a heating pad on a low setting.

Make Your Own Sourdough Starter

Day 2: The first 24 hours you may see bubbling or some growth activity. Discard half the starter and add 1 cup flour to the remaining starter with 1/2 cup cool water if your house is warm; or lukewarm water if it's on the cooler side. Mix well, cover, and let the mixture rest at room temperature for 24 hours. Discarding half the starter is necessary to prevent from having too much starter; keeping the starter volume the same helps balance the pH level; and the discarding makes the yeast have more food to eat each time you feed it for growth.

Days 3: By the third day you'll see more bubbling; a fresh, fruity aroma, and some evidence of expansion (growing).

Days 4 & 5: Now start two feedings daily, as evenly spaced as your schedule allows every 12 hours, i.e. 6am and 6pm or 8am and 8pm. Don't worry if it is not exactly 12 hours between feedings this is only general.

First feeding on day 4: Choose the time you want to start and thoroughly stir down the starter (remember No metal); remove and discard 1/2 starter. Add 1 cup flour and 1/2 cup water to the remaining starter. Mix the starter, flour, and water; cover and let the mixture rest at room temperature for approximately 12 hours. Repeat for the second feeding on day 4. Day 5: repeat day 4 feeding, or as many days as it takes for your starter to become very active.

Figure to the left is the starter 12 hours after feeding on day 6 which shows more vigorous activity. After about a week of consistent feeding, you actually have starter and it should be about 1¾ cups to 2 cups. You're now ready for **Sourdough Starter Care**.

Sourdough Starter Care

Never consume raw starter yourself. When feeding the starter, again I must reiterate:

- Use chlorine-free, filtered, distilled or purified water
- Always use organic einkorn wheat or emmer wheat when flour is referred to in this care
- Never use metal with any sourdough starter
- Use only wood or plastic utensils and ceramic, glass or plastic containers

1. Now that you have a starter from day 6, add ¼ cup lukewarm water to the starter container, and stir to partially dissolve the starter and loosen it from the container sides.
2. Transfer the starter to a bowl. Yield is about 2 cups.
3. Wash the normal sourdough storage container making sure it is well cleaned, well rinsed and soap free for later use.
4. In the bowl add 1¼ cup water and 2 cups flour and mix loosely, cover, and let it sit at room temperature (about 68°F to 70°F) for 8 to 12 hours. It should expand and become bubbly, or at least start to bubble.
5. Stir the starter and discard about half; this will bring the pH to the proper level. This should yield approximately 2 to 2 ½ cups of starter.
6. Mix in 1/2 cup water and 1 cup flour to remaining starter in the bowl. Let it sit for another 2 to 4 hours or until it starts to show bubbles again. This should yield approximately 4 cups of starter.
7. Divide the starter in half once more; you can give 2 cups to a friend or use it in a recipe or discard.
8. The remaining 2 cups is to be refrigerated in previously washed container. I know this all sounds overwhelming, but once your starter is made, you will get the hang of the maintenance and you will find that it is not as hard as described. It just takes practice.

Using Your Starter in a Recipe

Making "Fed" or "Ripe" Starter

If you have been storing the starter in a warm place, use the amount needed for the recipe and feed the remaining starter by mixing in 1/2 cup water and 1 cup flour. If your starter has been refrigerated, you need to feed it before you use it in a recipe.

1. Up to 12 hours before beginning a recipe, stir the refrigerated starter and discard 1 cup

2. Feed the remaining starter with 1/2 cup water and 1 cup flour. Let it sit for 4 to 12 hours. Yield: about 2 to 2 ½ cups.

3. Use however much "fed starter" the recipe calls for and feed the remainder with 1/2 cup water and 1 cup flour.

4. Let this remaining starter sit at room temperature for 2 to 4 hours, until bubbly, cover and refrigerate.

5. If you are not planning to use your starter for over a week, take it out of the refrigerator and feed it once a week as described above. Make sure you always discard half the starter. After mixing in more flour and water, you can return the starter to the refrigerator without waiting for it to get bubbly first if you don't plan to use the starter again soon.

Different methods of maintaining your starter

1. Sweetening a starter: If your starter is too sour, reserve one cup and discard the rest. Feed the reserved starter with 1 cup water and 2 cups flour. Mix well and let rest for 4 hours before using or refrigerating.

2. Increasing your starter: To grow a large amount of starter, simply feed it 1 cup of water and 2 cups of flour without discarding any. Feed again 2 to 4 hours later, and you'll have plenty on hand to use or to share.

3. Resuscitating a neglected starter: If your sourdough starter sits in the refrigerator for too long between feedings, it will develop a layer of liquid on top. It will smell very strong and will be sluggish (not produce many bubbles). If this happens, pour off most of the liquid, throw all but 1 cup of starter away. Transfer the 1 cup to a clean ceramic, glass or plastic bowl. (Wash the dirty container as previously instructed to use later.)

Using Your Starter in a Recipe continued

Feed the rescued cup of starter with 1 cup water and 1 cup flour. If the starter is still alive it will begin to bubble after a few hours. Discard half at this point and feed it again with ½ cup water and 1 cup flour and let it sit for another 2 to 4 hours to become active again; then use it or refrigerate it.

4. When to start over; If your sourdough starter begins to mold, or the odor is not the usual clean, sour aroma (an alcohol smell is OK), or if it develops a pink or orange color ton top, throw it out. It's very rare for this to happen so don't worry. Order more of the starter or make a new batch.

5. If you know you will be travelling and there is no one to feed the starter in your absence, freeze it in a clean glass, ceramic, or plastic container. Just make sure the lid is not metal and a 3 inch space is left at the top for freezing expansion. When you come home or want to use the starter, put it in room temperature for 12 hours or overnight. It may start to bubble on its own. Stir and discard half the starter and feed the remaining starter with 1/2 cup water and 1 cup flour. Let it sit for 4 to 12 hours before using in a recipe or place in the refrigerator for later use.

Notes

Sourdough Rye Bread

Yield: 1 large loaf or 2 small loaves

Ingredients

3¼ cups lukewarm water

1/2 cup "fed" sourdough starter

(See Using Your Starter in a Recipe)

1 teaspoon yeast

3¼ cups organic rye flour

3¼ cups organic unbleached einkorn flour

2 tablespoons organic black strap molasses

1 tablespoon organic fennel seeds

1 teaspoon organic anise seeds

1 teaspoon organic caraway seeds

1/2 teaspoon Himalayan or Celtic salt

Directions

1. Mix the starter and yeast with warm water in a medium sized bowl
2. Add the molasses and all the seeds and set aside
3. In a separate larger bowl combine the flours and salt
4. Gradually stir wet ingredients into the dry ingredients using a dough whisk or spoon until the flour is well incorporated; dough should be wet and sticky so do not add more flour
5. Cover the bowl with plastic and let rest for 15 minutes
6. After 15 minutes, using a dough whisk or spoon gently stir; cover bowl with plastic and let rest for another 15 minutes
7. After the last 15 minutes pour the dough onto a generously floured work surface; place a floured tea towel over the dough and cover the towel with plastic to prevent from drying out and let rest for 30 minutes

Sourdough Rye Bread continued

8. After 30 minutes remove cover and stretch out and fold the dough in half, then half again; do not knead the dough
9. Form dough into a ball and place in a baking dish and score the top of the dough with a razor or sharp serrated knife for the final rise in a warm place
10. The final rise should double in size for about 1 ½ to 2 hours
11. Preheat oven to 450°F a half hour before baking
12. Bake 10 minutes; reduce the heat to 350ºF; bake for another 40 minutes until the loaf reads at least 190 to 200ºF on a thermometer
13. Let cool completely for about one hour before cutting and eating

Description

It just takes time, but the rewards can't be beat. Rye lowers insulin response and improves blood glucose profile. In the fight against diabetes, cancer and obesity, foods that produce a low insulin response can be extremely helpful and rye can be very satisfying and filling when added to a meal. Rye may also reduce inflammation in people with metabolic syndrome.

Sourdough and Breads

Sourdough Extra Tangy Bread

Yield: 2 loaves

Ingredients

1 cup "fed" sourdough starter

(See Using Your Starter in a Recipe)

1½ cups lukewarm water

1/2 teaspoon Himalayan or Celtic salt

1 tablespoon organic sugar

5-6 cups organic unbleached einkorn flour

Directions

1. Pour the cup of starter into a large glass, plastic or ceramic mixing bowl
2. Add to starter warm water and 3 cups of flour and beat vigorously with a wooden spoon
3. Cover with plastic wrap and set it aside to rest at room temperature (68°F to 70°F) for 4 hours; refrigerate overnight or for about 12 hours
4. The next morning remove from refrigerator and reach room temperature; add salt, sugar and 2 cups flour; turn onto a well floured work surface; knead pushing and folding the dough; keep adding more flour a little at a time, if necessary, so dough no longer clings to the floured surface and is smooth and soft elastic dough
5. Place in a lightly olive oiled bowl, cover and let rise to very puffy though not necessarily doubled, about 5 hours
6. Divide the dough in half and shape into two oval loaves; cover and let rise until doubled, about 2 to 3 hours; preheat oven to 425°F; slash the tops of the loaves; bake in a for 30 minutes or until golden brown; remove and cool on a rack

Description

Extra rising time in a cool environment gives this bread a sour flavor and there's no added yeast in this recipe. Less yeast allows the dough to rise longer and slower, developing extra-sour flavor.

Sourdough and Breads

Sourdough Biscuits

Yield: 12 biscuits   Preheat oven to 400°F

Ingredients

2 cups "fed" sourdough starter

(See Using Your Starter in a Recipe)

2¾ cups organic unbleached einkorn flour

1/2 tablespoon organic aluminum free baking powder

or see homemade recipe-Condiments

1 teaspoon organic sugar

1/2 teaspoon organic baking soda

1/2 teaspoon Himalayan or Celtic salt

1/4 organic non-hydrogenated shortening or BGH free organic butter

1/2 cup milk, organic vitamin D

Directions

1. In a large bowl combine dry ingredients in a glass or ceramic mixing bowl
2. Mix soft shortening or butter into the dry ingredients until the mixture resembles cornmeal consistency
3. Stir in milk and mix well forming a ball
4. Turn dough onto floured work surface and knead gently for about 30 seconds adding additional flour if needed
5. Roll dough to about ½ inch thick
6. Cut into circles with a 1½" to 2" cutter
7. Place, not touching, on an ungreased parchment lined baking sheet
8. Cover lightly with a floured tea towel and let rest for 30 minutes
9. Brush tops lightly with melted butter or shortening and bake at 400°F for 15 minutes or until biscuits have puffed and are golden brown; remove and cool on a rack

Description

These biscuits are more "bread-like" than a traditional baking powder biscuit, but not as bread-like as the traditional yeast roll and they don't take as long to rise.

Sourdough and Breads

Sourdough Bread

Yield: 2 loaves   Preheat oven to 425°F

Ingredients

1 cup "fed" sourdough starter

(See Using Your Starter in a Recipe)

1½ cups lukewarm water

1 tablespoon organic sugar

1 teaspoons instant yeast

1/2 teaspoon Himalayan or Celtic salt

5 cups organic unbleached all purpose einkorn flour

Directions

1. Combine starter, water, sugar, salt and yeast in a large glass or ceramic bowl and mix well until all yeast is dissolved
2. Add flour a cup at a time to mix well with wet ingredients
3. When flour mixed in, turn onto a well floured work surface; knead pushing and folding the dough; keep adding more flour a little at a time, if necessary, so dough no longer clings to the floured surface and is smooth and soft elastic dough
4. Place dough in a greased (extra virgin olive oil) bowl; cover and let rise until doubled in size, 1 to 1½ hours
5. Pour dough onto well floured surface and divide the dough in half shaping into two loaves
6. Place loaves in lightly oiled and floured glass baking loaf pans
7. Cover and let rise until very puffy and double in size, 1 to 1½ hours
8. Bake in a preheated 425°F oven for 30 minutes or until golden brown
9. Remove from the oven and cool on a rack

Description

Because there is yeast in this sourdough bread recipe, the rise time is faster and is an easier bread to make. It still has the wonderful sourdough flavor.

Sourdough and Breads

Sourdough Buns

Yield: 12 buns   Preheat oven to 425ºF

Ingredients

1 cup "fed" sourdough starter

(See Using Your Starter in a Recipe)

1½ cups lukewarm water

1 tablespoon organic sugar

2 teaspoons instant yeast

1/2 teaspoon Himalayan or Celtic salt

5 cups organic unbleached all purpose einkorn

flour

Directions

1. Combine starter, water, sugar, salt and yeast in a large glass or ceramic bowl and mix well until all yeast is dissolved

2. Add flour a cup at a time to mix well with wet ingredients

3. When flour mixed in, turn onto a well floured work surface; knead pushing and folding the dough; keep adding more flour a little at a time, if necessary, so dough no longer clings to the floured surface and is smooth and soft elastic dough

4. Place dough in a greased (extra virgin olive oil) bowl, cover, and let rise until doubled in size, about 1½ hours

5. Pour dough onto well floured work surface and shape dough into a long oblong loaf; cut into 12 pieces

6. Place each, not touching to allow for expansion, on cookie sheet lined with parchment paper sprayed with olive oil; cover with a floured tea towel and let rise until very puffy and double in size, about 1 to 1 ½ hours

7. Bake in a preheated 425°F oven for 10 minutes and reduce to 350°F and continue to bake for an added 15 minutes or until golden brown

8. Remove from the oven and cool on a rack

Sourdough and Breads

Sourdough Baguettes or French Bread

Yield: 3 baguettes   Preheat oven to 425ºF

Ingredients

2 cups "fed" sourdough starter

(See Using Your Starter in a Recipe)

2 teaspoons dry yeast

1 cup warm water

3 teaspoons organic sugar

1/2 teaspoon Himalayan or Celtic salt

5-6 cups organic unbleached all purpose einkorn

flour

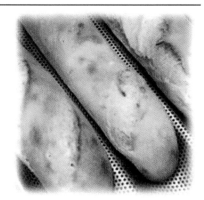

Baguette Directions

1. In a large glass or ceramic bowl combine starter with water, sugar, salt and yeast and mix well until all yeast is dissolved

2. Mix in 3 cups flour and allow the dough to rest about 20 minutes

3. Mix in 2 cups flour 1/2 cup at a time; turn onto a well floured work surface; knead pushing and folding the dough; keep adding more flour a little at a time, if necessary, so dough no longer clings to the floured surface and is smooth and soft elastic dough

4. Place dough into a well oiled bowl, turning to coat all sides

5. Cover and let rise until double in size, about 1½ to 2 hours

6. Turn onto a well floured surface; divide into three pieces

7. Knead each piece slightly while shaping into 3 long oblong shapes; place into a baguette pan; slash the tops of the loaves; cover with a floured tea towel and let rise until double in size, about 1½ hours

8. Bake at preheated 425°F oven for 30 minutes or until golden brown

9. Remove from the oven and cool on a rack

Sourdough Baguettes or French Bread continued

Yield: 2 loaves   Preheat oven to 350ºF

French bread loaves Directions

1. In a large glass or ceramic bowl combine starter with water, sugar, salt and yeast and mix well until all yeast is dissolved

2. Mix in 3 cups flour and allow the dough to rest about 20 minutes

3. Mix in 2 cups flour 1/2 cup at a time; turn onto a well floured work surface; knead pushing and folding the dough; keep adding more flour a little at a time, if necessary, so dough no longer clings to the floured surface and is smooth and soft elastic dough

4. Place dough into a well oiled bowl, turning to coat all sides

5. Cover and let rise until double in size, about 1½ to 2 hours

6. Turn onto a well floured surface; divide the dough in half and shape into two loaves

7. Place in a lightly oiled glass baking loaf pans; cover with lightly floured tea town; let rise to double in size, about 1 to 1½ hours

8. Carefully brush top with warm water and bake at 350° for 35 minutes and brush tops with water once again and bake and added 15-20 minutes until golden brown (this makes the top crust crunchy)

9. Bread is done when crust is brown and sounds hollow when tapped

10. Remove from the oven and cool on a rack

Description

There is more sourdough starter in this recipe which gives a stronger wonderful sourdough flavor and the yeast makes the rise time faster.

Sourdough and Breads

Sourdough Bruschetta

Preheat oven to broil

Ingredients

1 sourdough baguette

4 garlic cloves, finely minced

4 tablespoons extra virgin olive oil

1/2 pound organic cherry tomatoes, sliced

1/4 cup organic fresh basil leaves, chopped

1/4 cup goat cheese

Directions

1. Wash tomatoes and basil in vinegar water and pat dry; slice tomatoes; mince garlic; coarsely chop the basil (stems removed)
2. Slice bread to about ¾" thick
3. Brush both sides with olive oil; broil lightly toasting each side; set aside
4. Combine tomatoes, minced garlic and basil in a small bowl
5. Spoon onto each toasted bread piece
6. Dab the tops with cheese
7. Arrange on plates and serve immediately

Description

This is a wonderful appetizer that can be served with any meal or occasion.

Sourdough and Breads

Sourdough Pizza

Yield: 1 medium pizza

Ingredients

1 cup sourdough unfed starter

1 tablespoon extra virgin olive oil

1½ cups organic unbleached einkorn

1/2 teaspoon Celtic or Himalayan salt

Directions

1. Remove starter from refrigerator and let set at room temperature for 2 hours
2. Place sourdough starter, olive oil, salt, and flour in a glass bowl
3. Mix the dough until soft; if too dry add a little more water
4. Knead the dough on a well floured work surface until smooth and elastic; cover with floured tea towel and let rest for 30 minutes
5. While dough is rising preheat oven pizza stone or tiles at 450º F for 30 minutes
6. Sprinkle the top of the dough with additional flour; roll and stretch the dough into a large circle (if your dough is very elastic and wants to spring back, let it rest for a few minutes and then try rolling again)
7. Brush the dough with olive oil and layer with favorite organic pizza topping ingredients and carefully transfer to heated stone; bake for 15 minutes or until crust is golden brown

Description

Dough may be refrigerated and stored until ready to use. To store, place the dough in a plastic bag sprayed with olive oil. Store no longer than 7 to 10 days, or if frozen for up to 2 months. If refrigerated or frozen allow the dough to come to room temperature before rolling out.

Sourdough and Breads

Bisquick Mix, Homemade

Ingredients

8 cups organic unbleached all purpose einkorn flour

1¼ cups organic nonfat powdered milk or organic powdered buttermilk

1/4 cup homemade baking powder or organic non GMO aluminum free baking powder

1/2 tablespoon organic baking soda

2 cups non-hydrogenated shortening substitute like firm palm oil or organic butter

Directions

1. Combine flour, dry milk, baking powder, and baking soda in a very large bowl and mix in non-hydrogenated shortening well
2. Store in tightly closed container or in a one gallon zip lock bag and date contents
3. Makes about 10 cups and must be refrigerated

Description

Bisquick is a copyright name. However, with that being said, this recipe is lower in sodium and saturated fat. The ingredients in store-bought Bisquick Original consist of bleached wheat flour (enriched with niacin, iron, thiamine mononitrate, riboflavin and folic acid), corn starch, dextrose, partially hydrogenated soybean and/or cottonseed oil, leavening (baking soda, sodium aluminum phosphate, monocalcium phosphate), canola oil, salt, sugar, DATEM, and distilled monoglycerides mix with milk, shortening and sugar). The store-bought Bisquick is not a healthy choice.

Bisquick Drop Biscuits or Shortcake

Yield: 12 biscuits   Preheat oven to 450°F

Ingredients

2¼ cups homemade bisquick mixture

2/3 cup milk, whole organic Vitamin D

(For shortcakes: add 3 tablespoons extra

Non-hydrogenated shortening and 3 tablespoons

Organic unrefined sugar)

Directions

1. Stir all ingredients in a bowl
2. Using a spoon, drop onto ungreased or parchment lined cookie sheet
3. Bake for 8-10 minutes or until golden brown

Description

It is also fun and delicious to add a half cup of shredded natural organic cheddar cheese and chopped green onions.

Bisquick Dumplings

Ingredients

2 cups homemade bisquick mixture

2/3 cup milk, whole organic Vitamin D or

1 cup yogurt

Directions

1. Stir all ingredients in a bowl until a soft dough ball forms
2. Using a teaspoon; drop each scoop into boiling soup or stew (be careful not to overload and overpower the soup or stew with dumplings)
3. Reduce to a simmer and cook uncovered for 10 minutes
4. Cover and simmer an added 10 minutes and serve

Description

These dumplings are made with non-hydrogenated shortening. The American Diabetes Association states that non-hydrogenated shortening lowers the risk of cardiovascular disease, diabetes, and inflammatory biomarkers.

Bisquick Biscuits

Yield: 12 biscuits   Preheat oven to 450°F

Ingredients

2 ¼ cups homemade bisquick mixture

2/3 cup milk, whole organic Vitamin D

or 1 cup yogurt

(use 3/4 cup low-fat buttermilk for

buttermilk biscuits)

Directions

1. Stir all ingredients in a bowl and turn onto floured surface and knead gently to a semi smooth texture
2. Using hands, press dough to ½" thick and cut using a 1½ - 2" diameter cutter
3. Place on ungreased or parchment lined cookie sheet; bake for 8-10 minutes or until golden brown
4. Remove from the oven and cool on a rack

Sourdough and Breads

Maple Cornbread

Yield: 9 servings   Preheat oven to 400°F

Ingredients

1/2 cup organic yellow cornmeal, finely ground

1/2 cup organic yellow cornmeal, course ground

1 cup organic unbleached all purpose einkorn flour

1½ tablespoons homemade baking powder or organic

non GMO aluminum free baking powder

1/2 teaspoon organic baking soda

1 cup milk, whole organic Vitamin D

1/2 cup 100% pure maple syrup

2 tablespoons organic canola oil

2 organic free range eggs

Directions

1. Coat an 8 x 8 glass baking dish with oil; place in oven for 7 minutes to heat
2. While dish is heating combine all flours, baking powder and baking soda in a large bowl
3. Whisk together milk, syrup, oil and eggs in small bowl
4. Add milk mixture to flour mixture and mix until well incorporated
5. Pour batter into prepared preheated dish
6. Bake 20 to 25 minutes or until a toothpick comes out clean when inserted
7. Remove and let cool for 10 minutes before cutting into 9 squares and serve

Description

Also try adding 2 tablespoons pecans halves on top before baking or a cup of organic whole kernel corn for a nice texture

Healthy Breakfasts

Eating breakfast has been shown to help boost brainpower, manage weight, and improve nutrient intake. One theory about weight loss and diet maintenance is that eating breakfast is the most important meal of the day and it sets the tone for the rest of the day.

According to the American Dietetic Association, people who eat breakfast perform better in the school and work and have better concentration, problem-solving skills, and eye-hand coordination. Breakfast provides you with the energy and nutrients that lead to increased concentration. Studies show that breakfast can be important in maintaining a healthy body weight, can reduce hunger throughout the day, and help people make better food choices at other meals.

Start out with something that gives you nutrition like a bowl of oatmeal topped with fruit and nuts, or low-fat yogurt with berries and granola, or an omelet loaded with veggies and some rye toast on the side and of course a juice. If you are in a hurry, make the In a Hurry Breakfast Smoothie.

Breakfast Bars

Yield: 12-14 bars   Preheat oven to 350°

Ingredients

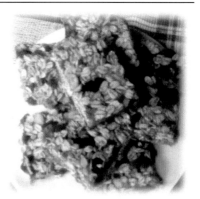

1 cup soaked organic pecans, chopped

1 cup soaked organic almonds, chopped

1/2 cup organic apricots, dried unsweetened
and unsulfured, chopped

1/2 cup organic fig, dried unsweetened
and unsulfured, chopped

1/2 cup organic dates, dried unsweetened
and unsulfured chopped

1/2 cup organic raisins, dried unsweetened unsulfured

3 cups rolled oats

4 organic free range eggs

1/2 cup 100% pure maple syrup or raw organic honey

1 teaspoon mace

1 teaspoon pure vanilla extract

1/2 cup filtered water

Directions

1. Heavily mist a 13x9 inch glass baking dish with extra virgin olive oil
2. In a large mixing bowl, whisk together eggs, syrup, mace, water and vanilla
3. Add oats and set aside covered to soften, 10 – 15 minutes
4. While oats are softening, chop soaked nuts, apricots, figs and dates (experiment with other unsulfured fruits or add seeds)
5. Transfer nuts, fruit and raisins to oats; mix well
6. Spread mixture to prepared dish and press down gently to cover bottom
7. Bake 20 minutes until lightly browned
8. Allow to cool before slicing into 3x3 inch bars

Breakfast Bars continued

9. Place bars covered in refrigerator or wrap individually to grab as a quick snack or a breakfast on the go.

Description

Sulfur dioxide gas is used as a preservative in dried fruit to prevent it from spoiling and to maintain the fruit's color. However, sulfur dioxide gas (sulfite) is toxic and too much exposure can cause serious illness or possibly even death. So make sure dried fruit is organic, sulfide and nitrate free.

Healthy Breakfasts

Breakfast Blintz

Yield: 8 Blintz   Preheat oven 200ºF

Ingredients

1½ cup milk, whole organic vitamin D

3 organic free range eggs

2 tablespoon organic butter, melted

2/3 cup organic all-purpose einkorn flour

Avocado oil spray

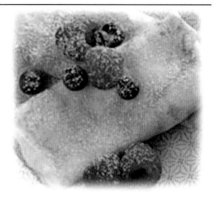

Filling:

1 cup low fat low sodium cottage cheese

3 tablespoons Greek yogurt

1 teaspoon honey, pure and natural

¼ teaspoon almond extract

2 cups each fresh blueberries and raspberries for topping

Directions

1. Wash berries in vinegar water, pat dry and set aside; melt butter
2. In a small bowl, whip milk, eggs and butter for crepe batter
3. Combine the flour to milk mixture and mix well; cover and refrigerate for 1 hour
4. In a blender, process cottage cheese and yogurt until smooth; add honey and extract; pulse the filling until well combined and set aside
5. Remove batter from refrigerator and stir
6. In a medium low heated stainless steel skillet pour 2 tablespoons of batter into center of skillet; lift and tilt pan to coat bottom evenly and cook until top appears dry
7. Spread 1 tablespoonful filling onto crepe and fold opposite sides of crepe over filling and roll together; remove blintz with wide spatula; place on a plate and set in warmed oven

Breakfast Blintz continued

8. Repeat with remaining batter, coating skillet with cooking spray as needed
9. Serve topped with berries and dust with organic confectioners' sugar if desired

Description

Greek yogurt has fewer calories and sodium with more nutrition coming from calcium and probiotics. The combinations of low fat low sodium cottage cheese and Greek yogurt have over 40 grams of protein per cup.

Breakfast Burrito

Yield: 4 servings   Preheat oven to 200°F

Ingredients

4 Lavash flat bread or low sodium organic tortillas

1 large organic red potatoes (about 1 cup), diced

4 tablespoon organic onion, mince

1 organic roma tomato (about 4 tablespoons), deseed and diced

1/2 cup organic low fat low sodium cottage cheese, well drained

4 organic free range eggs

2 tablespoons low fat yogurt

1 teaspoon Italian seasoning (see recipe-Condiments) or organic store-bought

2 tablespoons extra virgin olive oil

Instructions

1. Scrub potato in vinegar water and dice with skins into small bite size pieces
2. Par cook over medium heat with enough water just to cover potatoes
3. While potatoes are cooking, wash tomato, dice and deseed; mince onion
4. Place Flat bread on a plate covered with a damp paper towel to keep soft and pliable
5. Drain potatoes and add seasoning; gently mix together in pan to well coat; set aside covered to keep warm
6. Whisk eggs in a small bowl; add cottage cheese, yogurt and onion; mix well
7. Heat a stainless steel skillet with oil over medium low heat and add egg mixture
8. Cook egg mixture, stirring constantly until eggs are soft scrambled
9. Add eggs to potatoes and mix together
10. Place one Flat bread on parchment paper lengthwise in front of you keeping others covered with damp towel

Breakfast Burrito continued

11. Spoon 1/2 cup mixture in the center of flat bread; top with diced tomatoes; fold in the sides and roll up tightly; place on a plate in preheated oven to keep warm
12. Repeat steps 10 and 11 until finished
13. When ready to serve, place on warmed plate and cut in half

Description

These burritos are full of protein and also can be rolled in a paper towel whole to eat on the run. This is a very good source of protein and selenium.

Broiled Grapefruit

Yield: 2 Servings   Preheat oven to Broil

Ingredients

1 organic grapefruit, halved

1/2 teaspoon ground cinnamon or allspice

1/2 cup organic crushed pineapple

1/2 teaspoon organic raw sugar (if desired)

Direction

1. Wash grapefruit and cut in half
2. Spoon 1/4 cup crushed pineapple over each half
3. Sprinkle 1/4 teaspoon cinnamon over each half
4. Place on parchment covered cookie sheet and broil until pineapple is slightly browned
5. Serve with a slice of rye toast

Description

The pineapple seeps into the grapefruit which is still chilled in the middle. This is delightful change in serving grapefruit and is a very good source of Vitamin A and C.

Healthy Breakfasts

Granola Cereal

Yield: 4 ½ cups　　　　　　Preheat oven to 350°F

Ingredients

2 cups organic oats

1/3 cup organic flaxseed, ground

1/4 cup presoaked organic walnuts, chopped

1/4 cup presoaked organic pecans, chopped

2 teaspoons organic cinnamon, ground

1/3 cup orange juice, fresh squeezed

1/3 cup organic honey

1/4 cup organic sucanat (raw sugar)

2 teaspoons organic coconut oil

1 teaspoon pure vanilla

1/3 cup organic dried cranberries, raisins or other unsulfured organic dried fruit

Directions

1. Line cookie sheet with parchment paper, rub paper with coconut oil; chops nuts (add other nuts or seeds of choice)
2. Combine oats, flaxseed, nuts and cinnamon in a medium bowl
3. Heat juice, honey and sucanat in a small stainless steel saucepan over medium heat until sucanat dissolves; stir frequently
4. Remove from heat and add vanilla and coconut oil; pour over oat mixture and mix until well coated
5. Spread oat mixture in thin layer over prepared cookie sheet and bake for 12 minutes
6. Turn off oven and let sit in hot oven for 15 added minutes to continue to dry
7. Spoon dried granola into a bowl and add dried cranberries; cool completely and store in airtight container at room temperature up to 2 weeks

Description

Great for a fast, nutritious breakfast and served in a bowl with organic milk of choice

Mushroom Omelet

Yield: 2 servings   Preheat oven to 200°F

Ingredients

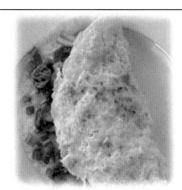

4 organic free range eggs

2 tablespoons organic sweet red pepper, diced and deseeded

1 cup organic mushrooms, sliced

2 tablespoon organic green onion, chopped

3 tablespoons Greek yogurt

4 tablespoons organic natural cheddar, shredded

Directions

1. Wash pepper, green onion and mushroom in vinegar water and pat dry
2. Place two plates in oven to warm
3. Chop onion; deseed and dice pepper and slice mushrooms and shred cheese
4. Beat eggs with yogurt in bowl and heat a stainless steel skillet with oil over medium low heat and add 1/2 egg mixture
5. Lift and tilt pan to coat bottom evenly and cook until top appears semi dry and reduce heat to low
6. Spoon half peppers, onion, mushrooms and cheese over one half of cooked egg mixture
7. With a large spatula, gently fold over the other half ; cover to melt cheese
8. When cheese melted, remove cover and lift onto warmed plate
9. Repeat for second omelet and serve immediately

Description

Mushrooms contain just as high an antioxidant capacity as carrots, tomatoes, green and red peppers, pumpkins, green beans, and zucchini. Selenium is a mineral that is not present in most fruits and vegetables but can be found in mushrooms. It plays a role in liver enzyme function, and helps detoxify some cancer-causing compounds in the body. Additionally, selenium prevents inflammation and also decreases tumor growth rates.

Oatmeal

Yield: 2 (1/2 cup servings)

Ingredients

3/4 cup organic old fashion thick rolled oatmeal

1¾ cups filtered water

Directions

1. Bring water and oatmeal to a boil in a 1 quart stainless steel saucepan
2. Reduce heat to medium low and cook for 3 minutes uncovered
3. Turn off heat, cover and rest for 15 minutes
4. Spoon into two bowls and top with favorite soaked nuts, banana, honey or fruit of choice

Description

Whole oats are the only source of a unique group of antioxidants called avenanthramides which is believed to have protective effects against heart disease, lowering blood sugar and cholesterol. The major protein in oats is called avenalin which is not found in any other grain, but is similar to legume proteins. Oats contain high amounts of many vitamins and minerals, such as manganese, phosphorus, and copper, B-vitamins, iron, selenium, magnesium and zinc. While microwaving this rapidly heats your food, what most people fail to realize is that it also causes a change in the food's chemical structure. This structural change causes food to lose most of the health benefits.

Pita Omelet

Yield: 2 servings

Ingredients

3 organic free range eggs

1 small organic roma tomato, diced and deseeded

1/2 cup organic spinach, chopped

2 tablespoon organic red onion, diced

2 tablespoons Greek yogurt

1 Pita

Directions

1. Wash tomato and spinach in vinegar water and pat dry
2. Chop spinach; deseed and dice tomato and chop onion
3. Beat eggs with yogurt in a bowl; add onion and transfer to a medium low heated skillet with avocado oil, 100% pure natural and lightly scramble
4. Turn off heat and gently fold in tomato and spinach and cover
5. Cut pita bread in half; spread open each half and spoon in half egg mixture to each half of pita and serve immediately

Description

Whole wheat pita is flat bread, originating in the Middle East and Mediterranean. When baked, it puffs up forming a pocket. Pita bread, though still a type of bread, is an excellent alternative to traditional sandwich bread, as long you pick the low sodium whole wheat variety.

Spinach Asparagus Breakfast Pie

Yield: 4 servings   Preheat oven 350°F

Ingredients

8 sheets organic fillo dough

2 cups fresh organic spinach

6 organic asparagus sprigs, chopped

2 tablespoons extra virgin olive oil

1/2 organic onion, finely chopped

2 organic garlic cloves, minced

1 teaspoon parsley, dried

1/2 teaspoon basil, dried

3 organic free range eggs

1 cup Greek Yogurt

1/2 cup low fat organic mozzarella cheese, shredded

1/2 cup low fat organic parmesan cheese, shredded

Directions

1. Wash spinach and asparagus and pat dry
2. Pinch stems off spinach; chop spinach and asparagus (or other veggies); set aside
3. Finely chop onions, mince garlic and shred cheeses
4. In a medium bowl whisk together eggs and yogurt and fold in cheese
5. Combine all ingredients to egg, yogurt and cheese and mix all ingredients together
6. Heavily spray a 6 cup glass baking dish with olive oil and line the sides and bottom with 8 sheets of fillo dough
7. Pour mixture in center and garnish with asparagus tips; bake for 35 to 40 minutes
8. Remove from oven when center is firm; let rest for 5 to 10 minutes before slicing
9. This can also be a meal for lunch or dinner that can be served with a green salad

Description

Asparagus is highest in fiber. A half cup serving contains nearly 3 grams. A half cup of spinach has 1.6 grams. Spinach and asparagus contain an extensive list of essential and non-essential nutrients, including B-complex vitamins, vitamins C and E.

Sourdough Pancakes, Basic Cakes

Yield: 20 small cakes

Ingredients

1½ cups "fed" sourdough starter (see Using Your Starter in a Recipe-Breads)

1/2 cup organic unbleached all purpose einkorn flour

1 tablespoon 100% pure maple syrup or organic honey

1 tablespoon melted organic butter

1 organic free range egg

2 tablespoons milk, whole organic vitamin D

1 teaspoon organic baking soda

Directions

1. This is important to avoid tough rubbery pancakes; place the starter in a warm bowl and add the flour and all dry ingredients first
2. Let all ingredients rest, covered to reach room temperature
3. In a separate bowl, beat the egg lightly and melt butter
4. Add milk to melted butter and egg mixture and stir it into the sourdough and flour batter
5. Heat a griddle to 400° with avocado oil
6. Just before ladling batter to heated griddle, add baking soda and stir; batter will bubble which will create a very light pancake
7. Ladle batter with a serving spoon or pour from a glass mixing cup; best pancakes are approximately 2 to 3 inches in diameter
8. If the top bubbles and undersides are browned, flip the pancake

Sourdough Pancakes, Basic Cakes continued

9. The second side cooks in about half the time the first side took and tends not to brown as evenly
10. Serve immediately with warmed organic 100% pure maple syrup, honey (however, be mindful of sugar intake) or other topping of your choice like peanut butter
11. Fruit and berry toppings enhance the flavor of the pancakes

Description

Sourdough often has a lower glycemic index–meaning; it doesn't spike blood sugar as dramatically. This is because it depletes damaged starches within it simply by its fermentative nature. Sourdough has the bacteria Lactobacillus in a higher proportion to yeast. With more Lactobacillus, the higher production of lactic acid, this means less of the potentially dangerous phytic acid and more mineral availability and easier digestion! (See Understanding of Rye and Wheat Breads under Breads)

Other Types of Sourdough Pancakes

Use the basic pancake recipe for many variations. The standard procedure for creating new and exciting types of pancakes is to stir in the added ingredients into the batter which makes the pancake different. These added ingredients can make a world of difference to prevent becoming tired of the same type of pancakes day after day.

Description

Sourdough Apple Pancakes

Use the basic Sourdough Pancake recipe but after adding the milk, stir in 1 cup sliced or grated apples, add 1 teaspoon nutmeg and 1 teaspoon vanilla, and add 1 teaspoon baking soda just before spooning on griddle.

Sourdough Banana Pancakes

Use the basic Sourdough Pancake recipe but after adding the milk, stir in 1 cup mashed or sliced bananas and add 1 teaspoon baking soda just before spooning on griddle.

Sourdough Blueberry Pancakes

Use the basic Sourdough Pancake recipe but after adding the milk, stir in 1 cup fresh or frozen organic blueberries; stir in 2 tablespoons honey or syrup to the batter and add 1 teaspoon baking soda just before spooning on griddle.

Veggie Mini Quiche

Preheat oven to 350°F

Ingredients

6 organic free range eggs

1 organic garlic clove, minced

2 cups organic carrots, shredded

1 cup organic spinach, chopped

1/2 cup low fat organic mozzarella, shredded

1 cup Greek Yogurt

Instructions

1. Wash carrots in vinegar water and shred
2. Shred mozzarella; finely chop spinach and grease a muffin tin
3. Beat eggs and garlic together in medium bowl; fold in shredded carrots, cheese and spinach
4. Divide egg mixture evenly in muffin tin
5. Bake egg muffins for 30 to 35 minutes or until eggs are fully set
6. Remove from oven and let cool at least 5 minutes before serving

Description

Eggs from organic free range ranch or farm hens yield 4 to 6 times more vitamin D as typical supermarket eggs and have one-third less cholesterol, quarter less saturated fat, two-thirds more vitamin A, two times more omega-3 fatty acids, three times more vitamin E and seven times more beta carotene.

Salads

Salads make a nutrient-rich meal. Greens have calcium, iron, potassium and vitamin B. Many salad basics, including tomatoes, sweet peppers and the greens, are chockfull of antioxidants. Vegetables in salads are good sources of fiber, which keeps the digestive tract healthy. Adding nuts, seeds or beans to the salad will boost fiber that helps lower cholesterol and keeps blood sugar balanced. This is our counter full of vegetables after our weekly shopping.

Apple Celery Salad

Yield: 4 servings

Ingredients

1 red organic apple, sliced

1 large organic granny smith apple, sliced

1 ½ cups organic celery stalks, sliced

1/4 cup low fat plain yogurt

2 teaspoons pure natural honey

1/4 teaspoon ground allspice

1 teaspoon fresh squeezed organic lemon juice

1/2 cup soaked walnuts or pecans, coarsely chop

Directions

1. Wash celery and apples in vinegar water
2. Slice celery, chop soaked nuts; core and slice apples discarding the core and squeeze juice
3. In a medium bowl whisk together yogurt, honey, allspice, and lemon juice
4. Stir in nuts, apples and celery
5. Garnish with ground allspice and serve as a side dish

Salads

Apple Pear Avocado Salad with Citrus Dressing

Yield: 4 salads

Ingredients

1 (10 ounce) package organic mixed salad greens

1/4 organic red onion, sliced

1/2 cup soaked walnuts, chopped

1/2 cup feta cheese, crumbles

1 teaspoon organic lemon zest

1 medium organic gala apple, cored and thinly sliced

1 medium organic pear, cored and thinly sliced

1 large organic avocado, peeled, pitted and sliced

Citrus Dressing:

1 organic fresh squeezed orange

1 organic fresh squeezed lemon

1 teaspoon lemon zest

1 teaspoon orange zest

1 organic garlic clove, minced

2 tablespoons flaxseed oil or cold pressed extra virgin olive oil

2 tablespoons pure natural honey

Directions

1. Wash and rinse citrus, apples, avocado and lettuce in vinegar water; pat dry
2. Zest and squeeze citrus and set aside; mince garlic; slice onion; core and slice apple; deseed, peel and slice avocado; chop nuts
3. Evenly place the washed fresh mixed greens onto four chilled salad plates
4. Top each plate with sliced onion rings, apples, pear and avocado; sprinkle each salad with crumbled cheese, chopped nuts
5. **For dressing**: In a small bowl whisk together juices, zests, garlic, oil, honey, and drizzle over salad and serve

Salads

Cannellini Bean and Tuna Salad

Yield: 4 servings

Ingredients

1 (15ounce) can organic white bean, well drained and rinsed

1 (6ounce) can wild Skip Jack tuna, low sodium, low fat, well drained

1/4 cup organic red onion, finely chopped

1/2 cup water chestnut; well drained, rinsed and finely chopped

1 large organic celery stalks, chopped

2 cups fresh organic baby spinach, chopped

2 tablespoons mayonnaise (see recipe-Condiments) or organic store-bought

1 tablespoon organic red wine vinegar

Directions

1. Wash celery and spinach in vinegar water; pat dry
2. Drained tuna; rinse and drain water chestnuts
3. Chop celery, water chestnuts and spinach
4. Prepare mayonnaise
5. In a bowl whip together mayonnaise and vinegar
6. Add tuna, onions, water chestnuts, celery and spinach and coat all ingredients well

Description

This is a perfect salad with various ways to serve: Serve over lettuce just as a salad, spoon into pita pouches adding tomatoes, roll up in flat bread as a wrap, or spoon into hollowed out tomato halves.

Cantaloupe Salad

Yield: 2 salads

Ingredients

1 organic cantaloupes, halved and deseeded

3 tablespoons Greek Yogurt

3 tablespoons mayonnaise (see recipe-Condiments) or organic store-bought

1 teaspoon organic fresh squeezed lemon juice

1/2 red or organic granny smith apple, diced

1/2 cup organic celery stalks, diced

1/2 cup organic cucumber, diced

1/2 cup organic zucchini, diced

1/2 cup organic Jerusalem artichoke macaroni, cold cooked al dente

1/2 cup organic raspberries

2 tablespoons organic green onions, finely chopped

4 tablespoons presoaked pecans, coarsely chopped

Directions

1. Cook macaroni al dente according to package directions; rinse and cool in the refrigerator
2. While macaroni is cooling, wash produce in vinegar water; pat dry and Prepare mayonnaise, juice lemon
3. In a large bowl whisk together mayonnaise, yogurt, and lemon juice
4. Core and dice apple, celery, cucumber and zucchini; chop onions and presoaked nuts and mix with mayonnaise mixture
5. Gently mix in the cold macaroni and berries until well coated
6. Cut cantaloupe in half; remove seeds; spoon mixture into cantaloupe halves and serve garnished with berries and mint if desired

Description

Or, cut up cantaloupe and mix all together and serve in bowls or on a plate of lettuce

Salads

Caramelized Pear Salad

Yield: 2 salads

Ingredients

2 firm ripe organic pears, cored and halved

2 tablespoons ghee (see recipe-Condiments)

2 tablespoons 100% pure maple syrup

2 tablespoon fresh squeezed organic lemon juice

1 teaspoon organic lemon zest

1 tablespoon balsamic vinegar

1 teaspoon Dijon style mustard

3 cups organic arugula lettuce

1/4 cup presoaked walnuts, chopped

2 ounces blue cheese, crumbles

Directions

1. Wash produce in vinegar water and pat dry; zest lemon and juice; halve pears
2. In large stainless steel skillet over low heat melt ghee with syrup and lemon zest and juice; stir about 2 minutes (ghee can be substituted for extra virgin olive oil)
3. Add pear halves and cook turning a couple of times, until pears just start to turn brown but keep firm
4. Divide lettuce to two cooled plates; remove pears, slice and place over lettuce, leaving sauce in pan
5. Add vinegar and mustard to skillet and caramelize over low heat; about 2 minutes
6. Drizzle sauce over salad
7. Sprinkle with blue cheese crumbles and nuts and serve

Description

Arugula, also known as garden rocket, is one of the nutritious green-leafy vegetable of Mediterranean origin and belongs within a family similar to mustard greens, cauliflower, and kale. Therefore, it is a natural anti-oxidant loaded with Vitamins A, C, K, and copper.

Salads

Celery Seed Dressing Salad and Variations

Yield: 1 cup

Dressing Ingredients

1/4 cup pure natural honey

2 teaspoons dry mustard

1 teaspoon celery seeds

1 tablespoon organic onion, chopped

1/3 cup organic red wine vinegar

1 cup flaxseed oil or cold pressed extra virgin olive oil

1/4 teaspoon thyme, dried organic

Mix together in a lidded jar and shake vigorously

Salad Variations Yield: 2 per salad

Salad Ingredients

VARIATION 1

1/2 head organic romaine lettuce, chopped

1 cup organic mandarin orange, well drained and chopped

1 head Belgian endive, chop

1 teaspoon organic green onion, chopped

1/4 cup presoaked walnuts, chopped

VARIATION 2

1/2 head organic romaine lettuce, chopped

1 organic pink grapefruit; peeled, sectioned and chop

1/2 cup organic escarole, chopped

1 teaspoon organic green onions, chopped

1/4 cup presoaked walnuts, chopped

Celery Seed Dressing Salad and Variations continued

Directions

For each salad:

1. Prepare Celery Seed Dressing ahead (see recipe-Salad Dressing) cover and refrigerate
2. Wash fruit and vegetables in vinegar water and pat dry
3. Peel fruit and section; chop all ingredients
4. Mix all ingredients together in a large bowl
5. Spoon into 2 separate chilled bowls or plates
6. Drizzle each salad with dressing

Salads

Coleslaw

Yield: 4 servings

Ingredients

3 cups organic Napa cabbage, shredded

1/4 cup organic medium carrot, shredded

3 tablespoons organic onions, finely chopped

3 tablespoons Greek Yogurt

1/4 cup flaxseed oil or extra virgin olive oil

3 tablespoons organic red wine vinegar

2 tablespoons pure natural honey

1 teaspoon celery seeds

1/2 teaspoon dry mustard

Directions

1. Wash vegetables in vinegar water and pat dry
2. Chop onions; shred cabbage and carrots
3. In a medium bowl, beat together oil, yogurt, honey, vinegar, celery seed, dry mustard and onion
4. Fold in cabbage and carrots until well coated
5. Chill for 1 hour before serving

Description

Napa cabbage is an amazing cabbage with a good source of Niacin, Calcium and Potassium, as well as Vitamin A, Vitamin C, Folate, Iron, Copper and Manganese.

Salads

Cranberry Grape Salad

Yield: 4 salads

Ingredients

4 cups organic mixed fresh lettuce

1 cup organic arugula lettuce

1 organic red or granny smith apple, diced

2 large organic celery stalks, diced

2 tablespoons organic raisins

2 tablespoons organic dried unsweetened cranberries

1 small organic cucumber, peeled, deseeded and diced

2 tablespoons feta cheese, crumbled

1/2 cup organic red seedless grape, halved

1/4 cup presoaked pecans, chopped

Directions

1. Prepare Sweet Tomato Dressing (See recipe-Salad Dressings)
2. Wash all produce in vinegar water at pat dry
3. Halve grapes; chop presoaked nuts; core and dice apple and celery; peel, deseed and dice cucumber
4. Mix lettuce, grapes, apple, celery, cucumbers, raisins and cranberries in a large bowl
5. Spoon into 4 separate chilled bowls or plates; sprinkle nuts, crumbled cheese and dressing over salads

Salads

Easy Spring Salad

Yield: 2 salads

Ingredients

2 cups organic romaine lettuce, chopped

1 cup organic mixed spring lettuce

2 tablespoons organic radishes, sliced

1 organic tomato, sliced

1 small organic red onion, sliced

2 tablespoons organic cooked chickpeas or canned
organic chickpeas, drained, well rinsed

Directions

1. Wash produce in vinegar water and pat dry; cook chickpeas or drain and well rinsed canned

2. Chop lettuce; slice radish, onion and tomato

3. Mix chopped romaine and spring lettuce together and spoon onto 2 chilled salad plates

4. Spoon chickpeas and chop radishes over each salad

5. Arrange red onion rings and tomato slices attractively over lettuce

6. Serve with your favorite dressing

Salads

Fruit Salad with Pineapple Dressing

Yield: 2 salads

Dressing Ingredients

1 organic pineapple, peeled, cored and sliced

1 tablespoon organic fresh squeezed lime juice

1 tablespoon organic fresh mint, finely chopped

1/4 teaspoon allspice, dried

2 tablespoons pure natural honey

8 organic romaine lettuce leaves

1 organic mango, peeled, cored and diced

1 cup organic raspberries

1 organic cantaloupe, peeled, deseeded and sliced

1 cup non fat low sodium cottage cheese

Directions

1. Core, peel and slice pineapple; purée quarter of the pineapple in food processor
2. Squeeze juice; chop mint
3. Add juice, fresh mint, allspice and honey puréed pineapple
4. Blend together and refrigerate dressing
5. Wash lettuce and fruit in vinegar water and pat dry; line 2 salad plates with lettuce leaves
6. Slice and arrange the remaining pineapple and fruit attractively upon the lettuce
7. Place 1/2 cup cottage cheese in the center of fruit and serve immediately with chilled dressing drizzled over the top

Grapefruit Orange Salad

Yield: 4 salads

Ingredients

3 cups organic mixed spring lettuce

1 tablespoon watercress, chopped

1 organic orange, peeled, sliced

1 small organic pink grapefruit, peeled, sliced

2 tablespoons presoaked almonds, sliced

2 tablespoons low fat plain yogurt

2 tablespoons French dressing

Directions

1. Prepare French dressing (see recipe-Salad Dressings) cover and place in refrigerator
2. Wash produce in vinegar water and pat dry
3. Peel and dice orange and grapefruit; chop watercress
4. Mix yogurt and dressing well in a large bowl, add all ingredients and mix all together
5. Serve into 4 separate chilled bowls or onto plates

Salads

Kale Salad

Yield: 2 salads

Ingredients

1 bunch organic kale, de-stemmed and cut

6 ounces organic baby greens

4 tablespoons sprouted, shelled pumpkin seeds

1 small organic grapefruit and/or medium organic
orange, sectioned and chopped

1/4 organic red onion, thinly sliced

3 tablespoons Pumpkin Vinaigrette Dressing

1 ounce Feta or low fat organic parmesan cheese

Directions

1. Prepare Pumpkin Vinaigrette Dressing (see recipe- Salad Dressings) cover and place in refrigerator
2. Wash produce in vinegar water and pat dry
3. Cut, de-stem kale; peel, section and chop orange; slice onion
4. Combine all ingredients in a bowl and mix well, adding dressing to taste
5. Serve into 2 separate chilled bowls or onto plates

Description

Change it up substituting citrus with 1 small organic granny smith apple, sliced and shredded golden or red beets.

Mango Avocado Salad

Yield: 4 salads

Ingredients

1 organic butter head lettuce, chopped

1 tablespoon organic watercress, chopped

1 organic mango, peeled and diced

1 organic avocado, peeled and diced

2 tablespoons organic dried cranberries

2 tablespoons low fat plain yogurt

2 tablespoons presoaked almonds, sliced

4 tablespoons French dressing

Directions

1. Prepare French dressing (see recipe-Salad Dressings) cover and place in refrigerator
2. Wash produce in vinegar water and pat dry
3. Peel and dice mango; peel de-seed and dice avocado; chop watercress
4. Mix yogurt and dressing well in a bowl, add remaining ingredients and mix until well combined
5. Serve into 4 separate chilled bowls or plates

Salads

Old Fashioned French Dressing Salads Variations

Yield: 1cup

Dressing Ingredients

1/4 cup distilled or filtered water

1/4 cup organic red wine vinegar

1 tablespoon organic fresh squeezed lemon juice

1 teaspoon Worcestershire sauce (without soy)

1 teaspoon dry mustard

1 organic garlic clove, minced

1 cup flaxseed oil or cold pressed extra virgin olive oil

Mix together in a lidded jar and shake vigorously

Salad Variations Yield: 2 each salad

Salad Ingredients

VARIATION 1

1/2 head organic romaine lettuce, chopped

1/2 cup organic green cabbage, shredded

1 organic red apple, finely chopped

1/2 cup organic fresh blueberries

1/4 cup presoaked almonds, sliced

VARIATION 2

1/2 head organic romaine lettuce, chopped

2 organic celery stalks, finely chopped

1 very ripe organic persimmon, chopped

1 cup low fat cottage cheese, well drained

1/4 cup presoaked pecans, chopped

Old Fashioned French Dressing Salads Variations continued

Directions

For each salad:

1. Prepare Old Fashioned French Dressing ahead (see recipe-Salad Dressing) cover and refrigerate
2. Wash fruit and vegetables in vinegar water and pat dry
3. Peel fruit; chop ingredients as indicated
4. Mix all ingredients together in a large bowl
5. Spoon into 2 separate chilled bowls or plates
6. Drizzle dressing over salads

Description

Persimmons can be eaten fresh, dried or cooked. To eat fresh VERY RIPE persimmons, cut or peel the skin and cut into quarters or eat whole like an apple. The skin is tough, therefore it is recommended to be peeled prior to consuming.

Peach Salad

Yield: 4 salads

Ingredients

4 large organic peaches, diced

3 cups organic mixed spring lettuce

1 tablespoon watercress, chopped

1 tablespoon hempseeds

2 tablespoons low fat plain yogurt

2 tablespoons Sweet Tomato dressing

Directions

1. Prepare Sweet Tomato dressing (see recipe-Salad Dressings) cover and place in refrigerator
2. Wash produce in vinegar water and pat dry
3. Peel and dice peaches and chop watercress
4. Mix yogurt and dressing well in a bowl; add peaches, lettuce and watercress; gently well coat
5. Serve into 4 separate chilled bowls or plates and top with seeds

Pumpkin Seed and Pear Salad

Yield: 2 to 4 salads

Ingredients

3 cups organic arugula lettuce

1 organic pear, sliced

1 tablespoon ghee (see recipe-Condiments)

1 ounce hard natural organic cheddar cheese

4 tablespoons sprouted shelled pumpkin seeds

Maple Dressing Ingredients:

3 tablespoons extra virgin olive oil

1 tablespoon balsamic vinegar

3 tablespoons 100% pure maple syrup

Directions

1. Wash produce in vinegar water and pat dry; slice pear
2. In stainless steel saucepan sauté sliced pears in ghee until pears are slightly browned and cool (ghee can be substituted for extra virgin olive oil)
3. Arrange lettuce on two chilled plates and spoon sliced pears over lettuce
4. Sprinkle pumpkin seeds and grate hard natural cheddar over salads
5. **For dressing:** Combine dressing ingredients in a jar with tightly fitted lid and vigorously shake until well mixed
6. Drizzle prepared dressing over salad and serve

Salads

Stuffed Tomato Salad

Yield: 3 stuffed tomatoes

Ingredients

3 ripe organic whole tomatoes

3 tablespoons Greek Yogurt

1/4 teaspoon celery seed

1 tablespoon organic onion, finely chopped

2 tablespoons organic carrots, finely chopped

2 tablespoons organic celery stalks, chopped

2 tablespoons organic frozen corn

3 tablespoons organic pineapple tidbits,
well drained

1 cup low fat cottage cheese, well drained

1 tablespoon organic red bell pepper, chopped

1 tablespoon organic green pepper, chopped

2 tablespoons presoaked pecans, finely chopped, if desired

Directions

1. Wash produce in vinegar water and pat dry
2. Quarter tomatoes, not cutting all the way through; hollow each and set aside
3. Chop onion, carrots, peppers, nuts and celery; drain pineapple tidbits
4. Beat together yogurt, celery seed and onion in a large bowl
5. Mix in, carrots, pineapple, corn and peppers until well coated
6. Fold in well drained cottage cheese
7. Scoop mixture into each of the hollowed out tomatoes and serve over a bed of favorite lettuce

Sweet Tomato Dressing Salad Variations

Yield: 1 cup

Dressing Ingredients

2 medium organic tomatoes

2 teaspoons pure natural honey or 100% pure maple syrup

1 tablespoon organic red wine vinegar

1/2 cup flaxseed oil or cold pressed extra virgin olive oil

1 teaspoon garlic powder

1 teaspoon onion powder

1 teaspoon ground, rosemary, dried

1 teaspoon oregano, dried

1 teaspoon ground thyme, dried

Mix together in a blender and store in a lidded jar; shake vigorously before use

Salad Variations Yield: 2 each salad

Salad Ingredients

VARIATION 1

1/2 head organic romaine lettuce, chopped

1 organic red delicious apple, finely diced

2 large organic celery stalks, finely diced

3 tablespoons organic raisins

1 small organic cucumber, peeled, deseeded and diced

2 tablespoons organic parsley, finely chopped

1/2 cup organic red seedless grape, halved

1/4 cup organic presoaked pecans, chopped

Sweet Tomato Dressing Salad Variations continued

VARIATION 2

1/2 head organic romaine lettuce, chopped

2 large organic celery stalks, finely chopped

3 tablespoons organic radishes, chopped

1 small organic, cucumber, peeled, deseeded and diced

1/2 cup organic strawberries, chopped

3 tablespoon organic dried cranberries

VARIATION 3

1/2 head organic romaine lettuce, chopped

1 organic red delicious apple, finely diced

2 large organic celery stalks, finely diced

3 tablespoons organic dates

1 small organic cucumber, peeled, deseeded and diced

1 small organic zucchini, diced chopped

1/4 cup organic presoaked pecans, chopped

VARIATION 4

1/2 head organic romaine lettuce, chopped

4 tablespoons organic spinach, fresh chopped

4 tablespoons organic raw peas

1 organic peach, slice

1 organic green onion, chopped

1/4 cup presoaked almonds, sliced

Sweet Tomato Dressing Salad Variations continued

Directions

For each salad:

1. Prepare Sweet Tomato Dressing (see recipe-Salad Dressing) cover and refrigerate
2. Wash fruit and vegetables in vinegar water and pat dry
3. Peel and chop or slice ingredients as indicated
4. Mix all ingredients together in a large bowl
5. Spoon into 2 separate chilled bowls or plates
6. Drizzle dressing over salads and serve

Salads

Thai Salad

Yield: 4 servings

Ingredients

1 cup vegetable or chicken broth (see recipe-Broth) or organic low sodium store-bought

1/2 cup organic brown basmati rice

1 organic red bell pepper, thin sliced strips

1/2 cup medium organic carrot, shredded

1/2 cup organic red onion, thin sliced

2 cups organic romaine lettuce, chopped

1 cup organic spinach leaves, chopped

1 cup organic mixed spring lettuce

Directions

1. Prepare Peanut Dressing ahead (See recipe-Salad Dressings) cover and refrigerate
2. Rinse rice under cold water until water runs clear
3. Bring the broth to boil in a saucepan large enough to accommodate rice expansion
4. When the broth begins to boil, stir in the well rinsed rice; reduce to a gentle simmer and cover
5. Simmer about 15 minutes or until rice is tender and liquid is absorbed
6. While rice is cooking, wash vegetables; pat dry and shred carrots, slice sweet pepper, and red onion; chop romaine
7. Mix lettuce, sweet pepper, carrots, and red onion together in a large bowl and divide among 4 serving plates
8. Spoon rice over greens and drizzle with dressing
9. Sprinkle with peanuts if desired

Vegetable Pasta Salad with Mustard Dressing

Yield: 4 servings

Ingredients

6 ounces organic Jerusalem artichoke macaroni or penne pasta

8 organic romaine lettuce leaves

1 cup organic frozen mixed corn, peas and carrots

1/2 cup organic cauliflower, florets

1/2 cup organic broccoli, florets

1/2 cup organic red onion, chopped

1/2 cup organic green onion, chopped

1/4 cup organic yellow pepper, chopped

1/4 cup organic green pepper, chopped

1/2 cup plain low fat plain yogurt

1/4 cup Greek Yogurt

1/4 cup organic dill weed, chopped

2 tablespoon Dijon style mustard

2 tablespoons organic fresh squeezed lemon juice

1 tablespoon red pepper flake

Directions

1. Wash produce in vinegar water and pat dry and defrost frozen vegetables
2. Chop fresh dill weed, onions, yellow and green peppers; cut cauliflower and broccoli florets into bit size pieces
3. Cook pasta according to package directions and just 5 minutes before al dente add corn, peas, carrots, cauliflower and broccoli; finish cooking; drain well; chill in refrigerator for 1 hour

Vegetable Pasta Salad with Mustard Dressing continued

4. While pasta and vegetables are chilling, whisk together yogurts, dill weed, mustard, juice, in a large bowl to make mustard dressing
5. Add onions, peppers and chilled pasta and vegetable mixture to mustard dressing; stir gently until well coated
6. Garnish individual chilled salad plates with lettuce and spoon salad over lettuce

Description

This salad is very filling and satisfying and is a good source of Protein (especially broccoli), and a very good source of Vitamin A, Vitamin C, Vitamin K, and Vitamin B6.

Salads

Waldorf Salad

Yield: 4 salads

Ingredients

1/4 cup Greek yogurt

1 teaspoon pure natural honey

1 tablespoon organic fresh squeezed lemon juice

1 organic gala or granny smith apple, core and dice

1/2 cup organic red seedless grape, halved

1/2 cup organic green seedless grape, halved

1/2 cup large organic celery stalks, chopped

1/2 cup organic raisins

4 tablespoons presoaked pecans, coarsely chopped

4 leaves organic butter head lettuce

Directions

1. Wash fruit and vegetables in vinegar water and pat dry; juice lemon
2. Whisk together yogurt, honey and lemon juice in a large bowl
3. Core and dice apple; chop celery and nuts; halve grapes and add to yogurt mixture
4. Toss gently to coat
5. Spoon onto lettuce leaf on 4 individual chilled salad plates

Salads

Yogurt Cucumber Dressing Salad Variations

Yield: 1 ½ cup

Dressing Ingredients

1 organic cucumber, finely chopped

1/2 teaspoon marjoram, dried

1/2 teaspoon dill weed, dried

1 teaspoon organic fresh squeezed lemon juice

1/2 teaspoon organic onion, finely chopped

1 tablespoon Greek Yogurt, more if thicker dressing is desired

Mix together in a blender and store in a lidded jar; shake vigorously before use

Salad Variations Yield: 2 per salad

Ingredients
VARIATION 1

1/2 head organic romaine lettuce, chopped

Handful organic kale

2 large organic celery stalks, finely chopped

1 organic red delicious apple, chopped

1 organic pear, chopped

1 organic peach, chopped

VARIATION 2

1/2 head organic romaine lettuce, chopped

Handful organic spinach

1/2 cup organic crushed pineapple, well drained

2 large organic celery stalks, finely chopped

1 cup low fat cottage cheese, well drained

1/4 cup presoaked hazelnut, chopped

Yogurt Cucumber Dressing Salad Variations continued

VARIATION 3

1/2 head organic romaine lettuce, chopped

Handful organic spinach

1 cup organic mandarin orange, well drained and chopped

1/4 cup organic dates, finely chopped

1 organic banana, sliced

1/4 cup presoaked pecans, chopped

VARIATION 4

1/2 head organic romaine lettuce, chopped

4 tablespoons organic spinach, fresh chopped

4 tablespoons organic raw peas

1/2 cup organic zucchini, shredded

1 cup low fat cottage cheese, well drained

1/4 cup presoaked almonds, sliced

Directions

For each salad:

Prepare Yogurt Cucumber dressing ahead (See recipe-Salad Dressings) cover and refrigerate

1. Wash fruit and vegetables in vinegar water and pat dry
2. Peel, slice and/or chop ingredients as indicated
3. Mix all ingredients together in a large bowl
4. Spoon onto 2 chilled plates
5. Drizzle dressing over salads and serve

Main Dishes

These recipes are primarily vegetarian. Neither vegetarians nor vegans eat meat. A vegan avoids all animal products, including eggs and dairy. Vegetarians tend to consume dairy products and eggs and maybe some fish. Therefore dairy products (milk, butter, yogurt, cottage cheese, etc.) are used in some of the recipes but should not be used if lactose intolerant. If there is no problem consuming these products, bear in mind that they should only be organic which are made from grass fed or flax meal fed cows or goats that have not been injected or fed BGH (Bovine growth hormone). Eggs used should be from organic free range chickens. Most of the recipes do not contain salt. Table salt should never be used and Celtic or Himalayan salts should only used sparingly. (refer to Dos and Don'ts of Certain Foods)

Main Dishes

Asian Dumplings

Yield: 40 dumplings   Preheat the oven to 200º F

Ingredients:

40 wonton wraps

2 tablespoon extra virgin olive oil

2 tablespoons organic Oshawa Nama Shoyu sauce

(organic fermented unpasteurized soy)

2 organic cloves garlic, finely minced

1 tablespoon organic fresh ginger, minced

2 tablespoons organic chives, finely chopped

2 tablespoons organic red pepper, finely chopped

1 organic free range egg

½ cup organic Napa cabbage, finely chopped

½ cup organic broccoli or cold slaw

½ cup carrots, coarsely grated

Directions

1. Wash onions, cabbage, carrots, peppers and broccoli slaw in vinegar water and pat dry

2. Mince garlic and ginger; deseed pepper and finely chop pepper, chives and cabbage; coarsely grate carrots

3. Whisk egg with oil and Nama Shoyu sauce in a large bowl and add with all ingredients and mix together

4. Remove 1 wonton wrapper from the package, covering the others with a damp cloth to keep from drying

5. Brush the edges of the wrapper lightly with water

6. Place 1/2 rounded teaspoon of the mixture in the center of the wrapper; fold wrapper up and pinch top together to seal

Asian Dumplings continued

7. Place in a well oiled steamer pan without touching each other; cover with a damp cloth; repeat until all of the filling is used
8. Bring 1 cup water to a simmer over medium heat; place steamer basket over boiling water and steam for 10 to 12 minutes over medium heat.
9. Remove the dumplings from the steamer to a heatproof platter, cover and place in oven to keep warm. Repeat until all dumplings are cooked.

Description

This goes great served in a bowl of plane vegetable or chicken broth and Stir Fry or Thai Salad recipe. Make this recipe interesting and change the vegetables to shredded zucchini, red cabbage or spinach.

These dumplings can be easily frozen:
1. Line a baking sheet with parchment paper
2. Place the dumplings uncooked on the baking sheet (do not stack) and place in the freezer
3. Once the frozen, transfer to a freezer bag
4. Can be frozen for up to 3 months
5. Cook the dumpling as usual without thawing (cooking time will be longer)

Asian Egg Rolls

Yield: 12 egg rolls   Preheat the oven to 425º F

Ingredients

12 egg roll wraps

2½ cups organic cabbage, shredded

2½ cups broccoli slaw

1 cup organic snow peas, chopped

1 medium organic carrot, shredded

1/4 cup bean sprouts

1 teaspoon extra virgin olive oil

1 teaspoon sesame oil

2 teaspoons organic ginger, minced

2 garlic cloves, minced

2 tablespoons fish sauce

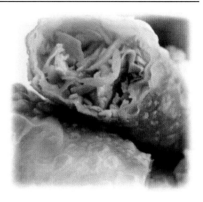

Directions

1. Place parchment paper over cookie sheet and set aside
2. Wash onions, cabbage, carrots, slaw, peas and sprouts in vinegar water and pat dry
3. Mince garlic and ginger; chop peas, shred cabbage and carrots
4. Heat oil in a large wok over medium-high heat; add garlic and cook for 30 seconds
5. Stir in cabbage, broccoli slaw, carrots, bean sprouts, and pea pods, fish sauce, sesame oil; cook for 5 minutes until soft-crisp; chill in refrigerator for 15 minutes
6. Place 1 egg roll wrapper onto work surface with 1 corner pointing toward you; spoon cooled filling into center of wrap; fold lower corner of wrapper up over filling; fold in corners; wet top corner with water and roll up wrap tightly; seal with top wet flap
7. Lightly coat egg rolls with olive oil and place, seam side down, on a baking sheet

Asian Egg Rolls continued

8. Bake for 10 minutes, turn and bake another 10 minutes or until golden brown on both sides.

Description

This goes great with the Easy Fried Rice recipe. Vegetables can also be changed for variety.

These egg rolls can be easily frozen:

1. Line a baking sheet with parchment paper
2. Place the egg rolls uncooked on the baking sheet (do not stack) and place in the freezer
3. Once the frozen, transfer to a freezer bag
4. Can be frozen for up to 3 months
5. Thaw in refrigerator and bake as usual

Broccoli Cauliflower Casserole

Yield: 6 servings   Preheat oven to 350° F

Ingredients

1/4 cup plain dry bread crumbs

1/4 cup plus 2 tablespoons low fat organic parmesan cheese, grated

4 tablespoons avocado oil, 100% pure natural

1½ Italian seasoning (see recipe-Condiments) or organic store-bought

2 cups organic broccoli, florets, bite size

2 cups organic cauliflower, florets, bite size

1 cup organic onion, chopped

1 tablespoon organic all-purpose einkorn flour

2 organic garlic cloves, minced

1/2 cup milk, whole organic Vitamin D

1/2 cup Greek Yogurt

Directions

1. In a small bowl mix bread crumbs with 2 tablespoons parmesan cheese, 2 tablespoons oil and ½ teaspoon Italian seasoning and set aside

2. Wash broccoli and cauliflower and break florets into bite-size pieces and set aside

3. Chop onion; mince garlic and sauté in remaining 2 tablespoons oil in large skillet over medium heat until tender

4. In a small bowl mix flour and remaining 1 teaspoon Italian seasoning, yogurt and milk; stir slowly into skillet and cook until mixture thickens

5. Add remaining ¼ cup parmesan cheese and cook until cheese is melted

Broccoli Cauliflower Casserole continued

6. Combine bite-size pieces of broccoli and cauliflower florets into skillet and gently coat
7. Spoon everything into a well-oiled 2 qrt baking dish
8. Sprinkle the top evenly with crumb mixture and bake 35-40 minutes or until heated through and top is lightly browned

Description

Broccoli and cauliflower are cruciferous vegetables and in the same family as cabbage, kale and Brussels sprouts and contribute to your overall vegetable intake and also offer health benefits due to their nutrient content. Both broccoli and cauliflower contain glucosinolates compounds that are found only in cruciferous vegetables. Eating glucosinolates might help lower your risk of cancer.

Main Dishes

Cabbage Steaks with Roasted Garlic Rub

Yield: 4-6 servings depending on size   Preheat oven to 400° F

Ingredients

1 large head green organic cabbage

1 ½ teaspoons organic extra virgin olive oil

3 fresh organic garlic cloves, minced

Salt and pepper to taste

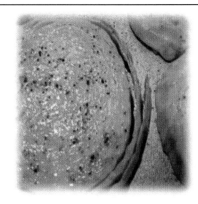

Directions

1. Wash cabbage and peel off outer layer and cut off root; discard
2. Cut cabbage starting from the root to the top in 1 inch thick slices
3. Mix garlic and oil in a small bowl
4. Brush both sides of the cabbage slices and sprinkle lightly with Himalayan or Celtic salt and cracked pepper
5. Place slices on cookie sheet lined with parchment paper and roast on middle rack for 30 minutes
6. Carefully flip cabbage steaks and roast an additional 30 minutes until the edges are brown and crispy

Description

This is a very good and easy vegetable to serve with any meal. It is also a very good source of manganese, dietary fiber, potassium, vitamin B1, folate and copper. Additionally, cabbage is a good source of choline, phosphorus, vitamin B2, magnesium, calcium, selenium, iron, pantothenic acid, protein, and niacin.

Main Dishes

Chili Made Easy

Yield: 4 servings

Ingredients

1 tablespoon avocado oil, 100% pure natural

1 organic onion, peeled and chopped

1/2 organic red bell pepper, chopped

1/2 organic green bell pepper, chopped

2 organic garlic cloves, minced

1 ½ cups organic tomatoes, crushed or (15oz)organic store-bought crushed tomatoes, no added salt

1 ½ cups kidney beans (see recipe-Beans) or (15oz) organic store-bought no added salt

1 ½ cups pinto beans (see recipe-Beans) or (15oz) organic store-bought no salt

1 ½ cups lentil beans (see recipe-Beans) or (15oz) organic store-bought no salt

1 ½ cups vegetable or chicken broth (see recipe-Broth) or organic low sodium store-bought

1 teaspoon paprika

1/2 teaspoon chili powder (see recipe-Condiments) or organic store-bought

1 teaspoon cumin, ground

Directions

1. Wash peppers in vinegar water and deseed; chop peppers and onion; mince garlic
2. In stainless steel 2 quart pan, sauté onion, garlic and peppers in oil until onions are transparent
3. Add crushed tomatoes and simmer for 5 minutes
4. Drain and well rinse beans; add all beans to the tomato mixture
5. Add broth and continue to simmer
6. Add paprika, cumin and chili powder
7. Simmer for 15 minutes
8. Serve hot in bowls with a green salad of choice

Main Dishes

Chili Taco Bake

Yield: 6-8 servings   Preheat oven to 350° F

Chili Ingredients

4 cups organic tomatoes, mashed or organic store-bought crushed tomatoes

1/2 cup organic red onion, chopped

2 organic garlic cloves, minced

2 tablespoons taco seasoning
(see recipe-Condiments) or organic store-bought

1/2 teaspoon cumin, ground

2 teaspoon chili powder (see recipe-Condiments) or organic store-bought

1 ½ cup organic cooked pinto beans or (15oz) organic store-bought no added salt

1 ½ cup organic cooked black beans or (15oz) organic store-bought no added salt

1 ½ cup organic cooked kidney beans or (15oz) organic store-bought no added salt

12 low sodium organic corn tortillas

1/2 cup organic cilantro, finely chopped

2 organic green onions, chopped

2 cup organic low fat mozzarella cheese, shredded

Directions

1. **For Chili:** Mash tomatoes; chop onion; mince garlic
2. Simmer onion with 2 tablespoons avocado oil until onions are transparent; add minced garlic and simmer 1 minute
3. Drain and well rinse beans if store-bought or refer to Advance Food Preparation Beans for cooked beans
4. Add tomatoes, taco seasoning, cumin, chili powder and all beans; simmer uncovered for 15 minutes stirring occasionally

Chili Taco Bake continued

5. **For Assembly:** Spray 13 X 9 oblong glass baking dish with avocado oil
6. Wash cilantro and green onions in vinegar water, pat dry and chop; shred cheese
7. Dip 6 corn tortillas in chili to coat both sides and place them on bottom of baking dish side by side forming 2 rows
8. Top with half chili mixture
9. Spoon half cilantro and half chopped green onion evenly over chili
10. Evenly spread 1 cup shredded mozzarella
11. Repeat for second layer, but do not add the final 1 cup mozzarella
12. Bake for 20 minutes
13. Remove from oven and top with the final 1 cup mozzarella
14. Return to oven until cheese melts being careful not to brown cheese
15. Remove from oven and set aside to cool 10 minutes
16. Slice and serve with fresh green salad

Description

Beans are a good source of protein and iron.

Main Dishes

Collard Greens, Kale and White Cabbage

Yield: 4 servings

Ingredients

1 teaspoon avocado oil, 100% pure natural

1 large organic red onion, chopped

3 organic garlic cloves, minced

1 cup organic collard greens, sliced

1 cup organic kale, sliced

1/2 head organic cabbage, chopped

3 cups vegetable or chicken broth (see recipe-Broth) or organic low sodium store-bought

2 organic tomatoes, raw

Directions

1. Wash vegetables well in vinegar water and pat dry
2. Cut off kale and collard ends; place leaf greens together and roll forming a cylinder shaped roll; slice entire roll
3. Remove outer layer of cabbage and discard, chop cabbage and onions; mince garlic
4. Sauté the onions and garlic in oil over medium heat in a medium stainless steel stock pot until onions are softened, about 2 minutes
5. Add all the greens and cabbage; cook another minute
6. Add the stock; cover and simmer until greens are tender, about 20 minutes
7. Chop tomatoes and add to greens; simmer until tomatoes are heated though but not mushy
8. Serve hot in bowls

Description

Kale is low in calories, high in fiber and has zero fat. It is great for aiding in digestion and elimination with its great fiber content. It's also filled with so many nutrients, vitamins, folate and magnesium. Collard greens have vitamin A, C, calcium, iron and vitamin B-6.

Main Dishes

Corn and Zucchini

Yield: 6 (1 cup) servings

Ingredients

1 tablespoon ghee (see recipe-Condiments)

3 cups organic corn kernels, fresh or frozen

1/2 cup organic onion, chopped

3 cup organic zucchini, diced

2 tablespoon parmesan cheese, shredded

Directions

1. Heat ghee in a skillet over medium heat; sauté onion until translucent (ghee can be substituted for extra virgin olive oil)
2. Cut kernels from the ears of corn
3. Add zucchini and corn; cook and stir until zucchini is tender, about 8 minutes
4. Sprinkle with parmesan cheese and serve hot

Description

This dish is also a good source of Dietary Fiber and Vitamin C.

Main Dishes

Corn Fritters

Yield: 14-16 Fitters

Ingredients

1½ cups organic corn, fresh or frozen well thawed

1/2 cup organic red bell pepper, finely chopped

1/2 cup organic green onion, finely chopped

2 teaspoons organic parsley, finely chopped

1¼ cups organic all-purpose einkorn flour

1 teaspoon baking powder (see recipe-Condiments) or non GMO aluminum free organic store-bought

1/2 teaspoon cumin, ground

3/4 cup milk, whole organic Vitamin D

1 organic free range egg

3 tablespoons avocado oil, 100% pure natural

Directions

1. Wash raw vegetables in vinegar water; pat dry and chop
2. Beat egg with milk in a medium bowl
3. Add flour, baking powder, and cumin to bowl and combine well; add fresh or thawed corn, peppers, onion, and parsley to mixture until well coated and well blended; batter should NOT be thin; add more flour if needed
4. Heat a stainless steel skillet with oil over medium heat; spoon batter into heated pan; press to flatten with spatula
5. Cook for 2 minutes on each side or until golden brown and place on paper towel
6. Add more oil if needed to complete all the batter
7. Serve hot with a salad

Main Dishes

Easy Fried Rice

Yield: 8

Ingredients

3 cups cooked organic basmati rice

2 tablespoons extra virgin olive oil

2 organic garlic cloves, minced

2 organic green onions, chopped

1 cup organic frozen peas and carrots, thawed

2 tablespoons Oshawa Nama Shoyu sauce
(organic fermented unpasteurized soy)

2 organic free range eggs, lightly beaten

Instructions

1. Cook rice according to package and set aside
2. Thaw frozen peas and carrots; mince garlic; chop onion
3. Preheat large stainless steel skillet over medium heat with oil
4. Add onion, peas and carrots and sauté until tender
5. Beat eggs while vegetables are sautéing
6. Slide the onion, peas and carrots to one side of pan and pour beaten eggs onto the other side to soft scramble
7. Mix vegetables and scrambled eggs together
8. Add the rice and Nama Shoyu sauce; stir the rice with the vegetable and egg mixture until heated through

Description

Both basmati and brown rice are fat free and are a good source of minerals like iron and B vitamins such as thiamine, niacin, folate and protein. This is excellent with Asian Dumplings in broth.

Eggplant and Bean Burger

Yield: 8 burgers   Preheat oven 450° F

Ingredients

1 organic red onion, diced

1 cup organic cooked white beans or (15oz) organic store-bought no added salt

1 cup organic cooled lentils or (15oz) organic store-bought no added salt

1/2 organic green bell pepper, deseeded, chopped

1 organic eggplant, peeled and chopped

1/4 cup organic parsley, fresh chopped

2 tablespoon pine nuts

1 organic garlic clove, minced

1 teaspoon cumin, ground

1/2 cup bread crumbs

2 teaspoons avocado oil, 100% pure natural

8 sourdough bun (see recipe if desired)

Directions

1. Wash produce in vinegar water and pat dry; peel and slice eggplant into 1/4" slices

2. Line cookie sheet with parchment paper and bake eggplant for 10 minutes; turning once half way through

3. While the eggplant is baking, sauté the onions in oil over medium heat until the onions soften and transparent

4. Remove the eggplant to paper towel and press out liquid; reduce oven to 400°F and place clean parchment paper on cookie sheet; spray with oil and set aside

5. Dice onion, chop peppers and mince garlic; drain and well rinse beans if store-bought or refer to Advance Food Preparation Beans for cooked beans

Eggplant and Bean Burger continued

6. Blend eggplant, onion, beans, peppers, parsley, pine nuts, garlic, and cumin in a food processor; blend together for about 15 seconds
7. Pulse in the breadcrumbs
8. Form patties (If unable to form a patty; add more breadcrumbs to thicken the mixture)
9. Place patties on cookie sheet and bake at 400° for 45 minutes, turning once halfway through
10. Remove the burgers from the oven and let sit for a few minutes before serving on a bun
11. Season to taste and top with fresh tomatoes, onion, mustard and aioli (see mayonnaise recipe-Condiments) lettuce or any desired topping

Description

Double or triple the batch and freeze burgers flat in freezer bag. Remove desired amount from freezer and thaw in refrigerator. Heat patties in skillet over medium heat until heated through.

Eggplant is a very good source of dietary fiber, vitamin B1, and copper. It is a good source of manganese, vitamin B6, niacin, potassium, folate, and vitamin K.

Eggplant Chickpea Burger

Yield: 8 burgers   Preheat oven to 400° F

Ingredients

1 organic eggplant, peeled and chopped

1 organic onion, chopped

2 organic garlic cloves, minced

3 cups cooked organic chickpeas or 2(15oz) organic store-bought no added salt, drained and well rinsed

3 tablespoons organic sundried tomatoes, chopped

3 tablespoons low fat organic parmesan cheese, shredded

2 tablespoons organic basil, dried

1/2 teaspoon organic oregano, dried

1 organic free range egg

1/4 cup organic flaxseeds, ground

1 ¾ cups breadcrumb

Avocado oil, 100% pure natural, as needed

8 sourdough bun (see recipe if desired)

Directions

1. Line cookie sheet with parchment paper and spray with oil

6. Wash, peel and chop eggplant; chop sundried tomatoes, onion; mince garlic; drain and well rinse chickpeas if canned or refer to Advance Food Preparation Beans for cooked beans

2. Sauté onion, garlic and eggplant in 2 tablespoons oil for 10 minutes over medium heat and cool

3. Place chickpeas in food processor with cooled eggplant mixture and pulse until well chopped

Eggplant Chickpea Burger continued

4. Pulse in sundried tomato, basil, oregano, egg, ground flaxseed, parmesan and 1/4 cup breadcrumbs; mixture will be soft and moist to form into patties
5. Place remaining 1½ cup breadcrumbs on a plate
6. Form patties and press both sides of each patty generously into breadcrumbs; place evenly on the prepared cookie sheet
7. Bake at 400° for 30 minutes, turning once (If frying is desired, drop the patties in a medium heated skillet with 2 tablespoons avocado oil; brown on both sides)
8. Transfer cooked patties to paper towel and allow cool for a few minutes before placing on a bun
9. Season to taste and top with fresh tomatoes, onion, mustard, aioli (see mayonnaise recipe-Condiments), lettuce or any desired topping

Description

Double or triple the batch and freeze burgers flat in freezer bag. Remove desired amount from freezer and thaw in refrigerator. Heat patties in skillet over medium heat until heated through. Chickpeas also known as garbanzo beans and contain healthy protein, fiber, vitamins and minerals.

Main Dishes

Eggplant Parmigianino

Yield: 4 - 6 servings   Preheat oven to 375° F

Ingredients

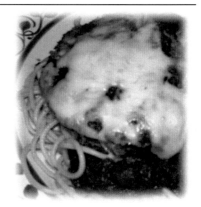

1 organic eggplant, peeled and sliced to 1/4" circles

1 organic free range egg

2 tablespoons filtered or distilled water

1/4 cup organic all-purpose einkorn flour

1/2 cup bread crumbs

1 tablespoon Italian seasoning

(see recipe-Condiments) or organic store-bought

2 cups spaghetti sauce (see recipe-Sauces and Dips) or

organic low sodium store-bought

1/2 cup low fat organic mozzarella cheese, shredded

1/4 cup low fat organic parmesan cheese, grated

3 tablespoons avocado oil, 100% pure natural

Pasta (see recipe-Main Dishes) or organic store-bought without refined flour

Directions

1. Wash eggplant in vinegar water, peel and slice to 1/4 inch slices and pat dry
2. Spoon breadcrumbs with seasoning on a small plate
3. Spoon flour onto a separate small plate
4. Beat egg and water together in a separate small bowl
5. Dip eggplant on both sides with flour
6. Dip both sides in egg mixture
7. Press both sides into the breadcrumb mixture
8. Heat oil in a stainless steel skillet over medium heat and cook eggplant until golden brown on each side

Eggplant Parmigianino continued

9. Transfer eggplant to 9 X 13 glass baking pan and bake at 375°; turn after 15 minutes and continue to bake another 15 minutes

10. While eggplant is baking, simmer spaghetti sauce over medium low until hot; cook organic pasta noodles (not made with refined flour) according to directions for al dented

11. Remove eggplant from oven and top with 2 tablespoons of heated sauce over each eggplant

12. Sprinkle mozzarella cheese over sauce coated eggplant and return to oven until cheese is melted

13. Drain pasta and portion onto 4 to 6 plates; spoon heated sauce over cooked pasta

14. Remove eggplant from oven and place on top pasta and sauce

15. Sprinkle with parmesan cheese and serve with a small salad of choice

Description

Eggplant parmesan can also be served without the noodles with a salad of choice. Eggplant is also a good source of manganese, vitamin B6, niacin, potassium, folate, and vitamin K.

Enchiladas with Eggplant

Yield: 6-8 servings   Preheat oven 350° F

Ingredients

6 cups red enchilada sauce (see recipe-Sauces) or 3(15 oz) cans organic low sodium store-bought

12 organic low sodium white corn tortillas

2 cups raw organic eggplant, peeled and chopped

1 cup cooked black beans or (15oz) organic store-bought no salt added

1 cup organic brown basmati rice, cooked

3 organic green onions, chopped

1/2 organic red bell pepper, chopped

1/2 organic yellow bell pepper, chopped

1/2 organic green bell pepper, chopped

2 organic garlic cloves, minced

1 cup low fat organic mozzarella cheese, shredded

Directions

1. Prepare enchilada sauce or heat organic store-bought sauce
2. Spread 2 cups of sauce over the bottom of a 9x13 oblong baking dish and set aside
3. Wash eggplant and peppers in vinegar water and pat dry
4. Peel and finely chop eggplant; deseed peppers and chop; chop onion; mince garlic
5. Simmer eggplant in stainless steel skillet over medium heat until soft, about 20 minutes
7. Drain and well rinse beans if canned or refer to Advance Food Preparation Beans for cooked beans

Enchiladas with Eggplant continued

6. While eggplant is simmering, cook brown basmati rice according to package; mash beans; shred mozzarella

7. Add garlic, mashed beans, cooked rice, peppers and onions to eggplant and simmer for 5 minutes

8. Tablespoon the mixture in the center of one tortilla; roll tortilla up tight and place seam side down in sauce covered baking dish

9. Repeat until all ingredients are used

10. Pour remaining sauce over the rolled tortillas and bake for 30 minutes

11. Remove from oven and sprinkle mozzarella over enchiladas, return to oven and bake until cheese has melted and serve with a salad

Description

To save time, double or triple batch and freeze enchilada flat in freezer bag without baking, adding sauce or cheese on top.

1. Remove desired amount from freezer and thaw in refrigerator. Preheat oven 350° F

2. Spread 2 cups enchilada sauce over the bottom of a 9x13 oblong baking dish and place thawed enchiladas over sauce seam side down.

3. Pour 2 cups sauce over the rolled tortillas and bake for 30 minutes

4. Remove from oven and sprinkle mozzarella over enchiladas, return to oven and bake until cheese has melted and serve with a salad

Main Dishes

Enchiladas with Vegetables

Yield: 6-8 servings   Preheat oven 350° F

Ingredients

6 cups red enchilada sauce (see recipe-Sauces) or 3

(15oz) organic store-bought no added salt

12 organic white corn tortillas, low sodium

2 cups organic cooked pinto beans or (15 oz)

organic store-bought no salt added

1 cup organic cooked brown basmati rice

2 organic green onions, finely chopped

1/2 organic red bell pepper, finely chopped

1/2 organic yellow bell pepper, finely chopped

1/2 organic green bell pepper, finely chopped

1 cup organic zucchini, finely chopped

1 cup organic cauliflower, finely chopped

2 organic garlic cloves, minced

1 cup low fat organic mozzarella cheese, shredded

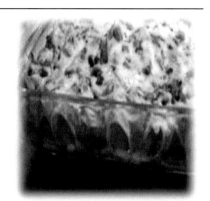

Directions

1. Wash onions, peppers, zucchini and cauliflower in vinegar water, pat dry
2. Drain and well rinse beans if canned or (refer to Advance Food Preparation Beans for cooked beans); mash beans
3. Prepare enchilada sauce or heat canned sauce; cook rice according to package directions
4. Deseed and chop peppers; chop onions, zucchini and cauliflower; mince garlic; shred mozzarella
5. Spread 2 cups of sauce over the bottom of an oblong baking dish and set aside

Enchiladas with Vegetables continued

6. Simmer garlic, mashed beans, cooked rice, onions, zucchini, peppers and cauliflower in a stainless steel sauce pan over medium low heat until heated through
7. Tablespoon filling mixture in the center of one tortilla; roll tortilla up tightly and place seam side down in sauce covered baking dish
8. Repeat until all ingredients are used
9. Pour remaining sauce over the rolled tortillas and bake for 30 minutes
10. Remove from oven and sprinkle mozzarella over enchiladas, return to oven and bake until cheese has melted
11. Serve on warmed plates with a salad of choice

Description

To save time, double or triple batch and freeze enchilada flat in plastic bag without baking or adding sauce on top.

1. Remove desired amount from freezer and thaw in refrigerator. Preheat oven 350° F
2. Spread 2 cups enchilada sauce over the bottom of a 9x13 oblong baking dish and place thawed enchiladas over sauce seam side down.
3. Pour 2 cups sauce over the rolled tortillas and bake for 30 minutes
4. Remove from oven and sprinkle mozzarella over enchiladas, return to oven and bake until cheese has melted and serve on warmed plates with a salad

Herb Garlic Sweet Potatoes

Yield: 4 servings   Preheat oven to 450° F

Ingredients

2 lbs organic sweet potatoes, sliced 1/4" thick

2 organic garlic cloves, minced

2 tablespoon ghee (see recipe-Condiments)

1 tablespoon balsamic vinegar

1 teaspoon pure natural honey

1/4 teaspoon organic basil, dried

1/4 teaspoon organic thyme, dried

1/4 teaspoon organic rosemary, dried crushed

1/4 teaspoon organic parsley, dried

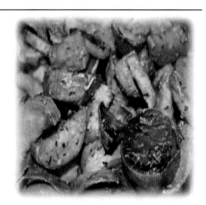

Directions

1. Line cookie sheet with parchment paper
2. Scrub sweet potatoes in vinegar water; slice to 1/4" thick pieces (do not peel); minced garlic
3. Melt ghee with honey and vinegar in a stainless steel skillet over medium low heat; combine minced garlic, herbs and potatoes to skillet; stir until well coated (ghee can be substituted for extra virgin olive oil)
4. Place potatoes on cookie sheet, bake for 15 minutes
5. Turn potatoes once and bake an added 15 minutes
6. Remove potatoes oven and serve hot

Description

Sweet potatoes are an excellent source of vitamin A and are also a very good source of vitamin C, manganese, copper, and vitamin B6.

Main Dishes

Herb Roasted Potatoes

Yield: 4 servings   Preheat oven to 425° F

Ingredients

1/2 lb organic potatoes, sliced unpeeled

1/4 cup organic sweet basil, chopped

1 teaspoon organic rosemary, dried crushed

1 teaspoon organic oregano, dried

2 tablespoons extra virgin olive oil

4 tablespoons low fat organic parmesan cheese, grated

Directions

1. Scrub potatoes in vinegar water and wash basil; pat dry; cut each potato into small wedges (do not peel); finely chop fresh basil
2. Place in a large bowl and combine all ingredients and stir until potatoes are well coated
3. Transfer potatoes to a cookie sheet lined with parchment paper and bake for 20-25 minutes or until tender and golden brown

Description

Potatoes are a rich source of fiber, iron, vitamin C and vitamin B-6, but to get the most nutrients you'll need to eat the whole potato. Potato skins are a rich source of iron.

Main Dishes

Mashed Potatoes with Cabbage

Yield: 8 (1/2 cup) servings

Ingredients

4 large organic potatoes

4 cups organic green cabbage, shredded

1 organic green onions, chopped

1 organic garlic clove, minced

1/2 cup vegetable or chicken broth (see recipe-Broth)

or organic low sodium store-bought

1/4 cup milk, whole organic Vitamin D

1/4 cup low fat plain yogurt

Directions

1. Scrub potatoes in vinegar water; cut into large cubes
2. Cook potatoes in a medium saucepan with enough water to cover potatoes for 20 minutes or until potatoes are tender
3. While potatoes are cooking, wash cabbage; discard outside layer; shred cabbage, chop onions; mince garlic
4. Bring broth and cabbage to a boil in a medium saucepan over medium heat; cover and reduce to simmer for 10 minutes
5. Uncover cabbage; add onion and garlic; cook until most of the liquid dissipates
6. Heat milk in small saucepan; stir in yogurt until smooth
7. Drain potatoes; add heated milk and yogurt to potatoes; mash until smooth
8. Add cabbage mixture to mashed potatoes; mash together until well combined and serve hot

Description

Adding cabbage to potatoes makes a very good source of manganese, dietary fiber, potassium, vitamin B1, folate and copper. Additionally, cabbage is a good source of vitamin B2, magnesium, calcium, selenium, iron, protein, and niacin.

Main Dishes

Old Fashioned Baked Beans

Yield: 14 to 16 ½ cups   Preheat oven to 350° F

Ingredients

2 cups organic dried navy beans

5 ½ qrts water, filtered or distilled

2 organic onions, chopped

2 organic garlic cloves, minced

1 cup ketchup (see recipe-Condiments) or organic low
sodium store-bought

6 tablespoons organic unsulfured molasses

1 tablespoon mustard (see recipe-Condiments
or organic low sodium store-bought

Directions

1. Sort beans for shriveled beans and undesirables and rinse
2. Transfer the cleaned beans to a large bowl; cover with water 2" over beans and leave them on the counter to soak overnight
3. The next day the beans will have absorbed most of the water; drain and rinse
4. Transfer the soaked beans to a large stainless steel stock pot and cover with water 2" over beans
5. Bring beans to a boil; reduce heat to a simmer
6. Chop onions and minced garlic; add to beans
7. Cover and simmer for 2 to 3 hours until beans are almost tender
8. Drain beans and reserve 2 cups of the liquid
9. Combine ketchup, mustard and molasses to beans; mix well
10. Transfer bean mixture into a 3 qrt well-oiled oven proof casserole dish and bake uncovered for 1 ½ hours or until beans are tender (If beans are too dry add reserved liquid, stir and continue baking another ½ hour) and serve with homemade corn bread (see recipe-Sourdough and Breads) if desired

Main Dishes

Pasta Dough

Yield: 6 servings or 1 pound

Ingredients

2 ½ cups organic all-purpose einkorn flour

4 organic free range eggs

1/4 cup extra virgin olive oil

1 to 2 tablespoons filtered or distilled water

or more if needed

Directions

1. Pour 2 cups of the flour into a mound on a clean surface and gently make a well large enough to hold the eggs in the center of the mound

2. Whisk together all of the eggs , olive oil and water in a small bowl; pour egg mixture into flour well

3. Using a fork gradually draw the flour into the center and stir it together with the egg-oil mixture, drawing in more flour until all of the flour is blended with egg

4. Begin kneading the dough by using clean hands and continue combining (If the mixture is too dry, wet hands and knead with wet hands)

5. Using the heels of your palms knead by pushing the dough down and away from you and turning it repeatedly (not breaking it but stretching the dough) until the dough feels smooth and satiny

6. Sprinkle more flour on surface if the dough becomes sticky or soft during kneading (kneading will take about 10 to 15 minutes)

7. When the pasta has been kneaded to the perfect smooth, satiny consistency, wrap it in plastic and let rest for 1 hour (can be stored in the refrigerator for 24 hours before cutting and cooking pasta)

Pasta Dough continued

8. Divide pasta into 4 pieces keeping each section separated and covered in plastic; roll out one quarter at a time, keeping the rest of the dough wrapped

9. Very lightly flour the work surface (no more than 1-1/2 teaspoons); shape the dough into a ball; roll out into a circle by stretching and pressing down by rolling the pin away from you; turn the disc a quarter turn and repeat adding a 1/2 teaspoon of flour to the surface; continue rolling the dough with a floured rolling pin working from the center of the dough outwards constantly moving and turning the dough and lifting it to make sure doesn't stick

10. When the dough is rolled to the desired thickness lightly fold one end of the dough over onto itself and roll forming a long cylinder; cut the pasta into desired thickness (I prefer Fettuccine, meaning "little ribbons", which is a flat thick pasta)

11. Cook fresh pasta noodles in a large pot of boiling water (Use about 6 quarts of water for 1 pound of pasta) for 1 to 3 minutes watching it carefully as fresh pasta cooks faster than dried

12. Pasta is best when cooked al dente (tender but firm to the bite) drain and serve immediately

Description

Spinach pasta dough:

1. Pour 2 cups of the flour into mound on a clean surface and gently make a well large enough to hold the eggs in the center of the mound

2. Wash about 3 cups of spinach leaves and purée in a food processor or blender until smooth; whisk 3 tablespoons spinach purée with all of the eggs, olive oil, salt and water in a small bowl; pour egg mixture into flour well

3. Follow the recipe above starting at 3

Main Dishes

Pasta and Pumpkin

Yield: 2-4 servings

Ingredients

1 small organic fresh pumpkin, deseeded

2 organic zucchini, chopped

1/2 organic onion, chopped

1 organic leek, sliced

6 organic asparagus spears slice into 1/2 inch pieces

1/2 cup organic snow peas

3 tablespoons organic basil, dried

2 teaspoons organic marjoram, dried

1/2 cup vegetable broth (see recipe-Broth) or organic low sodium store-bought

8 ounce (half 16oz) organic curly pasta, not from refined flour

Directions

1. Slice leek length wise in half and wash between sections with vinegar water; cut off and discard the tough greens and slice the remaining tender part of the leek; wash, peas, zucchini and asparagus in vinegar water
2. Slice asparagus into 1/4 " slices and slice leek; chop onion and zucchini
3. Halve pumpkin and discard seeds; cut entire pumpkin into quarters and place in a stainless steel pot with enough water to cover pumpkin and cook over medium heat
4. Just before pumpkin reaches boiling point remove, drain and set aside to cool
5. When cooled, peel and cut pumpkin into 1/2 " cubes and set aside
6. Add vegetable stock, leek, onion, zucchini, asparagus and herbs in a medium stainless steel saucepan and simmer over medium low heat
7. While vegetables are simmering cook pasta according package directions for al dente; about 7-8 minutes

Pasta and Pumpkin continued

8. Gently stir pumpkin into simmering vegetables until pumpkin is heated through
9. Drain pasta and transfer to simmering vegetables and gently mix together and serve immediately

Description

Pumpkin is not just good in pies but with imagination it can be combined in many dishes. Pumpkins are a good source of Thiamin, Niacin, Vitamin B6, Folate, Pantothenic Acid, Iron, Magnesium and Phosphorus, and a very good source of Vitamin A, Vitamin C, Vitamin E (Alpha Tocopherol), Riboflavin, Potassium, Copper and Manganese.

Main Dishes

Pasta Fettuccine with Vegetables

Yield: 2-4 servings

Ingredients

Fettuccine Pasta (see recipe-Main Dishes) or (16oz) organic store-bought not from refined flour

2 medium organic carrots

1 organic zucchini, sliced

1 organic crook neck squash, sliced

1 cup organic leek, sliced

1 organic garlic clove, minced

2 tablespoons organic green onions, chopped

1 tablespoon ghee (see recipe-Condiments)

1/2 teaspoon Italian seasoning (see recipe-Condiments) or organic store-bought

1/2 tablespoon potato flour

1/2 cup vegetable broth (see recipe-Broth) or organic low sodium store-bought

1 ½ ounces low fat organic parmesan cheese, shredded

2 tablespoons pine nuts, if desired

Directions

1. Slice leek length wise in half and wash between sections with vinegar water; cut off and discard the tough greens and slice the remaining tender part of the leek into ½ inch strips
2. Chop onions; mince garlic
3. Wash carrots, squash and zucchini in vinegar water and slice into ribbons with mandoline
4. Cook pasta according to package directions, al dente for about 8-10 minutes

Pasta Fettuccine with Vegetables continued

5. While pasta is cooking bring 1 cup water to a simmer over medium heat; place steamer pan over boiling water and steam carrots, squash and zucchini to just tender but still firm, about 5 minutes; drain and set aside covered

6. Sauté onion, garlic and leeks with ghee in a small stainless steel skillet over medium heat; add Italian seasoning and cook until onions are transparent (ghee can be substituted for extra virgin olive oil)

7. Stir in flour and coat to prevent broth from clumping

8. Add broth; cook stirring continually until sauce is thickened, about 5 minutes; pour over steamed vegetables

9. Drain pasta and combine with sauce and vegetables mixture stirring gently to coat all ingredients

10. Serve hot on warmed plates and top with parmesan and pine nuts if desired

Description

Eating a diet rich in vegetables as part of an overall healthy diet may reduce risk for heart disease, including heart attack and stroke as well as protect against certain types of cancers.

Main Dishes

Pasta Garlic Shrimp

Yield: 6-8 servings

Ingredients

Fettuccine Pasta (see recipe-Main Dishes) or organic store-bought without refined flour

1 organic onion, finely chopped

4 organic garlic cloves, minced

3 tablespoons ghee (see recipe-Condiments)

2 tablespoons organic all-purpose einkorn flour

1 cup milk, whole organic Vitamin D

1/4 cup white wine

1 cup low fat organic Romano cheese, grated or low fat organic mozzarella

1½ lbs fresh shrimp, peeled and deveined (about 25 shrimp)

3 ripe organic roma tomatoes, diced and deseeded

4 tablespoons low fat organic parmesan cheese, grated

Directions

1. Peel and devein shrimp and set aside covered in cold water
2. Wash tomatoes, deseed and dice; chop onion; mince garlic; grate cheese
3. Cook pasta according to package directions to al dente, for about 8 to 10 minutes
4. While pasta is cooking, sauté onion in ghee in a large skillet over medium low heat until onions transparent; stir in minced garlic and sauté another minute (ghee can be substituted for extra virgin olive oil)
5. Dissolve flour in milk in a small bowl and stir into garlic and onion mixture until well incorporated to prevent clumping; add wine continuously stirring until sauce thickens
6. Add shrimp to sauce; simmer stirring constantly for 4 minutes or until shrimp is pink in color

Pasta Garlic Shrimp continued

   7. Add Romano cheese to shrimp and sauce; drained pasta gently combine until evenly coated
   8. Serve hot garnished with parmesan cheese and tomatoes just before serving

Description

Shrimp is a unique source of carotenoids astaxanthin (astaxanthin is believed to be the most powerful carotenoid antioxidant that can help boost strength and stamina). It's also an excellent source of selenium and vitamin B12. This shellfish is a very good source of protein, phosphorus, choline, copper, and iodine. For added flavor if desired add ½ cup basil or tomato pesto to sauce (see recipes Advance Food Preparation)

Main Dishes

Penne Pasta with Asparagus

Yield: 4 servings

Ingredients

8 ounce (half 16oz) organic penne pasta, not from refined flour

1 tablespoon ghee (see recipe-Condiments)

1/4 teaspoon organic red pepper flakes

1/4 cup vegetable or chicken broth (see recipe-Broth) or organic low sodium store-bought

1/2 cup organic asparagus spears, cut into 1-inch pieces

2 organic garlic cloves, thinly sliced

1/4 cup organic onion, diced

1/2 cup organic ricotta cheese or organic low fat well drained cottage cheese

2 tablespoons low fat organic parmesan cheese, shredded

Directions

1. Wash asparagus in vinegar water; pat dry; cut into 1" pieces; dice onion; mince garlic
2. Cook pasta according to package directions to al dente, about 8 to 10 minutes
3. While cooking pasta, warm ghee in a large skillet over medium heat; sauté onions until transparent; stir in minced garlic and sauté another minute (ghee can be substituted for extra virgin olive oil)
4. Add broth and asparagus; cover and steam until the asparagus is just tender but still firm, about 5 minutes; add ricotta and combine
5. Drain pasta and add to asparagus mixture; add pepper flakes and fold ingredients together gently; serve hot garnished with parmesan cheese just before serving

Description

Asparagus is a very good source of fiber, folate, vitamins A, C, E and K, as well as chromium, a trace mineral that enhances the ability of insulin to transport glucose from the bloodstream into cells.

Main Dishes

Pizza Roll with Kale and Tomato

Yield: 2 Rolls   Preheat oven 425° F

Ingredients

2 Lavash flat bread, low in sodium

1 cup organic sundried dried tomato, chopped

2 cups fresh organic kale, coarsely chopped

2 organic green onions, chopped

1 package (3ounce) soft organic goat cheese

Organic sweet basil leaves

Directions

1. Gently wash basil and kale in vinegar water and pat dry; wash onion
2. Chop onions and sundried tomatoes
3. Pinch stems off basil and kale; coarsely chop the kale
4. Lay one flat bread on a clean work surface with long toward you; crumble half the cheese over each flat bread
5. Evenly spoon half sundried tomatoes, half chopped green onions and kale over tomatoes and cheese
6. Place desired amount of fresh basil leaves across the top
7. Roll the flat bread lengthwise away from you to form a long roll; repeat for second Lavash flat bread
8. Slice each roll into eight pieces
9. Place onto a parchment covered cookie sheet and bake for 10 minutes

Description

This is great to serve as a main dish with a salad or use as an appetizer. Quick and simple.

Main Dishes

Pizza with Healthy Flat Bread

Yield: 1 pizza   Preheat oven 425° F

Ingredients

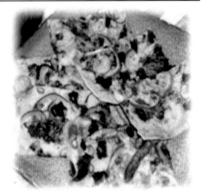

1 Lavash flat bread per pizza, low in sodium

3 tablespoons Caesar garlic dressing base or Tomato dressing base (see recipe-Salad Dressings) or organic low sodium store-bought

2 organic garlic cloves, thinly sliced

1/4 cup organic broccoli, bid size florets

1/4 organic red onion, thinly sliced

4 organic asparagus spears, diced

1/4 cup fresh organic sweet basil leaves

1/2 cup low fat organic mozzarella cheese, shredded or crumbled feta or goat cheese

Directions

1. Wash asparagus, broccoli and basil leaves in vinegar water and pat dry
2. Break broccoli into small bit size florets; thinly slice onion and garlic; dice asparagus; grated cheese
3. Place flat bread on a cookie sheet covered with parchment paper
4. Spread desired dressing base thinly over flat bread
5. Evenly place sliced garlic, broccoli, sliced onion, asparagus and desired amount of basil leaves over spread; top with cheese
6. Bake for 15 minutes until flat bread sides appear lightly toasted
7 Remove and slice into six pieces

Description

Many people seem to enjoy a good pizza. This is a healthier choice for a pizza and can be served as a main dish with a green salad of choice or as an appetizer. Also see Sourdough Pizza recipe Sourdough and Breads.

Main Dishes

Portobello and Caesar Avocado Sandwich

Yield: 2 servings

Ingredients

2 Portobello mushrooms caps

2 tablespoons extra virgin olive oil

1/2 teaspoon Italian seasoning (see recipe-
Condiments) or organic store-bought

3 tablespoons Caesar garlic dressing (see recipe- Salad
Dressings) or organic low sodium store-bought

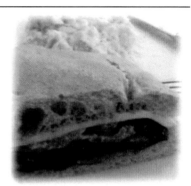

1 organic avocado, mashed

2 (1-ounce) slices low fat organic mozzarella cheese

1 organic medium tomato, sliced

Small bunch organic spinach leaves

1 sourdough bun (see recipe Sourdough and Breads if desired)

Directions

1. Prepare Caesar garlic dressing; wash tomato and spinach; pat dry
2. Slice tomato; clean mushrooms, remove stems and gills, peel cap and slice
3. Sauté mushrooms over medium heat with olive oil and seasoning
4. While mushrooms are sautéing, pit avocado and spoon out into small bowl and mash; add dressing and mix well
5. Slice bun in half lengthwise and spoon on warm mushrooms; top with avocado mixture
6. Top with desired amount of spinach, sliced tomatoes and 2 slices of mozzarella
7. Cut in half and serve each half with a small side of potato salad (see recipe this section) if desired or a green salad of choice

Description

Portobello mushrooms are a nutritional powerhouse. They provide antioxidants and are an excellent source of riboflavin, selenium and copper.

Main Dishes

Portobello Burger

Yield: 4 burgers

Ingredients

4 Portobello, mushrooms

1/4 cup balsamic vinegar

2 tablespoons avocado oil, 100% pure

1 teaspoon organic basil, dried

1 teaspoon organic oregano, dried

1 tablespoon organic garlic, minced

4 (1-ounce) slices low fat organic mozzarella cheese

4 sourdough bun (see recipe Sourdough and Breads if desired)

Directions

1. Clean mushrooms and remove stems; place caps on a plate with the gills up
2. Mince garlic; whisk together minced garlic, vinegar, oil, basil, and oregano (marinade)
3. Pour marinade into the mushroom caps; let stand at room temperature for 15 minutes, turning twice basting with marinade
4. Preheat stovetop grill to medium-high heat; brush grate with oil
5. Place mushrooms on the grill; brush with marinade frequently while grilling 5 to 8 minutes on each side, or until tender
6. Serve each mushroom on a sourdough bun garnished with cheese, lettuce, tomato, onions, mayonnaise or anything to your liking and desire

Main Dishes

Portobello Reuben

Yield: 2 servings

Ingredients

2 Portobello mushroom caps

2 tablespoons aioli (see mayonnaise recipe-
Condiments)

2 tablespoons extra virgin olive oil

1/2 teaspoon Italian seasoning

(see recipe-Condiments) or organic store-bought

1 cup sauerkraut, well drained

2 (1-ounce) slices low fat organic mozzarella cheese

4 rye bread slices, toasted (see recipe Sourdough and Breads if desired)

Directions

1. Clean mushrooms, remove stems and gills, peel cap and slice
2. Sauté sliced mushrooms in olive oil with seasoning over medium heat
3. When heated through, form two piles of mushrooms in skillet
4. Place a slice of cheese on each pile; turn off heat
5. Heat sauerkraut in saucepan over medium heat and thoroughly drain when heated through
6. Toast rye bread and spread aioli over slices
7. Spoon hot well drained sauerkraut onto 2 slices prepared rye toast
8. Spoon mushrooms over sauerkraut
9. Top each with remaining toast; slice in half and serve

Description

Sauerkraut contains high levels of dietary fiber, as well as significant levels of vitamin A, vitamin C, vitamin K, and various B vitamins and is a good source of iron, manganese, copper, sodium, magnesium, and calcium. Fermenting foods increases their nutritional content and makes them easier to digest and adds probiotics.

Main Dishes

Potato Parmesan Pancakes

Yield: 6-8 patties   Preheat oven to 200° F

Ingredients

2 cups leftover mashed, potatoes

1 small raw organic potato, shredded

1 organic green onion

1 small zucchini, shredded

2 organic free range eggs

1/4 cup breadcrumbs

1/2 teaspoon Italian seasoning (see recipe-Condiments) or organic store-bought

3 tablespoons low fat organic parmesan cheese, grated

2 tablespoons ghee (see recipe-Condiments)

Directions

1. If there are no leftover mashed potatoes, boil 3 potatoes, drain, mash and cool
2. Wash and shred raw potatoes and zucchini with skins and rinse; chop onions; grate cheese
3. Beat eggs in a large bowl; combine raw and mashed potatoes, zucchini, onions, grated cheese, seasoning and breadcrumbs; mix well with clean hands; form into patties
4. Heat stainless steel skillet with 2 tablespoons ghee and place patties into heated skillet; cook until golden brown, about 3-5 minutes on each side, turning once (ghee can be substituted in this recipe for avocado oil, 100% pure natural)
5. Transfer to a platter and place in preheated oven to keep warm until ready to serve
6. Serve cakes hot garnished with low fat yogurt, applesauce or cranberry sauce and a side of salad of choice

Main Dishes

Potato Patties

Yield: 4-6 patties   Preheat oven to 200° F

Ingredients

1 small organic yellow onion, finely chopped

2 organic garlic cloves, minced

1 organic free range egg

1/4 cup organic potato flour

4 tablespoons avocado oil, 100% pure natural

2 tablespoons parsley, chopped

2 organic potatoes, shredded

Directions

1. Wash and shred potatoes, rinse and set aside in large bowl
2. Chop onion; mince garlic
3. Sauté onion in 2 tablespoons oil over medium heat until tender; add garlic and sauté another minute
4. Transfer sautéed onions and garlic to shredded potatoes; add parsley and flour
5. Beat egg in a small bowl and combine to potato mixture and mix well with clean hands
6. Heat 2 tablespoons oil in a skillet over medium heat; scoop potato mixture making small mounds in heated skillet
7. Flatten mounds with spatula and cook until golden brown, about 3-5 minutes on each side, turning once
8. Transfer to a platter and place in 200º oven to keep warm until ready to serve hot with a Pear Salad (see recipe-Salads)

Main Dishes

Potato Patties with Spinach

Yield: 6-8 patties   Preheat oven to 200° F

Ingredients

1 small organic yellow onion, finely chopped

2 organic garlic cloves, minced

1 organic free range egg

1/4 cup bread crumbs

1/4 cup low fat organic parmesan cheese, shredded

2 tablespoons ghee (see recipe-Condiments)
100% pure natural

1/2 cup organic spinach, finely chopped

2 cups organic red potatoes, shredded

Directions

1. Wash and shred potatoes with skins; wash spinach and pat dry; finely chop spinach and onions; mince garlic; shred cheese
2. Rinse shredded potatoes and place in a saucepan; pour enough water in pan to cover potatoes
3. Par-cook shredded potatoes for about 8 minutes; drain well and set aside to cool
4. Add spinach, garlic, onions, cheese and bread crumbs to cooled potatoes
5. Beat egg in a separate small bowl and combine with potatoes and mix all ingredients together with clean hands
6. Heat stainless steel skillet with 2 tablespoons ghee (ghee can be substituted in this recipe for avocado oil, 100% pure natural)
7. Form potato mixture into patties and drop patties into heated skillet
8. Cook until golden brown, about 3-5 minutes on each side, turning once
9. Transfer to a platter and place in oven to keep warm until ready to serve
10. Serve patties hot with a salad of choice

Main Dishes

Potato and Veggies Bakers

Yield: 2 servings   Preheat oven to 400°F

Ingredients

2 organic russet potatoes

1 cup mixed vegetables, frozen

1/2 cup milk, whole organic Vitamin D

1/2 cup low fat plain yogurt

1/4 cup organic natural cheddar cheese, shredded

2 tablespoons low fat organic parmesan cheese, shredded

Directions

1. Scrub potatoes and slice through the top and bake for 1 hour
2. While potatoes are baking; shred cheese
3. Mix together milk, yogurt and vegetables over medium low heat until vegetables are heated through
4. Add cheddar cheese and stir until melted
5. Remove potatoes from oven and squeeze the sides until the potatoes split open
6. Pour vegetable mixture over potatoes; top with parmesan cheese and serve

Main Dishes

Potato Salad

Yield: 4-6 servings

Ingredients

6 organic red potatoes

1 organic onion, finely chopped

3 organic free range eggs, hardboiled

2 organic garlic, minced

1/2 organic red bell pepper, chopped

1 organic celery stalks, chopped

1/2 teaspoon organic celery seed

1 tablespoon organic dry mustard

1/2 cup Greek Yogurt

1/2 cup mayonnaise (see recipe-Condiments) or organic store-bought

2 tablespoons organic parsley, chopped

Directions

1. Prepare mayonnaise
2. Wash celery, pepper and potatoes in vinegar water
3. Cut potatoes into large cubes with skins and place in 2 qrt saucepan; add enough water to cover potatoes and cook over medium heat until done, but still firm; rinse with cold water; drain and refrigerate to cool for about 1 hour
4. While potatoes, hard boil eggs (see Advance Food Preparation–Hard Boiled Eggs); drain the water and let them set in ice water to stop the cooking; peel under cold running water and refrigerate covered in a bowl
5. Deseed pepper; chop pepper, onions, and celery; mince garlic; cut cold potatoes into smaller pieces; place all into a large bowl
6. Mix celery seeds, mustard, parsley, yogurt and mayonnaise in a small bowl and fold into potato mixture
7. Chop peeled cold eggs and fold gently with potato mixture until well coated; refrigerate until ready to serve

Main Dishes

Potato Salad without Eggs

Yield: 4-6 servings

Ingredients

6 organic red potatoes

1 medium organic onion, finely chopped

1/2 organic green bell pepper, finely chopped

1/2 organic yellow bell pepper, finely chopped

1/2 organic red bell pepper, finely chopped

3 organic garlic cloves, minced

2 organic celery stalks, finely chopped

1 cup mayonnaise (see recipe-Condiments) or organic store-bought

1 teaspoon Italian seasoning (see recipe-Condiments) or organic store-bought

Directions

1. Wash celery, peppers and potatoes in vinegar water
2. Cut potatoes into large cubes with skins on and place in 2 qrt saucepan
3. Add enough water in pan to cover potatoes and cook over medium heat; potatoes will be done when soft skewered but still firm
4. Rinse immediately with cold water, drain and refrigerate for about 1 hour to cool
5. While potatoes are cooling make mayonnaise; chop onions, peppers, celery; mince garlic
6. Fold mayonnaise, seasoning, onions, peppers, celery and garlic into cooked cold potatoes
7. Return to refrigerator until time to serve

Potatoes - Healthier Scallops

Yield: 6 servings   Preheat oven to 375°

Ingredients

4 cups organic potatoes, thinly sliced with skins

2 tablespoons avocado oil, 100% pure natural

1 organic onion, chopped

2 tablespoons potato flour

1 cup milk, whole organic Vitamin D

1 cup low fat plain yogurt

1/2 cup organic natural cheddar cheese, shredded

1/2 cup low fat organic parmesan cheese, shredded

1/4 cup bread crumbs

Directions

1. Scrub potatoes in vinegar water but do not peel; cut into thin slices (the thinner the better the potatoes will bake) to measure about 4 cups; rinse thoroughly and set aside
2. Chop onions and shred cheeses
3. Oil sides and bottom of 1 ½ qrt casserole dish and set aside
4. Sauté onions over medium heat in oil until transparent and tender
5. Stir in flour reducing heat to low
6. Whisk yogurt and milk together in a small bowl and add to onion mixture; stirring constantly while slow cooking
7. Stir in ¼ cup cheddar and ¼ cup parmesan cheeses; cook and stir until cheese is well melted; remove from heat and cover to keep warm
8. Spread ½ potatoes at bottom of prepared casserole dish
9. Pour ½ cheese sauce over the potatoes
10. Spread the remaining potatoes in casserole dish

Potatoes - Healthier Scallops continued

11. Pour remaining cheese sauce over all the potatoes
12. Bake covered in preheated oven for 1 hour
13. Remove from the oven and sprinkle the remaining cheeses and breadcrumbs over the potatoes
14. Return to oven and bake uncovered for another 15 minutes or until top is brown and bubbly

Description

Less cheese equals less fat. As with all cheese, pay attention to its frequent use. Serve with a green salad. (Make sure milk and cheeses are from animals not fed BGH, grass fed or flax fed)

Main Dishes

Potatoes with Asparagus and Bok Choy

Yield: 4 servings

Ingredients

4 organic red potatoes

1 small organic yellow onion, chopped

2 organic garlic cloves, minced

12 asparagus spears, organic

2 organic baby bok choy

1 tablespoon ghee (see recipe-Condiments)

1/2 cup vegetable or chicken broth (see recipe-Broth)

or organic low sodium store-bought

Directions

1. Wash all vegetables in vinegar water and pat dry
2. Break off the tough ends of the asparagus and separate the bok choy leaves
3. Slice potatoes into thin slices (do not peel)
4. Chop onions; mince garlic
5. Sauté onions in ghee over medium heat in a stainless steel skillet until onions are almost transparent; add garlic and cook 1 minute (ghee can be substituted in this recipe for extra virgin olive oil)
6. Add potatoes and broth to skillet
7. Cover and steam until potatoes are par cooked; add bok choy and asparagus over the potato mixture
8. Cover and continue to steam until the asparagus is cooked but still firm
9. Dish and serve immediately

Description

Bok choy has barely a trace of fat, yet delivers protein, dietary fiber and almost all the essential vitamins and minerals. This makes bok choy a nutrient-dense food that offers several health benefits.

Main Dishes

Quinoa and Black Beans

Yield: 2-4 servings

Ingredients

1 tablespoon avocado oil, 100% pure natural

1 small organic onion, chopped

2 organic garlic cloves, minced

1/2 cup organic quinoa, uncooked

1 cup vegetable or chicken broth (see recipe-Broth) or
organic low sodium store-bought

1/2 teaspoon cumin

1/2 cup organic corn kernels, fresh or frozen

1½ cups organic cooked black beans or (15oz) organic store-bought no salt added

1/4 cup cilantro (coriander), chopped

Directions

1. Chop onions and cilantro; mince garlic; thaw corn; drain and well rinse beans if using canned (refer to Advance Food Preparation Beans for cooked beans)
2. Sauté onions with oil over medium heat in stainless steel skillet until onions are almost transparent; add garlic and cook 1 minute
3. Add broth, quinoa and cumin to skillet
4. Bring the mixture to a boil; cover and reduce heat; simmer 20 minutes
5. Stir in corn and black beans; continue to simmer an added 5 minutes until corn and beans are heated through
6. Mix in cilantro and serve

Description

Quinoa is low in saturated fat and very low in cholesterol and sodium and contains a good source of folate, magnesium and phosphorus, and a very good source of manganese.

Main Dishes

Quinoa Stuffed Bell Peppers

Yield: 6 servings

Ingredients

3 organic quinoa, cooked

1 cup organic corn, kernels fresh or frozen

1/2 cup organic cooked black beans or organic store-bought no salt added

1/2 cup organic tomato, diced and deseeded

1/2 cup low fat organic mozzarella cheese, shredded

1/4 cup feta cheese crumbles

3 tablespoons organic cilantro (coriander), chopped

1 teaspoon cumin, ground

1 teaspoon garlic powder

1/2 teaspoon onion powder

1/2 teaspoon chili powder or more to taste

6 red bell peppers, bell peppers (red, green, yellow or orange) tops cut, stemmed and cored

Directions

1. Cook quinoa according to package directions and set aside covered
2. Line a 9×13 baking dish with parchment paper; wash peppers in vinegar water, slice off tops, hollow out and set aside
3. Shred mozzarella; crumble feta; deseed and dice tomatoes; drain and well rinse beans if using canned (refer to Advance Food Preparation Beans for cooked beans); combine and gently mix all ingredients into the cooked quinoa pan to make the filling
4. Spoon the filling into each bell pepper cavity
5. Place each filled pepper on prepared baking dish with filled cavity side up
6. Bake until the peppers are tender or until the filling is heated through, about 25-30 minutes and serve immediately

Main Dishes

Salmon Baked with Dill

Yield: 6 Servings   Preheat oven to 350ºF

Ingredients

1 whole wild salmon, 12 inches long

1 organic garlic, minced

1 organic lemon, thinly sliced

2 organic lemons, fresh squeezed

fresh tarragon and dill sprigs, as needed

Directions

1. Wash salmon in cold water and clean inside
2. Squeeze juice of 2 lemons; marinate the salmon in lemon juice for one hour
3. Remove and rinse salmon and discard juice
4. Stuff the center with fresh dill, tarragon, minced garlic and lemon slices.
5. Bake in glass dish for 45 minutes; slice and serve with salad of choice

Description

Not only does salmon have beneficial omega-3 and protein it may also slow the growth of atherosclerotic plaque and reduce the chance of developing dementia.

Main Dishes

Salmon Cakes

Yield: 2-4 servings

Ingredients

8 ounces wild fresh salmon filet, deboned

1/4 cup organic red bell pepper, diced and deseeded

1/4 cup organic scallion, coarsely chopped

1 organic garlic clove, minced

1/4 cup bread crumbs

1 tablespoon Worcestershire sauce (without soy)

1 tablespoon fresh squeezed lemon juice

1 tablespoon coconut oil

2 tablespoons mayonnaise (see recipe-Condiments) or organic store-bought

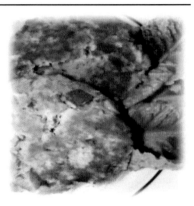

Directions

1. Rinse salmon and break apart with a clean fingers to debone; set aside covered
2. Wash peppers and onion in vinegar water; juice lemon; deseed and dice pepper; chop onion; mince garlic
3. In a medium bowl combine mayonnaise, peppers, onion, garlic, juice, bread crumbs and salmon pieces; mix well with clean hands
4. Shape into four ½ inch thick cakes
5. Dab stainless steel skillet with coconut oil over medium low heat
6. Cook cakes until lightly brown, turning only once; about 6-8 minutes on each side
7. Serve cakes garnished with romaine lettuce leaves and salad

Description

Salmon is responsible for most of the nutrients in this dish. It provides at least half of your daily protein and more than 20 percent of the recommended daily intake of all the B vitamins and calcium. It is heart-healthy with essential omega-3 fatty acids.

Main Dishes

Salmon Grilled with Citrus Marinade

Yield: 4 servings

Ingredients

4 (4ounce) 1 inch thick, wild salmon fillets

Marinade:

3/4 cup organic orange juice, fresh squeezed

1/4 cup organic lemon juice, fresh squeezed

1/4 cup organic lime juice, fresh squeezed

2 organic garlic cloves, minced

3 tablespoon orange marmalade, reduced sugar

2 tablespoon cilantro (coriander), finely chopped leaves

Directions

1. Rinse salmon and set aside covered in cold water
2. Wash citrus and cilantro in vinegar water and pat dry
3. Squeeze the juices; finely chop cilantro; mince garlic
4. Combine marmalade, juices, cilantro and garlic in a stainless steel skillet
5. Over medium heat bring mixture to a boil; immediately reduce to a simmer and stir until syrupy
6. Pour marinade into a shallow glass dish and roll the 4 salmon fillets into mixture until all sides are well coated
7. Cover and refrigerate 1 to 2 hours
8. Heat well-oiled grilling griddle over medium heat
9. Grill marinated salmon fillets for 4 minutes on each side brushing with remaining marinade
10. Serve with brown rice or salad of choice

Main Dishes

Salmon Flat Bread Wrap

Yield: 2 wraps

Ingredients

2 Lavash flat bread

Lemon Dill Yogurt Spread

1 cup organic arugula greens

4 oz wild smoked salmon

1/2 cup organic alfalfa sprouts

1 organic cucumber, thinly sliced length-wise

Directions

1. Prepare Lemon Dill Yogurt Spread (see recipe below)
2. Wash the arugula, sprouts and cucumber and pat dry
3. Slice the cucumber length-wise in thin slices with mandoline
4. Debone the wild smoked salmon if necessary breaking it with clean fingers
5. Place flat bread vertically in front of you; spread the Lemon Dill Yogurt Spread over the entire flat bread
6. Sprinkle half the arugula leaves into a neat row about 1" from the bottom of the flat bread; spoon half of the smoked salmon pieces over the arugula
7. Add half alfalfa sprouts over the salmon; cover salmon with cucumber slices
8. Fold the bottom of the flat bread over the ingredients and continue to roll the flat bread away from you wrapping all of the ingredients into a tight roll; repeat for second wrap
9. Cut the wraps in half diagonally and serve

Salmon Flat Bread Wrap continued

Lemon Dill Yogurt Spread Ingredients

4 tablespoons Greek yogurt

2 tablespoon organic cream cheese

1 organic lemon, fresh squeezed

1¼ teaspoon lemon zest

1 organic green onion, finely chopped

1 ½ tablespoon organic dill

Directions

1. Wash green onion in vinegar and lemon in vinegar water
2. Squeeze juice into a small bowl and set aside; finely chop onion
3. Grate the lemon for the zest to make 1¼ teaspoon
4. Whisk juice, zest, yogurt and cheese until blended smooth; mix in onion
5. Use immediately, or cover with plastic wrap and store in fridge until ready to use

Description

The spread can easily be made to accommodate more than two wraps to have on hand. Spread can be stored up to 7 days covered in the refrigerator. Arugula is a rich source of certain phytochemicals (chemical compounds that occur naturally such as carotenoids or flavonoids) that have been shown to combat cancer-causing elements in the body. It also adds a spicy element to this wrap.

Main Dishes

Salmon Spinach Roll

Yield: 4 servings   Preheat over 375º F

Ingredients

4 ounces fresh wild salmon fillet, deboned

1/2 cup organic cooked basmati rice

1/2 cup organic onion, finely chopped

3 organic garlic cloves, minced

1 tablespoon Worcestershire sauce (no soy)

2 tablespoons extra virgin olive oil or avocado oil, 100% pure natural

1/4 cup organic vegetable or fish broth

2 cups organic spinach, chopped

3/4 cup low fat organic mozzarella cheese, shredded

Directions

1. Cook rice according to directions and set aside to cool
2. While rice is cooking; shred cheese; finely chop onion; mince garlic; rinse salmon and debone breaking apart with clean fingers
3. In skillet over medium heat add oil and Worcestershire; sauté onions until onions are transparent; add garlic and sauté 1 minute
4. Add broth and fish; cover and steam for 5 minutes; add spinach and cover to steam an added 5 minutes
5. Remove from heat and cool enough to mix with clean hands
6. Mix in cooled cooked rice and cheese
7. Place a sheet of parchment paper over work surface; place 8 sheets of fillo dough onto paper with long end of dough near you; spoon fish mixture at end of dough nearest you

Salmon Spinach Roll continued

8. Fold sides over fish mixture; Roll the dough using the paper to guide dough making a long tight roll
9. Salmon roll should still be on paper; use paper to pick up and place salmon onto cookie sheet with parchment paper and bake for 35 minutes or until dough is lightly browned
10. While roll is baking make dill sauce (see recipe-Sauces and Dips)
11. Slice and spoon with hot dill sauce just before serving

Description

Salmon is one of the best sources of the essential omega-3 fatty acids which prevent systemic inflammation, lower blood pressure and reduce the risk of heart attack or stroke.

Main Dishes

Salmon, Herb Crusted

Yield: 2-3ounce servings   Preheat oven 350°F

Ingredients

1 (6 ounce) fresh wild salmon filet cut in half

1/4 cup fresh organic parsley, finely chopped

1 tablespoons rosemary, coarsely ground

1 tablespoons tarragon, ground

1 tablespoons oregano, coarsely ground

1 tablespoons extra virgin olive oil

2 organic garlic cloves, minced

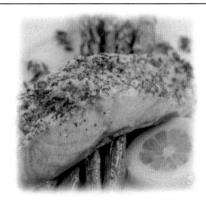

Directions

1. Chop and grind herbs; mince garlic
2. Rinse salmon and slice in half
3. Combine herbs in a shallow dish and press one side of salmon pieces into herbs
4. Heat oil in oven proof skillet and sauté garlic until tender but not brown
5. Place salmon, herb side down over garlic and cook 5 minutes
6. Turn salmon over in skillet and bake in preheated oven for 7 minutes
7. Serve on a bed of steamed asparagus

Description

Not only does this dish have the wonderful nutritional value of salmon but also that of asparagus. Asparagus is an excellent source of vitamin K, folate, copper, selenium, vitamin B2, vitamin C, and vitamin E. It is a very good source of dietary fiber, manganese, phosphorus, niacin, potassium, choline, vitamin A, zinc, iron, protein, vitamin B6, and pantothenic acid.

Main Dishes

Squash Bake

Yield: 4-6 (1/2 cup) servings   Preheat oven to 350°

Ingredients

1 large organic butternut squash

1 organic free range egg

1/4 cup bread crumbs

1 tablespoon ghee (see recipe-Condiments)

3 tablespoons organic onions, chopped

Directions

1. Wash squash and cut into large pieces; put into a large saucepan with enough water to cover 1" over squash and cook over medium heat
2. Once brought to a boil reduce heat and simmer until tender
3. While squash is simmering chop onions and sauté in a small skillet with ghee until transparent (ghee can be substituted in this recipe for extra virgin olive oil)
4. Drain squash in colander; cool enough to peel skin with hands
5. Return peeled pieces to sautéed onions and mash
6. Beat egg in small bowl and combine with squash; mash together
7. Transfer to a lightly oiled casserole dish
8. Top with a light layer of breadcrumbs and bake for 20 to 25 minutes or until lightly browned.

Description

Butternut squash is one of the most popular winter-squash vegetables. It contains no saturated fats or cholesterol. It is a rich source of dietary fiber, high in vitamin A and rich in B-complex.

Squash Sauté

Yield: 4 (1/2 cup) Servings

Ingredients

2 tablespoons ghee (see recipe-Condiments)

1/2 organic red bell pepper, chopped

2 medium organic yellow squash, sliced

2 medium organic zucchini squash, sliced

1/2 organic onion, sliced

2 tablespoons organic dried parsley

Directions

1. Wash pepper and squash with vinegar water; deseed pepper and chop; slice squash and onion
2. Over medium heat melt ghee; add red peppers, squash and onion; sauté 12 to 14 minutes until squash is tender but still firm; add parsley (ghee can be substituted in this recipe for extra virgin oil)
3. Serve hot with a fish dish if desired

Description

Any kind of squash can be made in this dish. Squashes have protein, vitamins A, B6, C and K, thiamin, niacin, phosphorus and copper, as well as a very good source of dietary fiber, folate, magnesium, potassium and manganese.

Main Dishes

Stir Fry

Yield: 6 servings

Ingredients

2 tablespoons avocado oil or extra virgin olive oil

1/2 cup organic carrot, sliced

2 cups organic celery stalks, sliced

1/2 cup organic broccoli, chopped to bite size pieces

1/2 cup organic snap peas

1/2 organic green pepper, sliced

1/2 organic red bell pepper, sliced

1 organic onion, sliced and separate rings

2 organic garlic cloves, minced

1/2 cup organic zucchini, sliced

1 tablespoon sesame seeds

1/2 cup vegetable or chicken broth (see recipe-Broth) or organic low sodium store-bought

1 teaspoon organic peanut butter

2 tablespoons Worcestershire sauce

2 teaspoons arrowroot

Directions

1. Wash and slice carrots, celery, peppers, onions and zucchini; wash and chop broccoli to bite size flowerets; mince garlic
2. Heat oil in a wok or large heavy stainless steel skillet; add onions and sauté for 2 minutes; add garlic and sauté 1 minute
3. Stir in broccoli, carrots, celery, snap peas, zucchini, and peppers; stir-for 7 minutes
4. In a small bowl, whisk together soy free Worcestershire sauce, broth, peanut butter and arrow-root until smooth
5. Stir sauce mixture into vegetables; cook 1 to 2 minutes or until sauce is thickened
6. If desired, serve over 1/2 cup hot cooked brown or wild rice garnished with sesame seeds

Main Dishes

Taco Salad

Yield: 2 Salads

Ingredients

3 cups organic romaine lettuce, chopped

1/2 cup organic spring lettuce

1 cup organic cooked black or pinto beans or organic store-bought no salt added

1 organic tomato

1 organic green onions, chopped

4 tablespoons Greek Yogurt

4 tablespoons salsa (see recipe-Sauces and Dips) or organic low sodium store-bought

1/2 cup low fat organic mozzarella cheese, shredded

1 organic avocado, sliced

1 organic lemon

Organic corn tortilla chips

Directions

1. Wash lettuce, onion, avocado and tomato in vinegar water and pat dry; drain and well rinse beans if using canned (refer to Advance Food Preparation Beans for cooked beans)
2. Chop romaine and onions; shred mozzarella; thinly slice tomato and set aside
3. Peel avocado and cut in half; cut lemon in half
4. Mash half the avocado in a small mixing bowl and squeeze half the lemon over avocado
5. Add salsa to mashed avocado and mix together; set bowl aside
6. Slice remaining avocado and squeeze the other half lemon over top and set aside
7. Arrange 6 to 8 tortillas chips at the bottom of 2 bowls, spoon lettuce over chips; spoon beans over lettuce and chips of each bowl

Taco Salad continued

8. Sprinkle green onions and mozzarella over each bowl
9. Arrange sliced tomato and sliced avocado over salad
10. Spoon the yogurt and the avocado/salsa on each dish
11. Serve immediately – no dressing needed

Description

This dish is light, fresh, bold and flavorful. Not to mention satisfyingly filling.

Main Dishes

Tacos

Yield: 12 tacos

Ingredients

1/2 cup organic cooked chickpeas or organic store-bought no salt added

1/2 cup organic cooked lentils or organic store-bought no salt added

2 organic roma tomatoes

6 tablespoons taco seasoning (see recipe-Condiments) or organic store-bought

12 organic low sodium white corn tortillas

1/2 cup organic green onion, chopped

1/2 cup Greek Yogurt

1 cup romaine lettuce, shred

1/2 cup low fat organic mozzarella, shredded

1/4 cup fresh cilantro, finely chopped

Directions

1. Wash lettuce, green onion, cilantro; slice lettuce; chop cilantro and green onion; shred cheese; deseed and dice 1 tomato; set aside in bowls for topping

2. Drain and well rinse beans if canned (refer to Advance Food Preparation Beans for cooked beans) and place in food processer with 1 tomato and taco seasoning; pulse to make into consistency of ground beef

3. Transfer beans to a stainless steel skillet at low heat; simmer uncovered for 7 to 10 minutes so tomato juice evaporates, stir occasionally

4. While beans are simmering heat tortillas over medium heated griddle for 30 seconds on each side, or until desired crispness

Tacos continued

5. Spoon bean filling onto each tortilla; top with desired amount ingredients reserved in bowls; fold each in half and serve

Description

Chickpeas are a legume, a good source of dietary fiber, protein and copper, and filling.

Main Dishes

Vegetable Pie

Yield: 6 – 8 servings   Preheat oven to 375°

Ingredients

1/2 cup mayonnaise (see recipe-Condiments)
or organic store-bought

2 tablespoons potato flour

1 cup milk, whole organic Vitamin D

1 teaspoon organic low sodium vegetable
or chicken bouillon

1/2 cup organic broccoli, bite size florets

1/2 cup organic carrots, diced

1/2 cup organic potato, diced unpeeled

1/2 cup organic corn, frozen

1/2 cup organic peas, frozen

1/2 cup organic green beans, frozen

Pie crust (see recipe-Desserts) or 1 organic store-bought with 2 crusts

Directions

1. Prepare mayonnaise
2. Wash vegetable in vinegar water and pat dry; dice unpeeled potato and carrots; break broccoli into bite size florets
3. Par cook all vegetables over medium heat, about 10 minutes (vegetables should be firm)
4. While vegetable are cooking, combine mayonnaise, flour and bullion in a medium saucepan
5. Stirring continually, combine milk and simmer until mixture is thick and bubbly
6. Drain par cooked vegetables; add to saucepan and simmer until heated through turn off heat and set aside covered

Vegetable Pie continued

7. Roll piecrust dough into 9 ½" circle and transfer into an ovenproof pie plate; spoon in par cooked vegetable mixture
8. Roll second piecrust dough into 9 ½" circle and place over vegetable mixture; fold the edges under; press edges down with a fork
9. Cut slices on top to vent while baking; bake in preheat 375° oven for 15–20 minutes or until lightly browned
10. Let stand 5 minutes before serving with a salad of choice

Description

This is a quick and easy pie that only takes an hour to prepare. It is perfect on those chilly days and is loaded with vitamins.

Main Dishes

Vegetarian Lasagna

Yield: 6-8 servings   Preheat oven to 350°

Ingredients

1 medium organic sweet onion, finely chopped

2 tablespoons extra virgin olive oil

8 ounces portabella mushroom, sliced

2 cups fresh organic spinach, chopped

2 organic zucchinis, sliced

2 organic yellow squash, sliced

15 ounces ricotta cheese, drained

2 organic free range eggs

1 ½ cups low fat organic mozzarella cheese, shredded

1/2 cup low fat organic parmesan cheese, grated

4 cups spaghetti sauce (see recipe-Sauces and Dips) or organic low sodium store-bought

Directions

1. Coat a 9X12 baking dish with oil
2. Wash mushrooms, squash and spinach in vinegar water and pat dry
3. Thinly slice squash lengthwise with mandoline to create flat noodles; set aside
4. Chop spinach; grate cheeses and set aside
5. Wash mushrooms; remove stems and gills and slice
6. Over medium heat, sauté onions in 2 tablespoons oil until translucent
7. Add sliced portabella mushrooms and continue to sauté until softened
8. In a bowl beat eggs and ricotta cheese together and transfer to onion and mushroom mixture and stir in spinach
9. Heat 4 cups spaghetti sauce in a stainless steel sauce pan and cover the bottom of baking dish with 2 cups of the sauce; set the remaining sauce aside
10. Layer of zucchini and squash noodles over the sauce

Vegetarian Lasagna continued

11. Spread a third of mushroom and spinach mixture across the squash
12. Sprinkle a third of the mozzarella cheese over mixture
13. Repeat the layers two more times
14. Top with crisscrossed final layer of squash noodles
15. Cover and bake 1 hour
16. Remove from oven and top with parmesan cheese
17. Return to oven and bake uncovered another 10 minutes or until parmesan is lightly browned
18. Let lasagna rest for 15 minutes prior to cutting and serving
19. Spoon warm spaghetti sauce at bottom of each warmed plate and top with lasagna and serve

Description

This has low carbohydrates and mushrooms are a good source of protein, thiamin, vitamin B6, folate, magnesium and zinc. Spinach is a good source of iron, calcium and vitamin A.

Main Dishes

Vegetarian Sausage/Meatball

Yield: 10 – 12 sausages or meatballs   Preheat oven to 425°

Ingredients

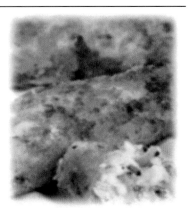

1 small organic onion, finely chopped

3 tablespoons extra virgin olive oil

4 tablespoons low fat organic parmesan cheese, grated

3 organic garlic cloves, minced

2 cup cold organic cooked basmati rice

1 cup cold cooked organic chickpeas or organic store-bought no salt added

1 cup cooked organic kidney or navy beans or organic store-bought no salt added

2 organic free range eggs

1 teaspoon dried organic thyme

1 teaspoon dried organic oregano

1 teaspoon dried organic sage

1/4 teaspoon dried organic cilantro

1/4 teaspoon cayenne pepper, (if desired)

1 cup bread crumbs

Directions

1. Well drain and rinse beans if store-bought (refer to Advance Food Preparation Beans for cooked beans); cook rice according to package directions and cool; grate parmesan cheese

2. In a large stainless steel frying pan, sauté onions in 1 tablespoons of the oil until onions are transparent; add garlic and sauté 1 minute

3. In food processor, mix cheese, cooled rice, beans, eggs, thyme, oregano, cilantro, sage and sautéed onion/garlic mixture (not pureed)

Vegetarian Sausage/Meatball continued

4. Form mixture into sausage shapes or meatball shapes and roll in the bread crumbs
5. Line a cookie sheet with parchment paper and brush with oil; place shapes on prepared cookie sheet; bake at 425° for about 15 minutes, turn and continue to bake another 15 minutes until browned and firm.

Description

These are excellent with spaghetti. Make extra to freeze flat and thawed later in the refrigerator. Heat thawed sausages or meatballs in skillet with a little oil.

Main Dishes

Vegetarian Sloppy Joes

Yield: 6 servings

Ingredients

2 teaspoons extra virgin olive oil

1 medium organic yellow onion, diced

1 organic green pepper, diced and deseeded

3 organic cloves garlic, minced

2 cups organic cooked lentils or organic store-bought no salt added

2 tablespoons chili powder

2 teaspoons organic dried oregano

Pinch of cayenne pepper

1 (16-ounce) can organic crushed tomato, no salt added

1/4 cup organic tomato paste, no salt added

3 tablespoons 100% pure maple syrup

2 tablespoons Dijon style mustard

Directions

1. Wash peppers in vinegar water and pat dry; dice pepper and onion; mince garlic
2. Heat oil in a large skillet over medium heat; sauté onions and pepper until onions are transparent; add garlic and sauté 1 minute
3. Well drain and rinse beans if store-bought (refer to Advance Food Preparation Beans for cooked beans) cooked lentils, chili powder, oregano and cayenne pepper
4. Season with salt and pepper to taste; stir in crushed tomatoes and tomato paste
5. Simmer for 10 minutes (If mixture is little dry, add extra crushed tomatoes)
6. Stir in maple syrup and mustard and remove from heat
7. Spoon a ½ cup of the Lentil Joes onto sourdough roll; slice in half and serve

Description

Lentils are a good source of protein, iron, phosphorus and copper.

Main Dishes

Zucchini Fritters

Yield: 6 fritters

Ingredients

3 tablespoons organic avocado oil, 100% pure

2 organic zucchini, grated

2 organic free range eggs, well beaten

1/4 cup organic potato flour

1/4 cup organic red bell pepper, diced

Directions

1. Wash zucchini and peppers in vinegar water and pat dry
2. Grate zucchini; wrap in paper towel and squeeze to remove excess moisture
3. Transfer zucchini to a bowl and mix all remaining ingredients
4. Form mixture into balls and drop into medium heated stainless steel skillet; flatten with a spatula
5. Cook for about 3 minutes on each side until brown
6. Remove and set on paper towel and serve with a salad

Description

Zucchini is a very good source of dietary fiber, protein, vitamin A, vitamin C, vitamin B6, folate and iron.

Main Dishes

Notes

Soups

Homemade soups are a better choice than canned. Store-bought soups often contain the chemical BPA and are high in sodium. A warm bowl of soup can hit the spot on a cold day and is a healthy meal as it tends to be high in vegetables and is filling.

Barley Tomato Soup

Yield: 4 servings

Ingredients

3/4 cup organic pearl barley

3 cups vegetable broth (see recipe-Broth) or organic low sodium store-bought

1 teaspoon dried organic basil

2 tablespoons extra virgin olive oil

1/2 organic onion, finely chopped

2 organic garlic cloves, minced

2 organic celery stalks, diced

2 organic tomatoes, diced and deseeded

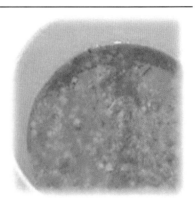

Directions

1. Wash celery and tomatoes in vinegar water; dice and deseed tomatoes; chop onion, celery and mince garlic; rinse barley until water runs clear
2. In a stainless steel stock pot boil vegetable broth and add barley; reduce heat to medium low for 20 minutes or until barely is tender
3. While barley is cooking, sauté onions and celery in olive oil over medium low heat until onions are transparent; add garlic and sauté 1 minute
4. Purée tomatoes in blender or food processor; add tomatoes, onion mixture and basil to cooked barley; cook until well heated through
5. If soup to thick, add 1 cup of broth
6. Serve hot with a salad of choice

Description

Vegetable barley soup is nutritious, full of fiber, vitamins A and C and is low in calories.

Soups

Corn and Potato Chowder

Yield: 6 servings

Ingredients

2 tablespoons extra virgin olive oil

1 large organic onion, diced

2 organic celery stalks, diced

3 organic garlic cloves, minced

6 organic potatoes, diced

2 cups organic sweet yellow, corn, (fresh or frozen)

4 cups low sodium organic vegetable or chicken broth (see recipe-Broth) or organic low sodium store-bought

1 teaspoon thyme, dried

1 cup milk, whole organic Vitamin D

2 tablespoons potato flour

Directions

1. Wash celery and potatoes in vinegar water and pat dry; dice unpeeled potatoes, celery and onion; mince garlic
2. Sauté onion and celery in oil over medium heat in a stainless steel stock pot until onions are transparent; add garlic and sauté 1 minute
3. Add broth, potatoes, thyme and corn to sautéed mixture
4. Bring to a boil; reduce immediately to a simmer until potatoes are tender
5. Whisk potato flour with milk and add to mixture slowly to prevent clumping
6. Stir soup while it thickens to prevent burning
7. Serve hot immediately with maple corn bread if desired

Description

Antioxidant activity, which helps protect the body from cancer and heart disease, is actually increased when corn is cooked. Sweet corn is loaded with lutein and zeaxanthin, the two photochemicals that promote healthy vision.

Soups

Fish Chowder

Yield: 6 servings

Ingredients

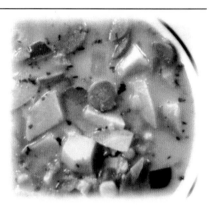

1½ lbs wild cod fillets or monkfish, 1 inch pieces

3 tablespoons extra virgin olive oil

1 large organic onion, diced

1 organic leek, sliced

3/4 cup organic celery root or 3 celery stalk, diced

3 organic garlic cloves, minced

1/2 teaspoon thyme, dried

1/2 teaspoon oregano, dried

1/4 teaspoon paprika

1/4 cup red wine vinegar

6 organic potatoes, diced

1 small organic carrot, sliced

1 organic green bell pepper, diced

1 cup organic sweet yellow corn, (fresh or frozen corn)

4 cups fish broth or vegetable broth (see recipe-Broth) or low sodium store-bought

1 cup milk, whole organic Vitamin D

2 tablespoons potato flour

2 tablespoons parsley, dried

Directions

1. Slice leek length wise in half and wash between sections with vinegar water; cut off and discard the tough greens and slice the remaining tender part of the leek; wash celery, peppers, potatoes and carrots with vinegar water

2. Deseed peppers; dice onion, celery, peppers, and unpeeled potatoes; slice carrots; mince garlic

Fish Chowder continued

3. Sauté onion and celery in oil in a stainless steel stock pot over medium heat until onions are transparent; add garlic and sauté 1 minute
4. Deglaze onion and garlic with red wine vinegar; add thyme, oregano and paprika
5. Add broth carrots, potatoes, corn, and peppers; bring to a boil and reduce immediately to a simmer for 20 minutes until potatoes are tender
6. Whisk potato flour with milk and add to mixture slowly to prevent clumping
7. Stir soup while it thickens to prevent burning
8. Add fish and simmer until fish is cooked through; add parsley
9. Serve hot immediately

Description

Fish, particularly cold water fish like cod, promotes cardiovascular health because it is a good source of blood-thinning omega-3 fatty acids as well as an excellent source of vitamin B12 and B6. Cod is also a very good source of niacin, another B vitamin that is often used to lower high cholesterol levels.

Soups

Hippocrates Gerson Soup

Yield: 6 servings

Ingredients

1 large or 2 small fresh organic leeks, sliced

1 pound fresh organic potatoes, chopped

1½ pounds fresh organic tomatoes, chopped

1 large organic onion, chopped

1 small organic celery knob or 4 organic celery stocks, chopped

1 small parsley root or 4 sprigs of organic parsley

2 organic garlic cloves, minced

Directions

1. Wash and scrub vegetables gently in vinegar water; slice leek length wise in half and wash between sections with vinegar water; cut off and discard the tough greens and slice the remaining tender part of the leek; coarsely chop all vegetables; do not peel any vegetables
2. Place vegetables into a stainless steel stock pot with enough filtered water to cover vegetables and bring to a boil
3. Reduce to a simmer immediately and cook for 2 hours until all vegetables are tender
4. Pass through a food mill in small portions and serve hot

Description

This soup is in the Gerson Therapy and is a vital component of the diet. Treating cancer alternatively involves eating Gerson's Hippocrates Soup that strengthens the immune system and kidneys as it contains large amounts of vitamins and minerals. The soup can be eaten on its own or used as a flavorful base for other vegetable dishes. With imagination there are multitude of ways that can be used and incorporate it into every meal.

Soups

Lentil and Creamy Tomato Soup

Yield: 4 servings

Ingredients

1 cup organic brown lentils

1 organic onion, coarsely chopped

2 organic garlic cloves, minced

3 organic tomatoes, deseeded and diced

4 cups vegetable or chicken broth (see recipe-Broth) or organic low sodium store-bought

1 tablespoon cumin

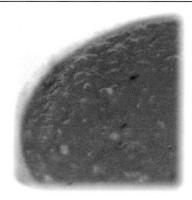

Directions

1. Wash tomatoes in vinegar water; rinse lentils until water runs clear; chop onions; deseed and dice tomatoes; mince garlic
2. Heat olive oil in stainless steel 2 quart pan; sauté chopped onions over medium heat until transparent; add garlic and sauté 1 minute
3. Add broth, lentils, cumin and tomatoes to sautéed onion mixture; cook for 20 minutes over medium low heat
4. Remove from heat and allow cooling; when cooled, purée half the soup in a food processer or blender until smooth
5. Pour puréed mixture back into pan and add more broth if soup is too thick and reheat
6. Served topped with a tablespoon of yogurt if desired

Description

Lentils are rich in dietary fiber, both the soluble and the insoluble type. They are undigested, which means they will pass out of our bodies. Insoluble fiber encourages regular bowel movement and prevents constipation and helps prevent colon cancer. The soluble fiber reduces the risk of heart disease and regulates blood sugar for people with diabetes.

Soups

Lentil Soup in 30 Minutes

Yield: 6 servings

Ingredients

1/2 cup organic brown lentils

1/2 cup organic green lentils

1 organic tomato, deseeded and diced

1/2 organic onion, finely chopped

2 organic garlic cloves, minced

1 medium organic carrot, chopped

1 organic celery stalks, chopped

6 cups vegetable or chicken broth (see recipe-Broth)

or organic low sodium store-bought

2 tablespoons extra virgin olive oil

Directions

1. Wash tomatoes, celery and carrot in vinegar water; rinse lentils until water runs clear; chop onions, celery and carrots; deseed and dice tomatoes; mince garlic
2. Heat olive oil in stainless steel 2 quart pan over medium heat and sauté onions, garlic, celery, carrot until onions are semi soft
3. Rinse dried lentils until water runs clear; add lentils and broth to sautéed mixture and cook for 20 minutes over medium low heat
4. Add more broth if soup is too thick
5. Serve hot with a fresh salad

Description

The soluble fiber in lentils helps stabilize blood sugar levels. If you have insulin resistance, hypoglycemia or diabetes, lentils are full of complex carbohydrates that can help control blood glucose and cholesterol levels, appetite and can lower the risk of getting type II diabetes.

Soups

Minestrone Soup

Yield: 8 servings

Ingredients

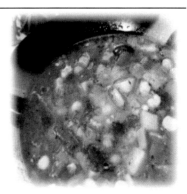

1 large organic onion, chopped

3 organic garlic cloves, minced

2 organic celery stalks, chopped

2 organic carrots, chopped

1 large organic potato, diced

3 organic tomatoes, deseeded and diced

1/2 cup organic frozen corn

1/2 cup organic frozen peas

4 cups organic cooked kidney beans or organic store-bought, no added salt

8 cups vegetable broth (see recipe-Broth) or organic low sodium store-bought

2 cups tomato sauce (see recipe-Advance Food Preparation) or organic low sodium

3 tablespoons organic parsley, freshly chopped

2 teaspoons oregano, dried

2 teaspoons thyme, dried

2 teaspoons rosemary, dried and crushed

4 teaspoons basil, dried

1 teaspoon cumin

1-2 teaspoon chili powder or to taste

3 tablespoons extra virgin olive oil

Directions

1. Wash all vegetables in vinegar water; deseed and dice tomatoes; chop onion, celery, carrots and unpeeled potatoes; mince garlic

2. In a stainless steel stock pot, sauté onions, celery, and carrots in 3 tablespoons oil over medium heat until onions are transparent; add garlic and sauté 1 minute

3. Add the remaining ingredients and bring to a boil; reduce heat immediately and simmer for 30 minutes stirring occasionally until potatoes are done but still firm and serve with a salad if desired or a slice of rye toast.

Soups

Onion Soup

Yield: 2 servings

Ingredients

2 large organic yellow onions, sliced

2 organic garlic cloves, minced

3 tablespoons potato flour

3 cups vegetable or chicken broth (see recipe-Broth) or organic low sodium store-bought

4 tablespoons low fat organic mozzarella, shredded

1 teaspoon marjoram

1 slice rye or sourdough toast

2 tablespoons hemp or avocado oil, 100% pure natural

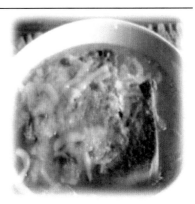

Directions

1. Peel and slice onions to desired thickness; separate rings and sauté onions with oil in a 2 qrt sauce pan until onions are soft and slightly browned; add garlic and sauté 1 minute

2. Sprinkle potato flour over cooked onions and garlic; stir until coated; add vegetable broth; simmer uncovered for 30-40 minutes until soup thickens; add marjoram

3. Toast 1 slice of rye or sourdough bread; slice into 4 pieces; divide soup into 2 oven-proof bowls with 2 pieces of toast over each soup

4. Sprinkle 2 tablespoons cheese over toast and place under broiler to melt cheese

5. Serve with a small dinner salad of choice

Description

Onions have incredible health benefits. The photochemicals in onions improve the working of Vitamin C in the body for an improved immunity. Onions contain chromium, which assists in regulating blood sugar and onions have been used to reduce inflammation and heal infections. And, onions have a powerful compound called quercetin which is known to play a significant role in preventing cancer.

Soups

Pinto Bean Soup

Yield: 6 servings

Ingredients

4 cups cooked organic pinto beans or organic store-bought no salt added, well rinsed and drained

1/4 cup organic green onion, chopped

4 organic garlic cloves, minced

1 medium organic carrot, diced

1½ cups organic frozen corn

2 organic tomatoes, deseeded and diced

6 cups vegetable or chicken broth (see recipe-Broth) or organic low sodium store-bought

2 tablespoons extra virgin olive oil

Directions

1. Wash all vegetables in vinegar water; chop onion; mince garlic; deseed and dice tomatoes; dice carrots
2. Heat oil in stainless steel 2 quart pan over medium heat and sauté green onions, minced garlic, corn and diced carrot for 2 minutes
3. Add broth, cooked beans (refer to Advance Food Preparation Beans for cooked beans) and tomatoes; simmer for 20 minutes over medium low heat
4. Add more broth if soup is too thick and serve with a salad of choice

Description

Typically beans are high in fiber, calcium, and iron. Beans and legumes are also a great source of protein. Combined with vegetables, beans and legumes not only make a delicious meal but often provide the full complement of essential amino acids.

Soups

Potato Leek Soup

Yield: 6 servings

Ingredients

4 organic potatoes, diced

2 organic leeks, sliced

3 organic garlic cloves, minced

1 organic yellow onion, chopped

3 tablespoons organic parsley, freshly chopped

4 cups vegetable or chicken broth (see recipe-Broth) or organic low sodium store-bought

1 organic cucumber or chives, chopped (for garnish)

Directions

1. Slice leek length wise in half and wash between sections with vinegar water; cut off and discard the tough greens; slice the remaining tender part of the leek; wash potatoes, parsley and chives

2. Dice unpeeled potatoes; chop onion, parsley and chives; dice unpeeled potatoes; mince garlic

3. In a stainless steel saucepan over medium heat sauté leeks, onions and garlic with a small amount of olive oil until the onions are transparent

4. Add broth and potatoes and bring to a boil; reduce to a simmer immediately; when potatoes are almost done add parsley and simmer for 10 added minutes over medium low heat

5. Serve garnished with a 1 teaspoon of chives

Description

Soup can be puréed in a food processer or blender for vichyssoise; garnish with 1 tablespoon chopped deseeded cucumbers

Soups

Potato Cream Soup

Yield: 6 servings

Ingredients

2 tablespoons extra virgin olive oil

4 medium organic potatoes, unpeeled and diced

1 organic onion, chopped

2 organic celery stalks, chopped

2 organic garlic cloves, minced

1/2 teaspoon thyme, dried

1/2 teaspoon rosemary, crushed dried

4 cups vegetable or chicken broth (see recipe-Broth)
or organic low sodium store-bought

1 cup milk, whole organic Vitamin D

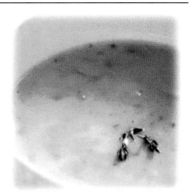

Directions

1. Wash vegetables in vinegar water; dice unpeeled potatoes; chop onion and celery; mince garlic
2. In stainless steel stock pot sauté onions and celery in olive oil over medium heat until onions are transparent
3. Add garlic, broth and potatoes and bring to a boil
4. After boiling point reached, reduce to a simmer until potatoes are tender
5. In a food processor, pulse soup until blended chunky, not smooth
6. Return to pan and add milk and seasonings; simmer for 5 additional minutes or until thickened. Serve hot with a salad of choice.

Description

The added fiber in potatoes slows the absorption of sugar into the blood to improve digestion and feel satisfied longer, which is great for weight-loss. The skins of many soup vegetables are naturally high in fiber, but are often removed during the processed canned soups. Homemade soups tend to have more nutritious value and have less sodium.

Soups

Split Pea and Barley Soup

Yield: 6 servings

Ingredients

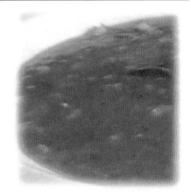

2 cups organic split peas, dried

10 cups vegetable or chicken broth (see recipe-Broth)

or organic low sodium store-bought

1/2 cup organic onion, finely chopped

3 organic cloves garlic, minced

1 teaspoon sucanat (organic unrefined sugar)

2 teaspoons lemon juice, fresh squeezed

1 teaspoon organic parsley, chopped fresh

1/2 teaspoon thyme, dried

1/2 cup organic pearl barley, dried

3 cups filtered or distilled water

1 cup organic carrot, diced

1 organic celery stalks, diced

Directions

1. Mince garlic; finely chop onion; juice lemon
2. Rinse dried peas and place them in a stainless steel stock pot with broth, onion, garlic, lemon juice, and Sucanat
3. Boil one minute; reduce heat and simmer for about 45 minutes or until peas are tender; add parsley and thyme
4. While peas are simmering, wash carrots and celery in vinegar water; dice carrots and celery
5. Combine barley with 2 cups water in separate saucepan; boil one minute; reduce heat and simmer for 45 minutes or until most of the water has been absorbed
6. Drain the barley mixture (peas and barley should be done about the same time)
7. Purée the peas in a food processer, blender or stick blender until smooth

Split Pea and Barley Soup continued

8. Add barley to the puréed split peas
9. Stir in chopped carrots and celery and simmer 15 minutes or until the carrots are tender, stirring occasionally
10. Remove from heat, cover, and allow sit at room temperature 15 minutes before serving

Description

Consuming split pea soup benefits your health due to its vitamin K content. Vitamin K maintains your health by helping the body respond to injury.

Soups

Split Pea Soup

Yield: 6 servings

Ingredients

2 organic leeks, sliced

3 organic garlic cloves, minced

1 large organic yellow onion, chopped

1/2 cup small organic celery root or celery stalks, chopped

2 large organic carrots, diced

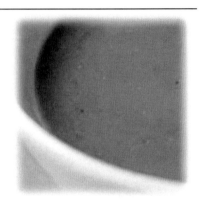

6 cups vegetable or chicken broth (see recipe-Broth) or organic low sodium store-bought

2 cups organic dried split peas (green or yellow)

2 teaspoons thyme, dried

1 teaspoon marjoram, dried

2 tablespoons extra virgin olive oil

Directions

1. Slice leek length wise in half and wash between sections with vinegar water; cut off and discard the tough greens and slice the remaining tender part of the leeks
2. Chop onion and celery; dice carrots; mince garlic
3. In a 6 qrt stainless steel pan heat olive oil over medium heat and sauté onions, leeks, carrots and celery root until onions are transparent;
4. Add broth, garlic, dried peas and herbs; bring to a boil
5. At boiling point, reduce to a simmer for 45 minutes
6. Remove from heat and blend in food processor or blender stick until smooth
7. Serve hot and garnished with 1 teaspoon yogurt if desired

Description

The healthy ingredients in split pea soup yield a nutrient-dense meal. Consuming the soup has a number of health advantages like the daily recommended intake of potassium as an essential mineral.

Soups

Tomato Basil Soup

Yield: 4 servings

Ingredients

8 organic tomatoes or 2 organic canned stewed

Tomatoes with no added salt

1 cup vegetable or chicken broth (see recipe-Broth) or

organic low sodium store-bought

1 organic celery stalk, chopped

1 organic onion, chopped

2 organic garlic cloves, minced

2 tablespoons fresh organic basil, chopped

2 tablespoons extra virgin olive oil

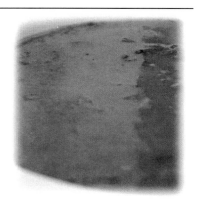

Directions

1. Wash all produce in vinegar water; chop basil, onion and celery; mince garlic
2. Purée tomatoes in a blender or food processer
3. In a stainless steel stock pot bring broth to a boil and add tomatoes and mash; reduce to medium heat
4. In a smaller stainless steel pan, while tomatoes are cooking in broth, sauté, celery and onions in oil until the onions are transparent; add garlic and sauté 1 minute
5. Combine sautéed ingredients and basil to tomato broth; reduce heat and simmer for 30 minutes; add freshly chopped basil or parsley
6. Serve hot immediately with a salad of choice

Description

Cooking tomatoes releases many benefits. Tomatoes don't lose nutritional value in the high heat processing. Making homemade tomato sauces (see recipe-Advance Food Preparation) are just as beneficial as fresh tomatoes. Try to buy organic tomatoes as they provide a higher dose of lycopene (a powerful antioxidant) than non-organic.

Soups

Vegetable Chowder

Yield: 6 servings

Ingredients

1 medium organic onion, diced

2 organic celery stalks, diced

1 large organic leek, sliced

2 organic garlic cloves, minced

6 organic potatoes, diced

2 cups mixed organic vegetables; peas, carrots, green bean, broccoli; fresh or frozen

4 cups vegetable broth (see recipe-Broth) or organic low sodium store-bought

1 cup milk, whole organic Vitamin D

1 teaspoon thyme, dried

3 tablespoons potato flour (optional to thicken)

2 tablespoons extra virgin olive oil

Directions

1. Slice leek length wise in half and wash between sections with vinegar water; cut off and discard the tough greens and slice the remaining tender part of the leek

2. Dice unpeeled potatoes, onion and celery; mince garlic

3. In a large stock pot, sauté leeks, onion and celery in olive oil until celery has softened but remains firm; add garlic and sauté 1 minute

4. Add potatoes, thyme and broth

5. Bring to a boil; reduce to simmer for 15 minutes or until potatoes are tender

6. Add milk and mixed vegetables; simmer another 10 minutes

7. If chowder is not thick enough mix 3 tablespoons potato flour with a little bit cold water dissolving lumps and add to chowder gradually to thicken; serve hot with a salad of choice.

Soups

Vegetable Rice Soup

Yield: 6 servings

Ingredients

1/2 cup organic onion, diced

2 organic celery stalks, diced

2 organic garlic cloves, minced

1/2 cup organic basmati rice

2 cups mixed organic vegetables; peas, carrots, corn, green bean; fresh or frozen

6 cups vegetable broth (see recipe-Broth) or organic low sodium store-bought

1 teaspoon dried thyme

2 tablespoons extra virgin olive oil

Directions

1. Rinse rice in cold water until it drains clear
2. Wash fresh vegetables in vinegar water; dice carrots, onion and celery; mince garlic; chop green beans
3. In a stainless steel stock pot, sauté rice, onion, garlic and celery in oil
4. Stir constantly until celery has softened but remains firm; add thyme and broth
5. Bring to a boil and reduce heat to medium; cook for about 10 minutes
6. Add vegetables and reduce heat to simmer; cook for another 10 minutes until rice is soft and vegetables are heated through
7. If the soup is too thick, add 1 more cup of broth. For a variation, experiment with different vegetables or substitute rice for favorite beans or barley

Description

Vegetables in soup contain many vitamins, such as A and C. Basmati rice can be beneficial and incorporating this grain into diets could be good as it very low in fat, but should be eaten in moderation.

Soups

White Bean and Barley Soup

Yield: 6 servings

Ingredients

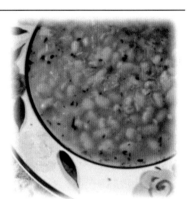

1 large organic onion, chopped

3 organic garlic cloves, minced

2 organic celery stalks, chopped

6 cups vegetable or chicken broth (see recipe-Broth) or organic low sodium store-bought

2 cups organic cooked white beans or organic store-bought, rinsed and well drained with no added salt

1/2 cup organic pearl barley

2 teaspoons oregano, dried

2 teaspoons thyme, dried

2 teaspoons rosemary, dried crushed

3 tablespoons extra virgin olive oil

Directions

1. Wash celery in vinegar water; chop onion and celery; mince garlic
2. In a stainless steel stock pot, sauté onions and celery in oil until onions are transparent; add garlic and sauté 1 minute
3. Rinse barley in cold water until it drains clear; add broth, herbs and barley to sauté mix; bring to a boil
4. At boiling point, reduce to a simmer for 30 minutes stirring occasionally until barley is tender
5. Well drain and rinse beans; add beans (refer to Advance Food Preparation Beans for cooked beans) and simmer another 5 minutes

Description

Barley, a whole grain, is an important source of dietary fiber, vitamins, and minerals that are not found in refined or "enriched" grains.

Desserts

The "health" aspect of desserts can be deceiving. Everyone has their own idea of what is a "healthy" dessert. Some think about low-fat desserts; others want fresh, seasonal, and organic ingredients; others check for recipes that have little or no added processed sugar. So face it, desserts are not always healthy, but here are some that could satisfy a desire for sweets and a bit healthier than what you may think.

Apple Cinnamon Cake - Gluten free

Preheat oven to 350ºF

Cake Ingredients

3¼ cups organic almond flour

1/2 teaspoon baking soda

1/4 cup organic arrowroot powder

2 teaspoon cinnamon

4 organic free range eggs

1/4 cup organic coconut oil, melted

1/2 cup pure natural honey

1 tablespoon pure vanilla extract

2 organic granny smith or tart apple of your choice, peeled, cored, and shredded

Cake Directions

1. Spread coconut oil on the sides of (2) 7-inch glass pans; sprinkle with almond flour; set aside
2. Wash apples, peel, core, and shred; melt oil and cool
3. Combine all dry ingredients in a medium-sized bowl
4. Whisk eggs, oil, honey and vanilla in a small bowl; pour into dry ingredients stirring until just combined; add apples
5. Stir gently to incorporate apples throughout batter
6. Pour equally into both pans and bake for 20 to 25 minutes or until a toothpick can be inserted into the center of the cakes and removed easily and clean
7. Allow cake to cool completely before icing (see recipe below)

Apple Cinnamon Cake - Gluten free continued

Cinnamon Icing Ingredients

1/2 cup organic coconut milk

2/3 cup organic arrowroot powder

4 tablespoons organic coconut manna

3 tablespoons pure natural honey

2 tablespoons 100% pure maple syrup

2 tablespoons cinnamon

1 teaspoon pure vanilla extract

Cinnamon Icing:

1. Whisk coconut milk and arrowroot powder in a small bowl until smooth
2. Continue whisking in remaining icing ingredients
3. Frost cooled cake; refrigerate leftovers

Apple Cake - Gluten free

Preheat the oven to 350°F

Ingredients

4 organic free range eggs

1/2 cup organic coconut oil, melted

1/2 cup pure natural honey

2 organic gala apple, peeled and diced

3 cups organic almond flour

1/4 teaspoon Himalayan or Celtic salt

1 teaspoon organic baking soda

Directions

1. Spread coconut oil on the sides and bottom of a 8 inch round baking dish; sprinkle with almond flour; set aside
2. Peel, quarter and deseed apples and slice into small pieces; melt oil and cool
3. Whisk the eggs, honey and cooled melted coconut oil in a small bowl
4. In a separate larger bowl, mix the almond four, salt and baking soda
6. Mix the wet ingredients, apples into the dry ingredients blending well; pour into the prepared baking dish
7. Bake 35 to 40 minutes and watch browning
8. Remove from the oven and let cool 30 minutes to an hour before slicing. Don't worry if your cake sinks in the center as this is a dense and heavy cake
9. Slice and serve; refrigerate leftovers

Desserts

Apple Pie Made Healthier

Preheat oven to 450°F

Ingredients

3/4 cup organic apple juice

5 medium organic granny smith apple, peeled, cored and thinly sliced

1 teaspoon ground cinnamon

1/2 teaspoon ground nutmeg

1/4 cup filtered water

1 tablespoon arrowroot powder

3 tablespoons organic butter

1 (15-ounce) package organic (2) pie crusts or see piecrust recipes this section

Directions

1. Wash apples in vinegar water; peel, core and slice thinly
2. Over medium heat add juice, apples, cinnamon, and nutmeg in a large saucepan; simmer for 7 minutes until juice is slightly reduced
3. Whisk water and arrowroot in a small bowl until smooth; stir into cooked apple mixture slowly; continue to simmer stirring constantly until mixture thickens
4. Remove from heat and set aside to cool
5. Place one 9½" piecrust dough at bottom of a glass pie pan
6. Spoon apple mixture onto dough covered pan and dot the top with butter
7. Place the 2nd 9½" piecrust dough, over the apple mixture; fold the edges under and flute with thumb and forefinger or press edges down with a fork
8. Cut slits in top to allow steam to escape while baking; bake for 10 min at 450°F then reduce to 350°F; bake an added 30 minutes or until crust is lightly browned
9. Remove from oven and allow to cool 30 minutes before serving

Directions

Non-hydrogenated shortening in the Shortening Free Pie Crust recipe is a better option and has healthier fat or try Shortening and Gluten Free Pie Crust.

Apple Spice Cake - Gluten free

Preheat oven to 350°F

Cake Ingredients

2 cups organic almond flour

1/2 teaspoon baking soda

1/4 cup arrowroot powder

1/4 teaspoon organic cinnamon

1/4 teaspoon organic ginger

1/4 teaspoon nutmeg

1/4 cup organic coconut oil, melted

1/2 cup pure natural honey

1 tablespoon vanilla extract, pure

1 tart organic apple, peeled, cored and diced

1 tablespoon organic almonds, finely chopped

Cake Directions

1. Use 1 tablespoon coconut oil to grease (2) 7-inch glass pans; sprinkle pans with almond flour and set aside
2. Wash apples in vinegar water, peel, core, and dice; melt oil; finely chop nuts
3. Combine all dry ingredients and nuts in a medium-sized bowl
4. Whisk oil, honey and vanilla in a small bowl; pour into dry ingredients stirring until just combined; add apples
5. Stir gently to incorporate apples throughout batter
6. Pour equally into both pans and bake for 20 to 25 minutes or until a toothpick can be inserted into the center of the cakes and removed easily
7. Allow cake to cool completely before icing (see recipe below)

Apple Spice Cake - Gluten free continued

Icing Ingredients

1/2 cup organic coconut milk

1/2 cup organic arrowroot powder

1 cup organic coconut manna

3 tablespoons pure natural honey

2 tablespoons 100% pure maple syrup

2 tablespoons organic mace

1 teaspoon vanilla extract, pure

Icing Directions

1. Whisk coconut milk and arrowroot powder in a small bowl until smooth
2. Continue whisking adding remaining icing ingredients
3. Frost cooled cake and store left over's in the refrigerator

Desserts

Fruit Parfait

Yield: 2 servings

Ingredients

1/4 cup organic strawberries

1/4 cup organic blueberries

1/4 cup organic blackberries

1/4 cup organic apple, diced

1/4 cup organic raspberries

4 tablespoons Greek Yogurt

1 tablespoon pure natural honey

Directions

1. Wash all fruit in vinegar water and pat dry
2. Combine all fruit in a bowl and spoon into 2 glasses
3. Mix yogurt and honey together in a small mixing bowl until well incorporated
4. Spoon over fruit

Description

Any fruit can be substituted. This is the easiest dessert ever and kids love it. It's even easy enough for them to help make too.

Desserts

Fruit Roll-Ups

Preheat the oven to 170°F

Ingredients

2 cups organic peaches or any fruit, sliced

2 tablespoons pure natural honey

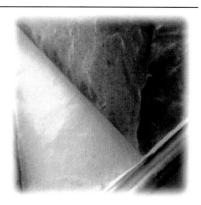

Directions

1. Wash fruit in vinegar water and cut off bruised portions, peel and dice
2. Purée fruit in a blender with honey and pour onto a baking sheet lined with parchment paper; coat with extra virgin olive oil spray
3. Dry in a 170° oven until the fruit sheets peel away easily from the baking sheet (about 6 to 8 hours)
4. Remove and roll lengthwise in parchment paper; cut roll into 1" wide sections
5. Keep in a covered container in the refrigerator

Description

Any fruit can be substituted. This is a wonderful healthy snack for kids.

Desserts

Kinda Guilt-Free Fudge

Ingredients

2/3 cup organic coconut manna

6 tablespoons organic extra virgin coconut oil

12 ounces 85% cacao chocolate

6 ounces organic hulled hempseeds

1½ cups organic almond slivers

1 cup organic dried cherries, chopped

1/8 teaspoon pure almond extract

Directions

1. Line an 8×8 baking dish with parchment paper
2. Evenly layer 1 ¼ cup almonds on baking pan
3. Evenly layer chopped dried cherries over almonds
4. Combine cacao chocolate chunks with the coconut oil and coconut manna in a stainless steel double boiler; melt stirring chocolate mixture to smooth and creamy
5. Add the pure almond extract and hemp seeds; stir for another minute
6. Gently pour the chocolate mixture over the almonds and dried cherries
7. Sprinkle the ¼ cup reserved almonds on top of the melted chocolate mixture and gently press into the warm chocolate
8. Refrigerate for approximately 2 hours
9. Remove the dish from the refrigerator; pull, lift and slide from the parchment and fudge onto a cutting board
10. Cut into 1" square chunks
11. Place fudge squares in a cover dish and store in the refrigerator

Kinda Guilt-Free Fudge continued

Description

Dark chocolate is loaded with nutrients that can positively affect your health. It is made from the seed of the cocoa tree, and is one of the best sources of antioxidants. Studies show that dark chocolate (must be at least 85%) can improve health and lower the risk of heart disease. The therapeutic benefits of hemp have an excellent 3:1 balance of omega-3 and omega-6 fatty acids, which promote cardiovascular health and have been proven to naturally balance hormones.

Shortening and Gluten Free Pie Crust

Yield: one 9" crust

Ingredients

1 cup organic millet flour

3/4 cup plus 2 tablespoons organic white rice flour

2/3 cup organic sweet rice flour

1/2 cup plus 1 tablespoon tapioca starch

2 teaspoons raw organic sugar (optional)

1 teaspoon xanthenes gum

1/4 teaspoon Himalayan or Celtic salt

2/3 cup organic non-hydrogenated shortening or BGH free organic butter

4 to 7 tablespoons cold filtered water

Directions

1. Make sure the shortening is cold
2. In food processor add dry ingredients and pulse to combine; pulse in shortening, about 10 pulses (mixture should crumbly with chunks of the shortening interspersed for a flakier crust)
3. Transfer mixture to large mixing bowl and add 4 tablespoons water and mix
4. If mixture is dry add more water one tablespoon at a time while mixing
5. Wrap with plastic wrap and chill for one hour in the refrigerator
6. Remove crust from the refrigerator (if butter is used, set out to reach room temperature before rolling out right away—rolled right out of the refrigerator the dough will crack due to the cold butter; if dough contains non-hydrogenated shortening it can roll it right away)
7. Place parchment paper on the working surface and place dough on generously floured paper; lightly flour the top of the dough as it is rolled to prevent it from sticking to the rolling pin

Shortening and Gluten free Pie Crust continued

8. When the desired 9½ inch size is reached, gently hold one end of the dough to the rolling pin and carefully roll the dough onto the pin pulling off the paper (this will help lift the dough to roll onto pie pan)
9. Press the dough carefully into the pan taking care that it doesn't tear (if it tears gently press the dough together in the pan)
10. Trim around the edges leaving 1" to overhang the edge of the pan and gently fold the excess dough under itself and stamp the edge with a fork or crimp them with your thumbs and forefinger.
11. Fill with your favorite pie filling and bake as directed.

Description

Double the recipe for a two crust pie—For a pie that requires a top, do not trim edge of excess dough and fill with your favorite pie filling and set aside. Roll the second half of the dough the same as instructed for the bottom and place over your pie filling then fold the excess dough under itself and stamp the edge with a fork or crimp them with your thumbs and forefinger.

This is a traditional gluten free pie crust that blends millet, white rice, and sweet rice flours plus a little tapioca starch. The millet provides the gluten-free pie crust with flavor, the white rice flour helps hold everything together, sweet rice flour aids in the flakiness, and tapioca starch makes is stick together. The trick to this crust is not to overwork the fat into the flour (do not over pulse). As soon as there are no large pieces of organic butter or non-hydrogenated shortening in the flour mixture, stop. You're done!

Desserts

Shortening Free Pie Crust

Yield: one 9" crust

Ingredients

1¼ cups organic unbleached all-purpose
einkorn flour

1/4 teaspoon Himalayan or Celtic salt

1/3 cup cold organic butter or non-hydrogenated
shortening

4-6 tablespoons filtered or distilled cold, water

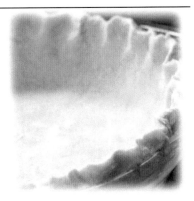

Directions

1. In medium bowl mix flour, salt, and non-hydrogenated shortening (make sure the non-hydrogenated shortening is cold and if using a food processor do not over-process as the mixture should be crumbly with chunks of the shortening or butter interspersed for a flakier crust)
2. Slowly add the cold water a tablespoon at a time until it forms a ball with your hands, but do not overwork the dough
3. Place parchment paper on the working surface and place dough on generously floured paper; lightly flour the top of the dough as it is rolled to prevent it from sticking to the rolling pin
4. When the desired 9½ inch size is reached, gently hold one end of the dough to the rolling pin and carefully roll the dough onto the pin pulling off the paper (this will help lift the dough to roll onto pie pan)
5. Press the dough carefully into the pan taking care that it doesn't tear (if it tears gently press the dough together in the pan)
6. Trim around the edges leaving 1" to overhang the edge of the pan and gently fold the excess dough under itself and stamp the edge with a fork or crimp them with your thumbs and forefinger

Shortening Free Pie Crust continued

7. Fill with your favorite pie filling and bake as directed or refrigerate covering with plastic wrap to keep from drying out until it is needed

Description

Double the recipe for a two crust pie—For a pie that requires a top, do not trim edge of excess dough and fill with your favorite pie filling and set aside. Roll the second half of the dough the same as instructed for the bottom and place over your pie filling then fold the excess dough under itself and stamp the edge with a fork or crimp them with your thumbs and forefinger.

Most pie crust recipes call for vegetable shortening which is bad hydrogenated fat. Use non-hydrogenated shortening substitute like firm palm oil or use organic butter from animals that have been grass fed or flax fed and not fed BGH. This is a better option and has healthier fat and therefore shortening free.

Desserts

Strawberry Shortcake

Preheat oven to 450°

Yield: 6 servings   Preheat oven to 450°F

Ingredients

2 cups organic strawberries, sliced

3 tablespoons pure natural honey

2 tablespoons organic low sugar strawberry jelly

1 cup Greek Yogurt

2¼ cups homemade bisquick mixture (see recipe-
Sourdough and Breads)

2/3 cup milk, whole organic Vitamin D

3 tablespoons extra non-hydrogenated shortening

3 tablespoons organic unrefined sugar

Directions

1. Mix Homemade Bisquick Using a spoon, drop 6 large biscuits onto a parchment lined cookie sheet

2. Bake for 8-10 minutes or until golden brown at 450°F; remove to cool

3. When cooled cut each in half lengthwise and set aside

4. In a bowl whisk 2 tablespoons honey and jelly together; add strawberries and mix gently until well coated

5. Spoon the strawberry mixture over the bottom halves of cut biscuits; replace the tops over the berry mixture

6. In a separate bowl mix together the yogurt and 1 tablespoon honey

7. Spoon the yogurt mixture over each cake

Strawberry Shortcake continued

Description

This recipe has less sugar and fat content than the traditional shortcake. Try blueberries with blueberry jelly too.

The ingredients in store-bought Bisquick Original consist of bleached wheat flour (enriched with niacin, iron, thiamine mononitrate, riboflavin and folic acid), corn starch, dextrose, partially hydrogenated soybean and/or cottonseed oil, leavening (baking soda, sodium aluminum phosphate, monocalcium phosphate), canola oil, salt, sugar, DATEM, and distilled monoglycerides mix with milk, shortening and sugar)

The store-bought Bisquick is not a healthy choice.

Index

Index

Index

Index

Index

Selected Bibliography

Charlotte Gerson: *Healing the Gerson Way, Defeating Cancer and Other Chronic Diseases* Obviously this book has had a positive impact on my life. It contains information a patient needs to utilize the Gerson Therapy. Additionally, it thoroughly details how the therapy works in the body and with many modern illnesses.

— *The Gerson Therapy: The Amazing Nutritional Program for Cancer and Other Illnesses* One of the first alternative cancer therapies, the Gerson Therapy has successfully treated thousands of patients for over 60 years and reveal the powerful healing effects of organic fruits and vegetables.

Charlotte Gerson and Morton Walker, D.P.M: *70 Years of Success! The Gerson Therapy The Proven Nutritional Program for Cancer and Other Illnesses.* This is a revised and updated edition of alternative medicine therapist Charlotte Gerson and medical journalist Morton Walker have collaborated to reveal the healing effects of organic fruits and vegetables. Not only can juicing reverse the effects of many degenerative illnesses-it can save lives.

Dr Max Gerson: *A Cancer Therapy: Results of Fifty Cases and the Cure of Advanced Cancer by Diet Therapy 6th Edition* Originally it was a reference for medical professionals and is a summary of thirty years of clinical experimentation. It is a Cancer therapy that explains the Gerson Therapy in detail and recounts 50 cases presented by Dr. Gerson. It is a medical dictionary of sorts and is very helpful for those on the Gerson Therapy.

David Servan-Schreiber, MD & PHD: *Anticancer: A New Way of Life* A remarkable story about a cancer survivor and scientist who changed his diet and lifestyle, learned to exercise regularly, manage stress and avoid contaminants in his body as best as possible. His research has led to the knowledge that a healthy immune system can keep the body's inflammation down which reduces cancer growth. The traditional Western diet is pro-inflammatory while a vegetarian diet, and Mediterranean diet as well as Indian and Asians cuisine are anti-inflammatory.

Suzanne Somers: *Breakthrough, Eight Steps to Wellness* Because of this book, I have learned the value of bioidentical hormone therapy and bioflavonoids. The book has a Q&A format with doctors who are curing cancer and using proven remedies and preventative care that most doctors just aren't talking about with patients. This book gave me HOPE and lead to much more.

Russell L. Blaylock, MD: *Natural Strategies for Cancer Patients* He is one of the doctors interviewed in Suzanne Somers: *Breakthrough, Eight Steps to Wellness.* His book is a must read to learn how to minimize the side effects of chemotherapy and radiation and increase the benefits of treatment programs to fortify the immune system and maintain strength and vitality. It explains which foods are uncommon cancer-fighting foods, which supplements can help and hurt, how certain fats and oils enhance the body and how flavonoids enhance the effectiveness of chemotherapy while adding a significant layer of protection to healthy cells.

Selected Bibliography

— *Health and Nutrition Secrets that Can Save Your Life* Discover how chemicals such as mercury, fluoride, food additives, heavy metals, pesticides and herbicides are destroying our bodies. Find out what we encounter every day that can lead to unexpected health complications and life-threatening disorders.

William Davis, MD.: *Wheat Belly* The author is a cardiologist and medical director for Track Your Plaque, an online heart disease prevention program. Lose the wheat, lose the weight, and find your path back to health. Understand that today's wheat is genetically modified and learn about the good wheat: einkorn and emmer.

Richard Béliveau, Ph.D. and Dr. Denis Gingras: *Foods That Heal Cancer: Preventing Cancer Through Diet*. Richard Béliveau, leading biochemist, has teamed up with Denis Gingras, a French researcher in the Molecular Medicine Laboratory of UQAM-Hôpital Sainte-Justine, to describe the science of food and which properties of particular foods are the active cancer-fighting elements. They precisely explain how different foods work to protect the body against different cancers and show which foods will be most effective. By understanding the science behind these therapeutic benefits, they have proven why it is so critical to add these cancer fighting foods to our diet and how easily it can be done.

Harold W. Manner, PhD.: *The Death of Cancer* Dr. Manner is a professor of Biology and Chairman of the Biology Department of Chicago's Loyola University. His treatment is based in research which builds on a controversial theory of nutrition therapy can contain, prevent, and cure cancer using laetrile. His book is about a metabolic program that claims cancer can be treated by being controlled through nutritional guidance, a positive attitude, and changes in lifestyle.

Esther and Jerry Hicks: *The Law of Attraction* This book helped me in my healing process with cancer and is continually helping me in my daily life. Here is an excerpt from the book that says it all. "Learn about the omnipresent *Laws* that govern this Universe and how to make them work to your advantage. The understanding that you'll achieve by reading this book will take all the guesswork out of daily living. You'll finally understand just about everything that's happening in your own life as well as in the lives of those you're interacting with. This book will help you to joyously be, do, or have anything that you desire!"

Cherie Calbom and Maureen Keane: *Juicing for Life* This book showcases the benefits of fresh fruit and vegetable juicing, including what juices can help with certain ailments. It contains fresh, vitamin-rich fruit and vegetable juicing recipes that can help you lose weight and improve your health by boosting your metabolism and cleansing your entire body.

Theodore A. Baroody, MA, DC, ND, L.M.T., PhD (Nutrition): *Alkalize or Die* Dr Baroody's book discusses how excess acids in the small intestines can negatively affect that vital organ and how overall health can be achieved by balancing the acidity in the body. The book describes and gives understanding how alkalizing the body can boost overall health and the health of specific areas of the body.

Selected Bibliography

Sally Fallon Morell and Mary G. Enig, Ph.D.: *Nourishing Traditions* Challenges politically correct nutrition and the diet "Dictorats" and includes information on how to prepare grains, health benefits of bone broths and enzyme-rich lacto-fermented foods.

— *Nourishing Broth* This book outlines the science behind broth's and their unique combination of amino acids, minerals and cartilage compounds. The book explains the benefits of fresh broth; healing of pain and inflammation, increased energy from better digestion, lessening of allergies and recovery from Crohn's disease. It explains how eating disorders are lowered because of the fully balanced nutritional broth program which lessens cravings that makes most diets fail. It outlines the diseases that bone broth can help heal such as osteoarthritis, osteoporosis, psoriasis, infectious disease, digestive disorders, and even some cancers.

Thomas Yarema, M.D., Daniel Rhoda, D.A.S. and Chef Johnny Brannigan: *Eat Taste Heal* Written by a medical doctor, a patient, and an acclaimed chef who utilizes humankind's most ancient system of healthy living. The book explores the field of holistic health and nutrition.

Marlo Morgan: *Mutant Message Down Under* A book about the simple truths of nature that can be applied in our modern society. It is an insight on how to get back in touch with nature, inner knowledge, inner guidance, and faith.

John Gunther: *Death Be Not Proud* An American journalist and author who is best known today for this book, a memoir about the death of his teenage son, Johnny Gunther, who was only seventeen years old when he died of a brain tumor. This is a deeply moving book about a father's memoir of a brave, intelligent, and spirited boy.

William Howard Hay MD: *Health Via Food* The author is a New York doctor and lecturer. This is his story of how he cured himself of Bright's disease which was unable to be cured using accepted medical methods of the time. Using alternative methods he came up with the concept of food combining (also known as the Hay diet). His concept was that certain foods require an acid pH environment in digestion, and other foods require an alkaline pH environment, and that both cannot take place at the same time, in the same environment.

Articles

Uhttp://cancerres.aacrjournals.org/content/68/21/8643.longU   A History of Cancer Chemotherapy by Vincent T. DeVita, Jr. or Edward Chu, Yale Cancer Center, Yale University School of Medicine

http://aseh.net/teaching-research/teaching-unit-better-living-through-chemistry/historical-sources/lesson-2/Merrill-Food%20Safety%20Regulation-1997.pdf   Richard A Merrill: *Food Safety Regulation-Reforming the Delaney Clause* is a forty page research document that outlines the potential threats to food safety regulations, cosmetic safety, and the regulations of added carcinogens in food. It reflects a distrust of the administration of food and the hold the US Congress has retained for itself as the primary authority to decide not only how food "safety" should be pursued, but what food "safety" means.

http://www.jvascsurg.org/article/S0741-5214(10)01727-1/fulltext *The History of Radiation Use in Medicine* by Amy B Reed, MD at the Heart and Vascular Institute, Penn State Hershey College of Medicine, Hershey, PA

Website Information

www.gerson.org The Gerson Therapy is a natural treatment that activates the body's extraordinary ability to heal itself through an organic, vegetarian diet, raw juices, coffee enemas, and natural supplements. The Gerson Institute is a non-profit organization in San Diego, California, dedicated to providing education and training in the Gerson Therapy, an alternative, non-toxic treatment for cancer and other chronic degenerative diseases.

www.burzynskiclinic.com The Burzynski Clinic was founded by Stanislaw R. Burzynski, M.D., PhD, cancer research and care has been inspired by the philosophy of the physician Hippocrates, *"First, do no harm."* The clinics treatments are based on the natural biochemical defence system of the body, which is capable of combating cancer with minimal impact on healthy cells.

www.foodmatters.tv   People at Food Matters are committed to helping people help themselves. They believe that your body is worthy of good care. Think of them as your nutritional consultants to a healthier life. Check out the website for all kinds of health tips, the pros and cons when purchasing juicers, and information about healing clinics.

www.mercola.com This natural health website has health articles and food facts. If you go to
http://articles.mercola.com/sites/Articledirectory.aspx you will see "Category" and under "Hot Topics" you can click on:
"Aspartame, Cancer, Fluoride, Fructose/Sugar, GMO, Mercury Free Dentistry, Nutritional Typing, Vaccines, and Vitamin D".

www.dr-gonzalez.com Dr. Nicholas Gonzalez does nutritional approaches to cancer and other degenerative diseases. Click on "Case Reports" to learn about patients diagnosed with cancer who have responded to our nutritional/enzyme treatment.

www.breastcancerfund.org This organization aims to help expose and eliminate the environmental causes of breast cancer. Stop this disease before it starts.

www.preventcancer.com Here you will find the article "The American Cancer Society, More Interested in Accumulating Wealth than Saving Lives" written by Samuel S. Epstein, M.D., Chairman of the Cancer Prevention Coalition. Dr. Epstein has been active in publicizing claims on the carcinogenic properties of chlordane pesticides, growth hormones in milk, nitrosamines in bacon, saccharin, beverage preservatives, and other food additives. However, his work has attracted criticism from the U. S. Food and Drug Administration, which claimed that his book *The Safe Shopper's Bible* misleads consumers by labeling safe products as carcinogenic. He is a strong critic of the American Cancer Society.

www.ewg.org Environmental Working Group is a non-profit, non-partisan organization dedicated to protecting human health and the environment. Find out answers to burning questions: Do you know what's in your tap water? What about your shampoo? What's lurking in the cleaners underneath your sink? What pesticides are on your food? How about the farms, fracking wells, and factories in your local area? Do you know what safeguards they use to protect your water, soil, air, and your kids? Which large agribusinesses get your tax dollars and why? What are GMOs? What do they do to our land and water?

Website Information

ww.cancer.gov/cancertopics/factsheet/Risk/BRCA. This website has a lot of information about cancer, BRCA1, BRCA2, and nutrition. However, it does focus primarily on chemotherapy and radiation cancer treatment. Nevertheless, it still offers a lot of valuable information.

www.cancer.org This site helped me learn and understand cancer. More than one million people in the United States get cancer each year. At this site you can find basic information about cancer, specific types of cancer, their risk factors, early detection, diagnosis, and treatment options.

www.russellblaylockmd.com I first learned about Dr. Russell Blaylock from Suzanne Somers: *Breakthrough, Eight Steps to Wellness*. Dr. Blaylock is a board certified neurosurgeon, author and lecturer and an expert on nutrition and toxins in food, cookware, teeth, and vaccines. His research discoveries have led to the idea that vaccines such as the H1N1 vaccine are dangerous or ineffective; that dental amalgams and fluoridated water are harmful to our health; and that aluminum cookware, aspartame, and MSG are toxic substances causing brain damage. Dr. Blaylock serves on the editorial staff of the Journal of the American Nutraceutical Association and is on the editorial staff of the Journal of American Physicians and Surgeons, official journal of the Association of American Physicians and Surgeons.

http://www.ams.usda.gov The U.S. Department of Agriculture's Agricultural Marketing Service administers programs that facilitate the efficient, fair marketing of U.S. agricultural products, including food, fiber, and specialty crops.

http://www.chrisbeatcancer.com At the age of 26 Chris Wark was diagnosed with stage III colon cancer in 2003. He had surgery, but refused chemotherapy. He is not a doctor but is an avid researcher on nutrition and natural therapies and he used nutrition and natural therapies to heal from cancer. He is alive and kicking, and cancer-free! It is wonderful site with all kinds of information about fluoride being a poison, cancer fighting food and natural therapies.

http://www.fluoridation.com   In depth views of fluoride poisoning and its effect on teeth, health, and the environment. The site also contains information about fraud, suppression, ethics and cover-ups.

http://fluoridealert.org/   More truth about fluoride regarding its poisoning attributes leading to death and brain damage and fifty reasons to oppose fluoridation.

http://www.naturalnews.com/002698_Ensure_food_marketing.html#ixzz2ycajO6c0 Nutritional values of Ensure

http://www.fakefoodwatch.com/2012/08/ensure-drink-sugary-fake-food-pseudo.html Nutritional values of Ensure

http:// www.naturalhealthschool.com on-line nutrition self study course in herbals, nutrition, natural health, and pH balance

DVDs

Beautiful Truth is a documentary from filmmaker Steve Kroschel. It is about a 15 year old boy, Garrett, who was raised in Alaska on a wildlife reserve, tries to cope with the death of his mother. He falls into depression and nearly flunks out of school. Because of his father's concerns, he makes a decision to begin home-schooling Garrett. As his first assignment his father gives him the controversial book written by Dr. Max Gerson, a physician to claims that diet is capable of curing cancer. The boy sets out to research Dr. Gerson's therapy to find out if it is truly legitimate.

Cancer: The Forbidden Cures is a documentary film by Massimo Massucco exposes all the successful cures against cancer discovered in the last 100 years, and the reasons why they were suppressed. Cancer is the only disease that has been defeated dozens of times without anyone knowing it. In the last 100 years, dozens of doctors, scientists, and researchers have developed diverse and effective solutions against cancer only to be thwarted by the political and propaganda power of the drug-dominated medical profession. This is the story of Essiac, Hoxsey, Laetrile, Shark Cartilage, Mistletoe, and Bicarbonate of Soda all put together in a stunning overview that leaves no doubt that inexpensive cures for cancer do exist but are systematically blocked by Big Pharma because they come from nature and cannot be patented.

Dying to Have Known is a movie about filmmaker, Steve Kroschel's 52-day journey to find evidence to the effectiveness of the Gerson Therapy—a long-suppressed natural cancer cure which led him across both the Atlantic and the Pacific Oceans. He presents the testimonies of patients, scientists, surgeons and nutritionists who testify to the therapy's efficacy in curing cancer and other degenerative diseases, and presents the hard scientific proof to back up their claims. You will hear from a Japanese medical school professor who cured himself of liver cancer over 15 years ago, a lymphoma patient who was diagnosed as terminal over 50 years ago as well as noted critics of this world-renowned healing method who dismiss it out of hand as "pure quackery." So the question that remains is, "Why is this powerful curative therapy still suppressed, more than 75 years after it was clearly proven to cure degenerative disease?" The viewers are left to decide for themselves.

Food, Inc. is an important movie from filmmaker Robert Kenner, who exposes how America's food supply is now controlled by a handful of corporations the put profit ahead of consumer health, the livelihood of American farmers, the safety of workers, and the environment. It reveals the shocking truths of what we eat, how it is produced, and who we have become as a nation.

Food Matters is a film about America's current state of health. This feature-length documentary film from Producer-Directors James Colquhoun and Laurentine ten Bosch sets about uncovering the trillion dollar worldwide sickness industry and gives people some scientifically verifiable solutions for overcoming illness naturally. The focus of the film is in helping people rethink the belief fed to us by our modern medical and health care establishments. The interviews point out that not every problem requires costly, major medical attention and reveal many alternative therapies that can be more effective, more economical, less harmful and less invasive than conventional medical treatments.

DVDs

Forks Over Knives by Lee Fulkerson and produced by John Corry is an American documentary film that advocates a low-fat, whole-food, plant-based diet as a way to avoid or reverse several chronic diseases and stresses that processed food should be avoided as well as food of animal origin.

Gerson Miracle examines many of the elements of the Gerson Therapy, explaining why we are so ill and how we have in our grasp the power to recover our health without expensive, toxic or mutilating treatments, using the restorative forces of our own immune systems. While the results seem miraculous, the real "miracle" lies within our own body and its healing processes. The documentary claims even the most advanced cases of cancer can be successfully reversed using this method which is NOT approved for use in the United States.

Second Opinion is a documentary by filmmaker, Eric Merola, about Ralph Moss, PhD who was Assistant Director of Public Affairs at Memorial Sloan-Kettering Cancer Center in New York City when he unveiled a cover-up of positive tests with America's most controversial anticancer agent, laetrile. He was ordered by Memorial Sloan-Kettering Cancer Center officials to falsify reports. He refused. Instead, he organized an underground employee group called Second Opinion to oppose this cover-up.

Made in the USA
Middletown, DE
05 July 2024

56931409R00215